Practical Music Theory

A Guide to Music as Art, Language, and Life

Textbook/Workbook

Practical Music Theory

A Guide to Music as Art, Language, and Life

Brian Dunbar

Factum Musicae

Published by *Factum Musicae*, U.S.A.
www.factummusicae.com

© 2015, 2010 by Brian Dunbar. All Rights Reserved. Seventh printing.

ISBN 978-0-578-06247-1

Portions of this book were previously published as *Music as Art, Language, and Life Volume I: Fundamentals*.
© 2009 by Brian Dunbar.

No part of this publication may be reproduced, stored in a retrieval system, or transmitted in any form or by any means—electronic, mechanical, photocopy, recording, or any other—except for brief quotations in printed reviews, without the prior written permission of the publisher.

Printed in the United States of America.

Contents

Prelude ix

PART ONE: Music Fundamentals

Pitch   1
    Range   1
    Middle C   1
    Hertz   1
    Notes   2
    Grand Staff   2
Timbre   2
    Overtones   3
    Harmonics   3
    Partials   3
    Fundamental   3
Intensity   3
    Amplitude   3
    Decibels   3
    Dynamics   3
Duration   4
    Rests   4

Chapter 1 - Pitch Notation   7
Pitches   7
Notes   7
Staff   7
Clef   7
    Treble Clef   7
    Bass Clef   8
    C Clefs   8
        Alto Clef   8
        Tenor Clef   8
Ledger Lines   9
Grand Staff   9
Ottava Sign   10
Octave   10
Loco   10
Interval   10
    Minor Second/Half Step   10
    Major Second/Whole Step   10
Scales   11
Scale Degrees   11
Accidentals   12
Bar lines   12
Measures   12
Ties   13
Note Components   13
Stem Length   13

Octave Identification   14
    Gamut   14
        Solfège   14
        Solmization   15
        Helmholtz System   15
        ASA System   15
        Midi Octave Designation   16
Enharmonic Notes   16

Assignments and Drills   17-25

Questions for Review   26

Assignments for Use with Anthology   27

Chapter 2 - Note Duration and Meter   29
Individual Note Durations   29
Individual Rest Durations   29
Ties   30
Rests   30
Dots   30
Double Dots   31
Beams   31
Beat   32
Meter   32
    Downbeat   32
    Duple Meter   32
    Triple Meter   32
    Quadruple Meter   32
    Quintuple Meter   32
Simple Meter   33
Compound Meter   33
Rhythm   33
Tempo   35
Time Signatures   35
Unit   36
Asymmetrical Meter   40
Borrowed Division   40
    Triplets   40
    Duplets   40
Irregular Division   40
Common Meter   42
Cut Time   42
Rhythmic Patterns   42
Anacrusis/Pick-up Note(s)   42
Basic Conducting Patterns   43
Syncopation   43
Accent Marks   44
Hemiola   44

Assignments and Drills   47-55

Questions for Review   56

Assignments for Use with Anthology   57

Chapter 3 - Intervals   59
    Interval   59
    Unison   59
    Octave   59
    Compound Intervals   59
    Harmonic Intervals   59
    Melodic Intervals   59
    Interval Quality   60
        Perfect Intervals   60
        Major Intervals   60
        Minor Intervals   60
        Augmented Intervals   61
        Diminished Intervals   61
    Unaltered Intervals   61
    Prime Unison   61
    Fourths   61
    Fifths   62
    Seconds   63
    Thirds   63
    Interval Inversion   63
    Enharmonic Intervals   64
    Tritone   64
    Doubly-augmented Fourths   65
    Doubly-diminished Fifths   65

    Assignments and Drills   67-78

    Questions for Review   80

    Assignments for Use with Anthology   81

Chapter 4 - Scales and Keys   83
    Scale   83
    Diatonic Scales   83
    Keys   83
    Tonic   83
    Tonality   83
    Modes   83
    Scale Degree Names   84
    Consonances   85
    Dissonances   85
    Transposition   87
    Tetrachords   87
    Key Signatures   88
    Order of Sharps   89
    Order of Flats   90

    Circle of Fifths (Major)   91
    Circle of Fifths (Major and Minor)   92
    Relative Keys   93
    Parallel Keys   93
    Natural Minor   94
    Harmonic Minor   94
    Melodic Minor   95
    Tonal Center   96
    Chromatic Scale   97
    Whole-Tone Scale   97
    Pitch Class   97
    Octatonic Scale   98
    Blues Scale   98
    Pentatonic Scale   99

    Assignments and Drills   101-118

    Questions for Review   120

    Assignments for Use with Anthology   121

Chapter 5 - Triads and Harmonic Analysis   123
    Triads   123
        Root   123
        Third   123
        Fifth   123
    Major Triads   123
    Minor Triads   123
    Diminished Triads   123
    Augmented Triads   123
    Harmonic Analysis   124
    Triad Charts   126
    Chorale Style   126
    Accompaniment   127
    Melody   127
    Harmonic Progression   127
    Arpeggio   128
    Root Position   129
    Close Spacing   129
    Open Spacing   129
    First Inversion   129
    Second Inversion   129
    Simple Position   129
    Pop-chord Symbols   132
    Lead Sheets   133
    Chord Charts   135

    Assignments and Drills   137-150

    Questions for Review   152

    Assignments for Use with Anthology   153

Chapter 6 - Beyond Pitch Notation 155

- Dynamics 155
- Articulation 156
- Ornaments 157
- Tempo Markings 158
  - Rallentando/Ritardando 158
  - Accelerando 158
  - A Tempo 158
- Percussion Notation 159
- Legend 159
- Repeat Symbol 159
- Two-bar Repeat Symbol 159
- Retrograde Repeat Symbol 160
- Da Capo 160
- Dal Segno 160
- Al Fine 161
- Al Coda 161
- Coda Sign 161
- Multiple Endings 161
- Measured Tremolo 161
- Undulating Tremolo 161
- Mixed Meter 162
- Substitute Notation 162
- Hemiola 163
- True Alternating Mixed Meter 163
- Fermata 164
- Cadence 164
- Transposition 165
- Transposing Instruments 165
- Concert Pitch 165
- Transposing Instrument Chart 166
- C Instrument Chart (Ranges/Clefs) 167
- Percussion Instrument Chart 167
- Vocal Ranges 168

Assignments and Drills 169-174

Questions for Review 176

Assignments for Use with Anthology 177

PART TWO: Diatonic Melody and Harmony

Chapter 7 - Seventh Chords and Figured Bass 181

- Sonority 181
- Seventh Chords 181
  - Major Seventh Chords 181
  - Minor Seventh Chords 181
  - Dominant Seventh Chords 181
  - Diminished Seventh Chords 181
  - Half-diminished Sevenths 181
  - Seventh Chord Inversions 184
- Textural Reduction 186
- Figured Bass 188
- Figured Bass Realization 191
- Outer Voices 193
- Inner Voices 193

Assignments and Drills 195-205

Questions for Review 206

Assignments for Use with Anthology 207

Chapter 8 - Nonharmonic Tones 209

- Passing Tones 209
- Neighboring Tones 210
- Escape Tones 210
- Appoggiaturas 211
- Anticipations 211
- Changing Tones 212
- Pedal Tones 212
- Suspensions 214
  - 9-8 Suspensions 215
  - 7-6 Suspensions 215
  - 4-3 Suspensions 215
  - 2-3 Suspensions 215
  - Decorated Suspensions 216
- Retardations 216
- Free Tones 219

Assignments and Drills 221-230

Questions for Review 232

Assignments for Use with Anthology 233

Chapter 9 - Harmonic Progression 235

- Harmonic Progression 235
- Inactive Tones 235
- Active Tones 235
- Cadence 237
  - Authentic Cadence 237
    - Perfect 237
    - Imperfect 237
  - Deceptive Cadence 238
  - Half Cadence 238
  - Plagal Cadence 239
- Circle Progressions 241
- Retrogression 242
- Harmonic Rhythm 242

      Assignments and Drills   247-251

      Questions for Review   252

      Assignments for Use with Anthology   253

Chapter 10 - Melody and Texture   255

      Motif   255
      Sequence   257
      Contoural Inversion   258
      Retrograde Motion   259
      Rhythmic Diminution   259
      Rhythmic Augmentation   259
      Retrograde Inversion   259
      Real Sequence   259
      Tonal Sequence   259
      False Sequence   259
      Modified Sequence   260
      Phrase   260
      Period   160
          Parallel Period   260
          Contrasting Period   260
      Texture   261
          Monophony   261
          Heterophony   261
          Homophony   262
              Block Chords   262
              Jump Bass   263
              Broken Chords   263
              Alberti Bass   263
              Arpeggiation   264
              Chorale Style   264
              Homorhythm   264
          Polyphony   265
          Stretto   265

      Assignments and Drills   267-273

      Questions for Review   274

      Assignments for Use with Anthology   275

Chapter 11 - Voice Leading   277

      Voice Leading   277
      Cantus Firmus   277
      Parallel Motion   278
      Similar Motion   278
      Contrary Motion   278
      Oblique Motion   279
      Laws of Voice Leading   279

      Regulations of Voice Leading   280
      Voice Crossing   280
      Voice Overlapping   280
      Uneven Fifths   281
      Doubling Principles   281
      Resolving Seventh Chords   283
      Prime   284
      Direction of Inflection Principle   284

      Assignments and Drills   287-297

      Questions for Review   298

      Assignments for Use with Anthology   299

PART THREE: Chromatic Harmony

Chapter 12 - Tonicization   303

      Tonicization   303
      Secondary Dominants   303
      Resolution of Secondary Dominants   307
      Secondary Cadence   308
          Secondary Authentic   308
          Secondary Half   308
          Secondary Deceptive   309
      Secondary Leading Tone Chords   309
          Resolutions   310

      Assignments and Drills   313-322

      Questions for Review   324

      Assignments for Use with Anthology   325

Chapter 13 - Borrowed Chords   327

      Borrowed Chords   327
      Modal Mixture   328
      Picardy Third   328

      Assignments and Drills   333-341

      Questions for Review   342

      Assignments for Use with Anthology   343

Chapter 14 - Augmented Sixth Chords   345

      Augmented Sixth Chords   345
      Italian Sixth   345

German Sixth   345
French Sixth   345
Resolution of Augmented Sixths   347

Assignments and Drills   351-359

Questions for Review   360

Assignments for Use with Anthology   361

Chapter 15 - Neapolitan Chords and Altered/ Expanded Dominants   363

Neapolitan Chord   363
Neapolitan Sixth   363
Phrygian II   363
Altered Dominants   366
Expanded Dominants   366
Augmented Dominants   366
Ninth, Eleventh, Thirteenth Chords   367

Assignments and Drills   371-381

Questions for Review   382

Assignments for Use with Anthology   383

Chapter 16 - Chromatic Mediants   385

Chromatic Mediants   385
Doubly-chromatic Mediants   385
False Relation   389
Complete Chart of Roman Numeral
   Identification   390

Assignments and Drills   391-394

Questions for Review   396

Assignments for Use with Anthology   397

Chapter 17 - Modulation   399

Modulation   399
Change of Mode   399
Closely-Related Keys   399
Common Chord Modulation   400
Phrase Modulation   401
Chromatic Modulation   401
Foreign Keys   402
Interhcange of Mode   402
Enharmonic Pivot Chords   402

Master Chord   403
Common Tone Modulation   408

Assignments and Drills   411-417
Questions for Review   418

Assignments for Use with Anthology   419

Postlude   421

Index   425

Prelude

Music Theory

Music theory is the study of the "grammar" of music. It is the examination of music's structure and form, from its tiniest components (foreground analysis) to its overall construction (background analysis). Just as a study of a language includes the alphabet, word formation, the parts of speech, and syntax, so music theory explores pitch, melody, harmony, and texture. Further, writing in a language involves developing thematic material throughout paragraphs, chapters, and an entire body of work. Similarly, to compose and analyze music, one must clearly understand the principles of the medium.

In the same way that various rules govern writing according to accepted practices of any language, there are also important regulations that preside over musical composition. Because this book explores music of Western cultures exclusively, it may be considered the music theory equivalent to a study of a Western language (English, for instance) and its literature. In Western music, these principles have been developed over a substantial period of time known as the ***common practice era***.

The Common Practice Era

The common practice era spans roughly from 1650 to 1875, encompassing most of the Baroque, Classical, and Romantic periods of music history when customs of tonal composition were cemented in Western music. Successful composers ranging from this historical stage to the present have generally employed the same set of musical principles, despite the presence of a vast array of musical styles and innovations. Since these principles have not only stood a significant test of time, but have transcended style as well, the rules of music theory are valuable tools for those who are serious about studying, performing, and composing music.

The Art of Music

Because music is an artistic form of human expression, the study of its theory enhances appreciation of the art. In fact, this is partly the purpose of studying music from a theoretical perspective. While learning music theory may often seem like a purely academic endeavor, one should keep in mind that a skilled music theorist is better equipped to perform, compose, and even simply enjoy music.

Inspired Musicianship

The study of theory is not a study in inspiration. It gives the musician tools needed to act upon the inspiration that is already present. Those inspired to make music, but possessing inadequate understanding of structure, are those for whom a study in theory is most beneficial.

Music Making - Work or Play?

Creating music is a pleasurable experience. Even though the discipline of practice is necessary to skilled music making, the work of practicing should not be perceived as drudgery or as a "necessary evil." Observing a child seriously at play reveals that the child is working hard, concentrating all energy on the chosen task. Similarly, musicians can enjoy both the "journey" and the "destination" of music making by devoting themselves to their craft. The study of music theory can be an enjoyable part of the journey toward meaningful and competent musicianship. It is the concept of work as play that prompted one of the editorial committee members of this book to remark that "drinking a cup of coffee in Starbucks while working on this book is one of the most relaxing, enjoyable things ever." For an outstanding treatise on the subject of the pleasure of work, see Madeleine L'Engle's book *Walking on Water: Reflections on Faith and Art* (Wheaton, IL: Harold Shaw Publishers, 1980), pages 167-168.

Getting the Most from This Book

Ideally, this textbook will be used in a classroom or in a one-on-one setting with an instructor. While the concepts in this book may be understood merely from reading the text and completing the assignments, the book is designed for classroom use where concepts are explained in detail, illustrated visually, and heard aurally.

Supplemental Material

Audio excerpts of musical examples used in this text are available online at no charge from the publisher. To access these materials, visit www.practicalmusictheorybook.com. The **assignments and drills** at the end of each chapter are available for download for those who prefer not to write in their textbook. For access to the download site, contact info@practicalmusictheorybook.com. **Instructor aids** such as graphic files for handouts or presentations are also available at no charge. Email info@practicalmusictheorybook.com for details on how and where to download supplemental teaching materials.

It is highly recommended that a collection of printed musical examples be used in conjunction with this textbook. A*ssignments for use with anthology* appear at the end of each chapter. These assignments are keyed to Schirmer Publishing's **Anthology for Musical Analysis, seventh ed.** by Charles Burkhart and William Rothstein.

Acknowledgements

This book could not have been written without my editorial committee: Polly Blanshan, Emily Heller, Louisa Jobes, Crystal Swan, and Amanda Walston. Their thorough scrutiny and countless excellent suggestions, contributions, revisions, and amendments have improved this book significantly. A special thank you is also in order for Andrew Parfenov, a gifted photographer and graphic designer whose art on the cover is a small sample of his enormous talent. I am deeply grateful to Brian Zylstra, director of information technology at Crossroads College, who rescued me from computer woes numerous times throughout the writing of this book. I am indebted to all my colleagues at Crossroads College, past and present, who have unknowingly influenced this work in many ways. Their role in the joyous journey of this book has been significant and their presence is found on these pages.

I cannot adequately articulate my appreciation for the extraordinary theory teachers who have guided me on my musical journey: Dottie Savoy, Mike Bennett, Richard Unfried, Barry Liesch, Stan Friedman, Edwin T. Childs, and especially Linda Duckett, who spent so much time mentoring and encouraging me. My parents, Robert and Gloria Dunbar, invested in me and always encouraged me to pursue my dreams. My wife, Cindy, and my sons, Jason and Derek, have been so gracious, allowing me extra time away from home to complete this project. I am overwhelmed by their constant love and support. I owe so much to the people of Cypress Park Community Church in Cypress, California, who lovingly endured my initiation as a professional musician, subjecting themselves to my new musical arrangements on a weekly basis. Mostly, however, I wish to express my deep gratitude to my students - those card-carrying theorists - whose hunger for knowledge and love of the musical art never cease to inspire me.

Jesu Juva

PART THE FIRST: MUSIC FUNDAMENTALS

Music is the artistic organization of sound and time.

All sounds are created by vibrations that travel via **sound waves** to the ear. Most vibrations are created by striking, plucking, rubbing, or blowing into an object. Other vibrations are manufactured electronically and are produced through a vibrating speaker.

Example F.01 is a visual representation of a sound wave.

Example F.01

Sound has four properties:
- Pitch
- Timbre
- Intensity
- Duration

Pitch has to do with the element of music called **range** and is, in the simplest of terms, the *highness* or *lowness* of sound. The speed, or *frequency*, of vibration determines the pitch. A vibration at 262 Hz produces the pitch known on the piano as **Middle C**. Hz is the abbreviation for **Hertz**, which literally means *cycles per second*. Thus, Middle C vibrates at 262 cycles every second.

As the cycles per second increase, the pitch rises; as they decrease, the pitch falls. Modern instruments are tuned to 440 Hz, which is the pitch **A** above Middle C. A tuning fork produces this pitch when struck, creating a vibration of 440 Hz. The lowest key on the piano is the pitch **A**, four *octaves* below 440 Hz. That pitch vibrates at a rate much slower than A440 – only 27.5 Hz.

Below is a diagram of the 88 keys of a piano. Each key that represents the pitch *A* in various *octaves*[1] includes its frequency designation. Middle C, 262 Hz, is also identified.

Example F.02

Middle C
262 Hz

27.5 Hz   55 Hz   110 Hz   220 Hz   440 Hz   880 Hz   1760 Hz   3520 Hz

Notice that the frequency of a pitch doubles as it moves up each octave. Conversely, it is reduced by half as it moves down each octave. Knowing this, it can be deduced that the *C* above Middle C vibrates at 524 Hz, and the C below Middle C vibrates at 131 Hz.[2]

These same pitches are represented by **notes** in the diagram of the **grand staff** below.

Example F.03

***

Timbre (pronounced *TAM-ber*), describes the **quality** of the sound. Some musicians refer to this as the *color* of the sound. *Timbre* is what distinguishes the sound of various instruments or voices, regardless of the pitch. A violin, a clarinet, and a piano may all play an identical pitch, such as A440, but it is the *timbre* of the instruments that helps the listener differentiate between them.

---

[1] *The term octave is explained in chapter one on Pitch Notation and chapter three on Intervals.*
[2] *Technically, Middle C is 261.626 Hz, so the C an octave above that is closer to 523 Hz than 524.*

Timbre is affected by a number of variables including the method of producing the sound, the materials used to create the instrument, and the size of the instrument. The timbres of a violin, a clarinet, and a piano are different because a violin is played by rubbing a bow on a string (or by plucking the strings), a clarinet is played by blowing on a reed, producing vibrations through a hollow cylindrical column, and a piano is played by pressing keys which cause small hammers inside the instrument to strike strings. Two vocalists of the same gender have differences in timbre (and range) because of dissimilarities in their vocal cords, throats, mouths, and nasal passages.

Each sound that is created also produces a series of less-audible **overtones**, called **harmonics**. Within each Hertz are sub-cycles that vibrate in fractions (halves, thirds, fourths, etc.) of the original Hertz. The harmonics are called **partials**, and the first partial is called the **fundamental**. All of the partials constitute the sound of the overall tone, but the *fundamental* gives the tone its basic pitch. Harmonics are an important part of timbre, as the strengths of various overtones contribute to the *color* of the sound.

Intensity is the *loudness* or *softness* of sound (not to be confused with *highness* or *lowness*, which designates pitch range), and refers to the amount of power or energy applied to the vibration, thus affecting its *volume*. **Amplitude**, another word for *intensity*, is measured in **decibels**. In music notation, intensity is indicated by markings called **dynamics**. *See example 6.01 in chapter six for a chart that matches approximate decibel levels with dynamic markings.*

Example F.04 demonstrates two identical pitches at different amplitudes.

Example F.04

These are the same pitch because they represent an identical number of cycles per second. The second one, however, is at a greater intensity (louder volume) than the first.

Example F.05, conversely, shows two different pitches at identical amplitudes.

Example F.05

These pitches are, in fact, an octave apart. The second one is an octave higher than the first one because it has twice as many cycles per second as the first.

Duration is the property of sound that deals with time. It is the length of sounds and silence. In music, pitch durations are indicated by *notes* of varying lengths. Silence durations are indicated by symbols called **rests**.

At the beginning of this introduction to the fundamentals of music, music was defined as *the artistic organization of sound and time*. Composers and performers have a vast palette from which to work, creating music of various pitches, timbres, intensities, and durations in their creative organization of sound and time within a space.

Musicians who devote themselves to *mastering* the fundamentals of music in this section will find success and enjoyment in the adventurous study of music theory that is to follow. Whether these rudiments are being learned for the very first time or merely reviewed, there is nothing more essential for continued success in music theory than intimately knowing the basics. Just as athletes who consistently execute the very fundamentals of their sport excel, so do musicians who consistently demonstrate mastery of the fundamentals of music.

Chapter 1
Pitch Notation

Example 1.01

Ut qué-ant láxis re- soná- re fíbris

Mí-ra gestó- rum fámu-li tu-ó- rum,

Sól-ve pollú-ti lábi– i re-á-tum, Sáncte Jo-ánnes.

Plainchant hymn
Ut qué-ant láxis

Composed by
Guido d'Arezzo
circa A.D. 1015

Pitches are actual sound frequencies, and ***notes*** are the visual representations of those pitches. Therefore, pitches are *heard*, while notes are *seen*. Notes are placed on a ***staff*** where their corresponding pitches are visually characterized.

The staff consists of five lines and four spaces, <u>numbered from bottom to top</u>.

Example 1.02

The notes are named by the first seven letters of the English alphabet (A through G), and are determined by the ***clef*** that is used. Clefs are symbols that are placed on the staff to identify each line and space.

The ***treble clef*** is also called the "G clef" for two reasons:

1. Its symbol is a stylized letter "G."
2. It designates the specific line on the staff that represents the note "G."

7

Example 1.03

↑ Treble clef ↑ Looks like "G" ↑ Identifies 2nd line of staff as G ↑ All other notes follow alphabetically

The **bass clef** is also called the "F clef" for two reasons:

1. Its symbol is a stylized form of the Gothic letter "F."
2. It designates the specific line on the staff that represents the note "F."

Example 1.04

↑ Bass clef ↑ Looks like "F" ↑ Identifies 4th line of staff as F ↑ All other notes follow alphabetically

There are several other clefs known as **C clefs**, most notably the alto clef and the tenor clef. The symbol for the C clef indicates where *Middle C* is on the staff. If the C clef appears on the third line of the staff, it is called the **alto clef**. If it appears on the fourth line of the staff, it is called the **tenor clef**.

Example 1.05

↑ Alto clef   ↑ Tenor clef

Instruments that employ music for the tenor clef are the bassoon, contra-bassoon, and trombone, though those who play each of these instruments must read bass clef as well. The viola uses the alto clef primarily, but violists also read treble clef. *See example 6.25 in chapter six for a chart that identifies the instruments that use these clefs.*

Regardless of the clef, when the music exceeds the boundaries of the staff, ***ledger lines*** are needed to extend the range of the staff. Example 1.06 demonstrates the use of ledger lines both above and below the staff.

Example 1.06

It is evident from this example that ledger lines extend the staff so that *spaces* above or below the actual ledger lines may be used as well.

The note that appears in the *treble clef* on the *first ledger line below* the staff is Middle C.
The note that appears in the *bass clef* on the *first ledger line above* the staff is Middle C.
The note that appears in the *alto clef* on the *third line of the staff* is Middle C.
These are shown below in example 1.07.

Example 1.07

When a treble clef and bass clef appear together and are connected by a vertical line and a bracket as shown in example 1.08, they constitute a ***grand staff***. The notes that appear on the grand staff below are identical. They are both Middle C.

Example 1.08

"Beautiful music is the art of the prophets that can calm the agitations of the soul; it is one of the most magnificent and delightful presents God has given us."
- theologian and musician Martin Luther

In order to reduce the need for excessive ledger lines in a passage of music where several ledger lines would be used in a row, or to accommodate a single note that exceeds the range of the staff by a significant amount, the *ottava sign* may be used instead of ledger lines.

The **ottava sign** indicates that the note should sound an **octave**[1] above or below where it is written. The abbreviation **8va** is used *above* the staff to indicate that the pitch should actually sound an octave *above* where written, and the abbreviation **8vb** is used *below* the staff to indicate that the pitch should sound an octave *lower* than written. These symbols are then followed by a dashed line to indicate the duration that the ottava designation remains in effect. For *extended regions*, the dashed line is often omitted and the word **loco** is used to indicate a *return* to the exact octave register of the notation.

For *two* octaves above or below, the symbol is **15ma** or **15mb** respectively. Examples 1.09 and 1.10 demonstrate how the ottava sign may be used to avoid using ledger lines.

Example 1.09

"This is a world in which people have, in countless ways, celebrated their existence in sound, searching for something for which, in the words of Ken Medema, 'There is no other way of saying it.'"

— *composer and author Harold Best*

Example 1.10

An **interval** is the distance between pitches. The smallest interval in Western tonal music is called a **minor second (m2)**. It is also known as a **half step**. A **whole step**, or a **major second (M2)**, is comprised of *two* half steps. The interval from one key to the next *adjacent* key on the piano, regardless of whether it is a white key or a black key, is a half step.

---

[1] *The term octave describes the interval of an 8th. An octave is the next occurrence of a specific note in a higher or lower register.*

Example 1.11

Half steps (m2) may be
black-to-white or
white-to-black
so long as *no* other
keys are in between.

Whole steps (M2) may be
black-to-white or
white-to-black
if another white
key *is* in between.

Whole steps
(M2) may be
black-to-black.

Half steps (m2) may
be white-to-white
if *no* black key
is in between.

Whole steps (M2) may
be white-to-white
if a black key
is in between.

It is important to note that *the staff is deceptive*. It falsely appears that the distances between all notes on the staff are the same, but in fact they are *not* all equidistant. The distance from B to C is a *half step* and the distance from E to F is a *half step*. All other adjacent intervals are *whole steps* apart. The location of the clef on the staff will cause the incidences of *half steps* and *whole steps* to be in different places.

For instance, in the C Major **scales** shown in example 1.12 in bass clef, alto clef, treble clef, and tenor clef, half steps always occur between the *third and fourth* notes of the scale, called **scale degrees,** and between the *seventh and eighth* scale degrees. In each case, arrows are used to point out where the half steps occur – between E to F and between B to C. All of the other adjacent intervals of the scale are whole steps.

Example 1.12

space 3 to line 4 and space 5 to line 6

line 4 to space 4 and line 6 to space 6

line 1 to space 1 and line 3 to space 3

space 1 to line 2 and space 3 to line 4

Without a clef, it is impossible to identify any note names on the staff or determine where the half steps and whole steps are. *Any* adjacent line/space combination has the *potential* to be either a whole step or a half step. The presence of a clef identifies the notes that appear on each line and space, thus indicating where the half steps and whole steps are.

It is easier to see the relationships between half steps and whole steps on the piano keyboard. The arrows in example 1.13 are again pointing to the half steps **B-C** and **E-F**.

Example 1.13

Accidentals are alterations that raise or lower notes.

> A ***sharp*** (♯) *raises* the pitch by a *half step*.
>
> A ***flat*** (♭) *lowers* the pitch by a *half step*.
>
> A ***double sharp*** (𝄪) raises the pitch *two* half steps (one whole step).
>
> A ***double flat*** (𝄫) lowers the pitch *two* half steps (one whole step).
>
> A ***natural*** (♮) cancels a previous accidental and returns the pitch to its unaltered form.

Bar lines are vertical lines on the staff that divide the music into ***measures***. Accidentals that occur *within a measure* remain in effect throughout that measure, but are cancelled by bar lines.

Example 1.14

If a note is altered by an accidental and then appears in the same measure *in a different octave,* that note is *not* affected by the accidental.

Example 1.15

E-flat   E   E-flat   E   E-flat   E-flat

Ties are symbols used to connect and sustain two notes of the same pitch, thus increasing their duration. Notes affected by accidentals that are tied *across a bar line* remain altered by the accidental.

Example 1.16

still F-sharp

"Where words fail, music speaks."
 - author Hans Christian Andersen

Notes consist of up to three parts: the **head**, the **stem**, and the **flag**. These will be dealt with in detail in chapter two on note durations and meter. At present, however, potential music theorists should familiarize themselves with the following music notation basics.

- The length of a note's stem should be *about an octave*.[2]
- The *third line of the staff* determines the direction and side of the stem.
- If the note is *above* the third line, the stem will go *down* from the left side of the head.
- If the note is *below* the third line, the stem will go *up* from the right side of the head.
- If the note is *on* the third line, the *context* of the notes around it will help determine which side the stem should go. If the context does not prove helpful in making a determination, the preferred practice is to put the stem *down* from the left side of the note head.

Example 1.17

head only   head and stem   head, stem, and flag

---

[2] *An exception occurs when ledger lines are used. Refer back to example 1.10. For ledger lines, extend the stem to the third line of the staff.*

Example 1.18

below third line, stem up on right

on or above third line, stem down on left

"The aim and final end of all music should be none other than the glory of God and the refreshment of the soul."

– composer J.S. Bach

Example 1.19

Accidentals are *always* to the left of a note on the same line or space as the note.

Flags are *always* to the right, regardless of the direction and side of the stem.

Musicians often find it necessary to identify a note in a particular octave. There are currently three common systems of **octave identification**, but unfortunately, none of them is accepted as the standard. Guido d'Arezzo, an eleventh-century Italian monk, developed the predecessor to these systems with a method called **gamut** (from the lowest note in the scale, *gamma ut*).

Guido is the father of the modern **solfège**[3] system often used in ear training, sight singing, and vocal/choral instruction. He composed a chant in honor of John the Baptist that he used to teach the scale degrees to his students. The chant, based on a six-note scale and shown in its original neumatic notation back in example 1.01, appears in modern chant notation here.

Example 1.20

Ut qué-ant lá - xis re - so - ná - re fí - bris Mí - ra ges - tó - rum

fá - mu - li tu - ó - rum, Sól - ve pol - lú - ti lá - bi - i re - á - tum, Sánc - te Jo - án - nes.

---

[3] *The term solfege draws its name from the Latin syllables "sol" and "fa" from measures five and four of the chant in example 1.20.*

The note beginning each phrase is one scale degree higher than the note that began the previous phrase. Thus, each phrase begins one step above the beginning of the preceding phrase. The Latin syllables that begin each phrase are *ut, re, mi, fa, sol,* and *la*. The technique of associating syllables with degrees of a scale is called **solmization**.[4] Over time, *ut* was replaced with *do*, and the syllable *ti* was added to accommodate the eight-note scale. Therefore, the modern-day solfège syllables are *do, re, mi, fa, so, la,* and *ti*, with *do* (an octave above the original *do*) completing the scale. The distance between each adjacent syllable is a whole step with the exception of *mi - fa* and *ti - do*, which are both half steps.

The *gamut* system of octave identification gave way over time to the **Helmholtz system** (named after the nineteenth-century German acoustician Hermann von Helmholtz). The Helmholtz system (which designates octaves as *sub-contra, contra, great, small, one-line, two-line,* and so forth) is still used in some circles but is losing popularity to the ASA system.

The ASA (Acoustical Society of America) system is illustrated in example 1.21 on both the grand staff and the piano keyboard.

Example 1.21

Middle C is C4. The range of each octave *begins with **C** and ends with **B***.

---

[4] *The term solmization draws its name from the Latin syllables "sol" and "mi" from measures five and three of the chant in example 1.20.*

A third, and most recent system, is the **MIDI Octave Designation System**.[5] In this purely numerical system, Middle C is given the designation *60*. For each note *below* Middle C, a number is *subtracted*, and for each note *above* Middle C, a number is *added*.

Notes that *share the same pitch* but are *spelled differently* when written are called **enharmonic notes** (or *enharmonic equivalents*). The term *enharmonic* denotes more than one possible spelling, and may be applied to intervals as well as individual notes.

Example 1.22

Although they share the same pitch, the two notes in example 1.22 are distinctly different notes. One is F-sharp, the other is G-flat. In composition, it is often obvious which spelling should be used and which spelling should be avoided; the context will determine which note to use. For the time being, it is important simply to be aware of enharmonic equivalents.

The notes in each measure in example 1.23 below are also enharmonic with each other, but trickier to spot because only *one* of the notes in each measure requires an accidental. The notes in measure one are B-sharp and C. Because **B** and **C** were only a half step apart to begin with, the **B** became enharmonic with **C** when it was raised a half step to B-sharp.

Example 1.23

This concludes the introduction to pitch notation. Note durations, an important aspect of pitch notation, will be covered in chapter two.

The first rule of music theory:
ALWAYS USE A **PENCIL**.

"Both ends of the pencil are useful."
– *unknown*

---

[5] *MIDI is an acronym for Musical Instrument Digital Interface. The MIDI system of facilitating universal communication between electronic musical devices, regardless of their manufacturer, was developed in the early 1980s.*

Assignments and Drills

Assignment 1.01

The objective of this assignment is legible and efficient clef writing.

1. Write ten treble clefs on the staff below. Make sure the "G" of the "G clef" symbol intersects with line one and line three of the staff. REFER BACK TO EXAMPLE 1.03 IF NECESSARY.

2. Write ten bass clefs on the staff below. Make sure you begin on line four and that the "F" of the "F clef" symbol intersects with line five, and that the two dots are on spaces three and four. REFER BACK TO EXAMPLE 1.04 IF NECESSARY.

3. Write ten alto clefs on the staff below. REFER BACK TO EXAMPLE 1.05 IF NECESSARY.

4. Write ten tenor clefs on the staff below. REFER BACK TO EXAMPLE 1.05 IF NECESSARY.

Assignment 1.02

The objective of this assignment is efficient note recognition in treble clef.

Instructions: Write the name of each note in the space provided. Measures one and twenty-one are done for you. Try to complete the assignment in less than five minutes. REFER BACK TO EXAMPLE 1.03 IF NECESSARY.

[Measures 1–30 of treble clef notes. Measure 1 is labeled "G". Measure 21 is labeled "A-sharp".]

Assignment 1.03

The objective of this assignment is efficient octave recognition in treble clef.

Instructions: Go back through assignment 1.02 and add the ASA octave designation for each note. For example, the answer to measure one is G4, measure two is E5, etc. Try to complete the assignment in less than two minutes. REFER BACK TO EXAMPLE 1.21 IF NECESSARY.

Assignment 1.04

The objective of this assignment is efficient note recognition in bass clef.

Instructions: Write the name of each note in the space provided. Try to complete the assignment in less than five minutes. REFER BACK TO EXAMPLE 1.04 IF NECESSARY.

Assignment 1.05

The objective of this assignment is efficient octave recognition in bass clef.

Instructions: Go back through assignment 1.04 and add the ASA octave designation for each note. For example, the answer to measure one is B2, measure two is A3, etc. Try to complete the assignment in less than two minutes. REFER BACK TO EXAMPLE 1.21 IF NECESSARY.

Assignment 1.06

The objective of this assignment is efficient note recognition in alto and tenor clefs.

Instructions: Write the name of each note in the space provided. Try to complete the assignment in less than six minutes. Be careful to watch for clef changes at the beginning of each system. REFER BACK TO EXAMPLE 1.05 IF NECESSARY.

Assignment 1.07

The objective of this assignment is efficient octave recognition in alto and tenor clefs.

Instructions: Go back through assignment 1.06 and add the ASA octave designation for each note. Try to complete the assignment in less than three minutes. REFER BACK TO EXAMPLE 1.21 IF NECESSARY.

Pitch Notation

Assignment 1.08

The objective of this assignment is efficient note recognition in all clefs.

Instructions: Write the name of each note in the space provided. Try to complete the assignment in less than five minutes. REFER BACK TO EXAMPLES 1.03, 1.04, AND 1.05 IF NECESSARY.

Assignment 1.09

The objective of this assignment is efficient octave recognition in all clefs.

Instructions: Go back through assignment 1.08 and add the ASA octave designation for each note. Try to complete the assignment in less than four minutes. REFER BACK TO EXAMPLES 1.09, 1.10, AND 1.21 IF NECESSARY.

Assignment 1.10

The objective of this assignment is legible and efficient pitch notation.

1. Create a treble clef at the beginning of the staff below.
2. Write notes on the staff in this order:
   line 1, space 4, space 1, line 4, line 2, space 3, line 3, line 5, space 2, 1 ledger line above.
3. Add a stem to each note.
4. Identify the notes by writing their names below them under the staff. It is not necessary to indicate octave designation, but you may include that if you wish for additional practice.

   REFER BACK TO EXAMPLES 1.02, 1.03, 1.06, AND 1.18 IF NECESSARY.

5. Create a bass clef at the beginning of the staff below.
6. Write notes on the staff in this order:
   line 1, space 4, space 1, line 4, line 2, space 3, line 3, line 5, space 2, 1 ledger line above.
7. Add a sharp to each appearance of the notes G, C, and F. For notes that are on a line, be sure the box created by the sharp symbol has the line clearly going through it. For notes that are on a space, be sure that the box does not have a line inside it.
8. Add a flat to each appearance of the notes E, A, and B. Again, for notes that are on a line, be sure that the rounded portion of the flat symbol clearly shows the line going through it. For notes on a space, be sure that the rounded portion of the flat symbol does not have a line going through it. The lines and spaces apply equally to accidentals as they do to note heads.

   REFER BACK TO EXAMPLES 1.02, 1.04, AND 1.06 IF NECESSARY.

9. Create an alto clef at the beginning of the staff below.
10. Write notes on the staff in the order prescribed below. If a note requires more than two ledger lines, use the ottava sign.

    REFER BACK TO EXAMPLES 1.05, 1.06, 1.09, 1.10, AND 1.21 IF NECESSARY.

    C4   C3   C5   A2   F#3   G5   E3   B1   Db4   F1

Assignment 1.11

The objectives of this assignment are note reading/writing in various clefs, octave identification, and legible notation with accurate stem/flag directions.

Instructions: Below are three systems with two staves each. In each system, write the notes from the upper staff into the lower staff so that the notes in the lower staff are in the identical octave register as the notes in the upper staff. Do not use the ottava sign or enharmonic spellings. Be sure to write notes with accurate stem and flag directions. Numbers 1, 11, and 21 have been done for you. REFER BACK TO EXAMPLES 1.07, 108, AND 1.19 IF NECESSARY.

Assignment 1.12

The objectives of this assignment are efficient note reading, recognition of accidentals, and interval identification (Major seconds and minor seconds only).

Instructions: In each measure, identify the interval by writing H for half step and W for whole step. If the interval is neither a half step nor a whole step, do not fill in the blank. Numbers 1, 11, and 21 are done for you. Try to complete the assignment in less than five minutes. REFER BACK TO EXAMPLES 1.11, 1.12, AND 1.13 IF NECESSARY.

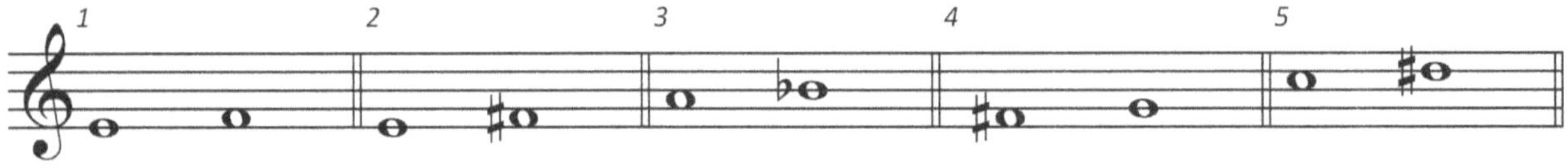

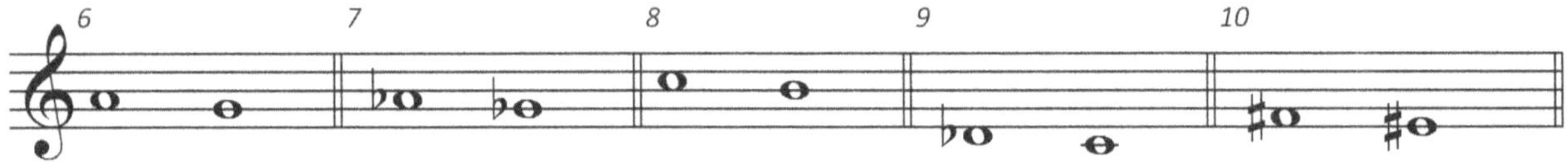

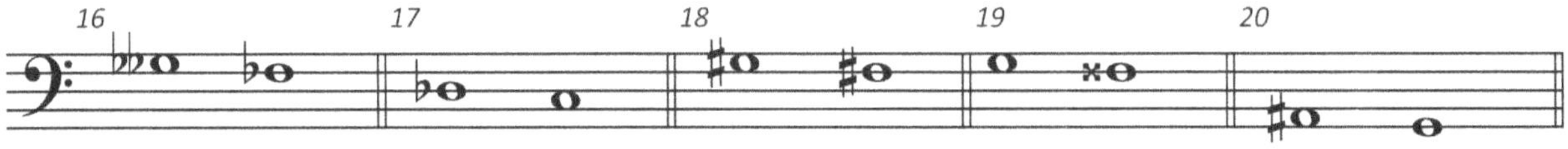

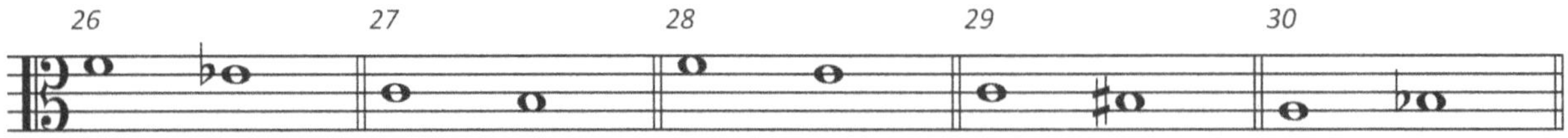

Assignment 1.13

The objective of this assignment is to create and identify enharmonic equivalents.

1. In measures 1 through 15, create one enharmonic equivalent for the note provided. Do not use double sharps or double flats. The first two measures are done for you.
2. In measures 16 through 30, circle each measure that includes an enharmonic equivalent.

   REFER BACK TO EXAMPLES 1.22 AND 1.23 IF NECESSARY.

Questions for Review

1. Why is the treble clef also called the G clef?

2. The alto and tenor clefs are both C clefs. What is the difference between them?

3. What is the grand staff?

4. What word is used as the plural of "staff"?

5. What is the technical term for the interval of a half step?

6. What is the technical term for the interval of a whole step?

7. What is the purpose of the ottava sign?

8. Explain why the staff is deceptive.

9. Which two sets of notes, unaffected by accidentals, are only a half step apart?

10. Do double sharps and double flats really exist in music? Speculate as to why they may be necessary.

11. If two notes appear simultaneously in different octaves, and one of them is altered by an accidental, is the other one affected by the accidental as well?

12. What is the proper length of a note stem? What is the exception?

13. How do you determine which way a stem should go and on what side of the note the stem should be?

14. In the ASA system of octave identification, what is the designation of Middle C?

15. Define the term *enharmonic notes*.

Assignments for Use with Anthology

A1.01 Identify each note below, as well as an *enharmonic equivalent* for each. It is not necessary to include octave designation.

- The note that is double-sharped on page 145, measure 42.

- The double-flatted note on page 360, measure 81.

- The double-flatted note on page 360, measure 87.

- The first note on page 368, measure 14, top staff.

- The double-sharped notes on page 385, measure 54.

A1.02 Identify the sharped note and the flatted note on page 324, measure 120. Include the ASA octave designation for both.

A1.03 Identify the note on page 287, measure 73, bottom staff.

A1.04 Is the last note in the top staff on page 294, measure 209 *A-natural* or *A-sharp*? Why?

A1.05 There are three *B-flat* notes in the top staff on page 294, measure 222. A *flat symbol* is used each time. Why is the flat symbol used more than once in this measure?

A1.06 Identify the last note in the top staff on page 210, measure 25. Include octave designation.

Chapter 2
Note Duration and Meter

While placement on the staff in a given clef identifies the pitch of a note, the presence (or absence) of stems and flags gives notes their durations in relation to other notes.

Example 2.01 shows note durations from longest to shortest.

Example 2.01

| breve | whole note | half note | quarter note |

| eighth note | sixteenth note | thirty-second note | sixty-fourth note |

The **breve** (also called a **double whole note**) and the **sixty-fourth note** are very rare.

A **rest** is a symbol that indicates silence, and therefore only specifies *duration*. Example 2.02 shows rest durations from longest to shortest.

Example 2.02

| double whole rest | whole rest | half rest | quarter rest |

| eighth rest | sixteenth rest | thirty-second rest | sixty-fourth rest |

A whole note or rest is equal in duration to two halves, four quarters, eight eighths, sixteen sixteenths, and so on. Because of this, a *half* note or rest is equal in duration to two quarters, four eighths, eight sixteenths, etc. Therefore, a *quarter* note or rest is equal in duration to two eighths, four sixteenths, eight thirty-seconds, and so on. Example 2.03 shows how *each note is exactly half the duration of its predecessor*. The same principle applies to rests.

Example 2.03

As mentioned in chapter one, **ties** are used to extend the duration of notes. Using ties, example 2.04 demonstrates several combinations of notes whose durations equal one whole note.

Example 2.04

Rests may not be tied because ties only extend actual sound. **Rests** *are the absence of pitch.*

Dots are added to notes or rests to extend their lengths without having to add a tied note or an additional rest. A dot extends the duration of a note or rest by half of its original duration. This is shown in example 2.05.

Example 2.05

When writing dotted notes on the staff, the dot *always* goes on the space to the *right* of the note or rest to which it is added. If the note is on a line, the dot goes in the space *above* that line, to the right of the note. Dots for *rests* go *on the third space*. Various dotted notes and rests are shown in example 2.06.

Example 2.06

"Music and silence combine strongly because music is done with silence, and silence is full of music."
— mime Marcel Marceau

Composers occasionally use a **double dot** to extend the duration of a note. A double dot adds *half* the value of the *first dot* to the note. So, the *full value* of a double dotted note is the duration of the original note *plus* half of its value (the first dot) *plus* a quarter of the original value (the second dot).

Example 2.07

Notes with flags are often *beamed* together in groups. **Beams** take the place of flags.

Example 2.08

Notice that the beams are always *straight lines*, even though they may be *slanted* at an angle.

When notes are beamed together, careful attention must be given to *stem direction*. In measures two and three of example 2.08, one might deduce that the *majority* of stems were going a certain direction, so the stems should take that same direction when beamed. This is *not* the determining factor, however. Notice in measure four that although the *majority* of stems are going downward in the un-beamed version, the correct notation when beaming is to put the stems *upward*. *The determining factor is the* farthest *note from the third line*. In measure four, the note on line 1 is farther from the third line than the note on space 4. The stems for the entire beamed group must, then, go *up*. In the case of measure two where all notes are equally distant from the third line, the preferred practice is to put the stems *down*.

"Music expresses that which cannot be said and on which it is impossible to be silent."

- author Victor Hugo

In music, the ***beat*** is a series of equal pulsations.

Example 2.09

time ▼ ▼ ▼ ▼ ▼ ▼ ▼ ▼ →

Meter is a recurring beat pattern. These recurring beats are *equal in duration* (as above), but *unequal in emphasis* (see examples 2.10—2.13). The *first* beat of each measure, called the ***downbeat***, is always the *strongest* beat.

The most basic meter is a two-beat sequence known as ***duple meter***; each strong beat is followed by a weak beat, which is in turn followed by another strong beat, and so on.

Example 2.10 duple meter

time ▼ U ▼ U ▼ U ▼ U →
     strong weak strong weak . . .

Triple meter results when a strong beat is followed by two weak beats before repeating the pattern.

Example 2.11 triple meter

time ▼ U U ▼ U U ▼ U U →
     strong weak weak strong weak weak . . .

All other metrical patterns are variants of duple and triple meter.

Quadruple meter is similar to duple meter. The third beat of the pattern is a strong beat, but not *as* strong as the downbeat.

Example 2.12 quadruple meter

time ▼ U ▽ U ▼ U ▽ U →
     strongest weak strong weak . . .

Quintuple meter has *two* forms, as shown below.

Example 2.13 quintuple meter

time ▼ U ▽ U U   or   ▼ U U ▽ U →

Bar lines are used to divide the meter into measures according to their beat patterns. This is illustrated in example 2.14 in duple, triple and quadruple meters.

Example 2.14

```
duple      ▼    U  | ▼    U  | ▼    U  | ▼    U  |
           1    2    1    2    1    2    1    2

triple     ▼  U  U | ▼  U  U | ▼  U  U |
           1  2  3   1  2  3   1  2  3

quadruple  ▼   U   ▽   U  | ▼   U   ▽   U  |
           1   2   3   4    1   2   3   4
```

In any meter, each beat may *divide* into either two equal parts or three equal parts. When a beat divides into *two* equal parts, the result is called **simple meter**. When a beat divides into *three* equal parts, the result is **compound meter**. Duple, triple, quadruple, and quintuple meters may all be either simple or compound *depending on how each beat divides*.

Example 2.15 illustrates *duple-simple* meter using the song, *Jesus Loves Me*.[1] The meter is *duple* because there are two beats per measure. The meter is *simple* because each beat divides into *two equal parts*.

Example 2.15 duple-simple

```
Je-  sus  loves me! |This  I   know,── |for  the  Bi-  ble |tells me  so.──
▼         U         |▼         U       |▼         U        |▼         U
1    +    2    +    |1    +    2    +  |1    +    2    +   |1    +    2    +
```

Three factors are at work in this example: the *beat*, the *division of the beat,* and the *rhythm* of the lyrics. **Rhythm** is the *duration of notes and rests in relation to the beat*. As an exercise to help distinguish between the *beat*, the *division of the beat*, and the *rhythm*, tap the *beat* with one hand, tap the *division of the beat* with the other hand, and speak the *rhythm*.

The rhythms in the verses of *Jesus Loves Me* are nearly identical to the division of the beat. Example 2.16 shows the *chorus* of this song, where the rhythms do *not* parallel the beat division.

---

[1] *Jesus Loves Me: Lyrics by Anna Bartlett Warner, 1860; music by William Batchelder Bradbury, 1862. Public Domain. Tune name: China.*

Example 2.16

```
Yes,——— Je-  sus |loves me,———— |yes,    Je-  sus |loves me ————|
 ▼      U     ▼     U            ▼       U      ▼      U
 1  +   2  +  |1 +  2  +         |1  +   2  +   |1  +  2  +     |
```

Again, tap the *beat* with one hand (making sure to give more emphasis to the downbeat), tap the *division of the beat* with the other hand, and speak or sing the *rhythm*.

Example 2.17 illustrates *duple-compound* meter using the song, *Oh, How I Love Jesus*.[2] The meter is *duple* again because there are two beats per measure. However, this time, the meter is *compound* because each beat divides into *three equal parts*.

Example 2.17   duple-compound

```
Oh,———    how I love |Je-———  sus,——— |oh,——— how I love |Je-———  sus,———|
 ▼        U           ▼        U       ▼       U          ▼        U
 1 + a  2 + a  |1 + a  2 + a  |1 + a  2 + a  |1 + a  2 + a |

Oh,———    how I love |Je-———  sus,— be|cause— He first — lov'd me.———|
 ▼        U           ▼        U       ▼       U          ▼        U
 1 + a  2 + a  |1 + a  2 + a  |1 + a  2 + a  |1 + a  2 + a |
```

Tap the *beat* with one hand (making sure to give more emphasis to the downbeat), tap the *division of the beat* (now *three* equal parts) with the other hand, and speak or sing the *rhythm*.

When counting the *division of the beat* in *simple* time (*two* equal parts), count "*one and two and,*" and so forth. When counting the *division of the beat* in *compound* time (*three* equal parts), count "*one and a two and a,*" etc.

Sometimes beats are not only *divided*, but even *subdivided*. In *simple* time, the beat *sub*divides into *four* equal parts, and in *compound* time, the beat *sub*divides into *six* equal parts. The excerpt from the *Hallelujah Chorus*[3] in example 2.18 shows beat *sub*division in simple time.

Example 2.18

```
Hal-——————— le — lu— jah! — |Hal-——————— le — lu— jah! —  Hal-le-|
 ▼         U      ▽      U    ▼         U      ▽       U
 1 e + a 2 e + a 3 e + a 4 e + a |1 e + a 2 e + a 3 e + a 4 e + a|

lu-— jah! —  Hal-le-lu-— jah!— Hal- |le-——————— lu-— jah!————|
 ▼         U      ▽      U    ▼         U      ▽       U
 1 e + a 2 e + a 3 e + a 4 e + a |1 e + a 2 e + a 3 e + a 4 e + a|
```

---

[2] *Oh, How I Love Jesus: Lyrics by Frederick Whitfield, 1855; music—19th century American melody. Public Domain. Tune name: Oh, How I Love Jesus.*
[3] *Hallelujah!: Lyrics from Revelation 19:6, 11:15, and 19:16; Music by George Frederick Handel, 1741. Public Domain. From the Oratorio, The Messiah.*

In this case, the *meter* is classified as *quadruple-simple* because there are *four* beats in each measure (strongest, weak, strong, weak), and the beat *divides* into *two* equal parts (and further *sub*divides *into four* equal parts). Tap the *beat* with one *foot* and speak the *rhythm*. Then tap the beat with one foot, tap the *division of the beat* with *one hand,* and speak the rhythm. Then tap the beat with one foot, tap the division of the beat with one hand, tap the *subdivision* with the *other hand,* and speak the rhythm. You will likely need to slow the *tempo* in order to effectively tap the subdivision. **Tempo** is the term for the *speed* in which the music is taken. *See example 6.05 in chapter six for a chart that describes specific tempo designations.*

To summarize, *meter* is classified using two designations: the *number of beats per measure* and *the way those beats are divided*. The most common time classifications are duple-simple, duple-compound, triple-simple, triple-compound, quadruple-simple, and quadruple-compound.

Time signatures are detailed, specific explanations of the meter. The time signature consists of two numbers, one above the other like a fraction, but *without* a line between the numbers. There are two types of time signatures—those that indicate *simple meter* and those that indicate *compound meter*. The *upper* digit alone indicates whether the meter is simple or compound. All *multiples of three* in the *upper* digit are compound, except for the number three itself. All other digits are simple.

Example 2.19

Simple Meter	Compound Meter
2/2 3/2 4/2 5/2	6/2 9/2 12/2 15/2
2/4 3/4 4/4 5/4	6/4 9/4 12/4 15/4
2/8 3/8 4/8 5/8	6/8 9/8 12/8 15/8
2/16 3/16 4/16 5/16	6/16 9/16 12/16 15/16

"If a composer could say what he had to say in words he would not bother trying to say it in music."
  - *composer* Gustav Mahler

In *simple meter*, the *top number* of the time signature *directly equals the number of beats* per measure. The *bottom number* represents the *unit*. The **unit** *is the type of note whose duration is equal to one beat*. The number 2 represents a half note, 4 a quarter note, 8 an eighth note, and so on.

Example 2.20

This example is a representative sample of simple meter and is not a comprehensive list of all possible time signatures in simple time.

duple-simple	triple-simple	quadruple-simple	quintuple-simple
2/2 = 2 half notes	3/2 = 3 half notes	4/2 = 4 half notes	5/2 = 5 half notes
2/4 = 2 quarter notes	3/4 = 3 quarter notes	4/4 = 4 quarter notes	5/4 = 5 quarter notes
2/8 = 2 eighth notes	3/8 = 3 eighth notes	4/8 = 4 eighth notes	5/8 = 5 eighth notes
2/16 = 2 sixteenth notes	3/16 = 3 sixteenth notes	4/16 = 4 sixteenth notes	5/16 = 5 sixteenth notes

Example 2.20 illustrates two important concepts. First, *any type of un-dotted note may represent the unit in simple time*. Quarter notes are the most common, but other notes may also serve as the unit. Second, *time classification* (such as duple-simple), is not the same as *time signature*. Triple-simple, for example, could be represented by $\frac{3}{2}$, $\frac{3}{4}$, $\frac{3}{8}$ or $\frac{3}{16}$.

In simple time, with the top digit indicating the number of beats per measure and the bottom digit signifying the unit, it can be deduced that *all the notes and/or rests placed within a measure will add up to the duration of the time signature*. For example, in $\frac{4}{4}$ time, all the notes/rests in each measure will equal the same duration as four quarter notes. There will be four beats in each measure, and the quarter note will represent each of those beats.

Compound meter is more complicated. Because each beat divides into three equal parts, *the unit must always be a dotted note in compound time*. Refer back to example 2.03, which shows that *un*-dotted notes naturally divide into *two* equal parts. Since a dot adds half of a note's value to that note, *dotted* notes naturally divide into *three* equal parts. Example 2.05 shows how a dotted quarter note, for example, equals a quarter note tied to an eighth note. Since a quarter note is equal in duration to two eighth notes tied together, a *dotted* quarter note equals *three* eighth notes tied together. A dotted whole note, then, equals the same duration as three tied half notes, a dotted half note equals three tied quarter notes, a dotted eighth note equals three tied sixteenth notes, etc.

In *compound* meter, the *top* digit of the time signature equals *three times the number of beats per measure*. Therefore, to determine the actual number of beats in the measure, *the top number must be divided by three.*

The *bottom* digit in compound meter represents the *division of the unit*. Since *the unit must be a dotted note* (able to divide into three equal parts), *the type of note represented by the bottom digit is one third of the unit*. In compound meter, if the bottom digit is 4, for example, representing a quarter note, it will take *three* quarter notes to equal *one* unit. Three tied quarter notes are equal in duration to one dotted half note. Thus, whenever the bottom digit is 4 in compound meter, the unit is a dotted half note.

Example 2.21

This example is a representative sample of compound meter and is not a comprehensive list of all possible time signatures in compound time.

	duple-compound	triple-compound	quadruple-compound	quintuple-compound
	6/2 = 2 dotted whole	9/2 = 3 dotted whole	12/2 = 4 dotted whole	15/2 = 5 dotted whole
	6/4 = 2 dotted half	9/4 = 3 dotted half	12/4 = 4 dotted half	15/4 = 5 dotted half
	6/8 = 2 dotted quarter	9/8 = 3 dotted quarter	12/8 = 4 dotted quarter	15/8 = 5 dotted quarter
	6/16 = 2 dotted eighth	9/16 = 3 dotted eighth	12/16 = 4 dotted eighth	15/16 = 5 dotted eighth

Example 2.21 indicates that *any type of dotted note may represent the unit in compound time*.

In compound meter, as in simple meter, *all the notes and/or rests placed within a measure will add up to the duration of the time signature*. For example, in 6/8 time, all the notes/rests in each measure will equal the same duration as six eighth notes (or two dotted quarter notes).

Example 2.22 further illustrates the difference between simple and compound meter, as well as a very important concept in rhythmic notation. In the two measures presented in this example, a time signature is *not* included. Both measures contain six eighth notes, but the notes are *beamed* differently. Knowing that the *unit* in *simple meter* divides into *two* equal parts and knowing that the *unit* in *compound meter* divides into *three* equal parts, both the time classification and the meter of each measure may be deduced.

Example 2.22

In the first measure of example 2.22, the notes are beamed together in groups that clarify that there are *three* beats, each dividing into *two* equal parts. The time classification, then, is triple-simple. Further, since each beat adds up to the duration of a quarter note, the time signature is $\frac{3}{4}$.

In the second measure of example 2.22, the same notes are beamed together in groups that clarify that there are *two* beats, each dividing into *three* equal parts. The time classification, then, is duple-compound. Further, since each beat adds up to the duration of a dotted quarter note, the time signature is $\frac{6}{8}$.

Using the song that was used in example 2.15 to illustrate the beat, the division of the beat, and rhythm in duple-simple meter, actual *notes* may now be used to illustrate these concepts.

Example 2.23

Je - sus loves me! This I know, for the Bi - ble tells me so.

There is still one strong beat and one weak beat in each measure, divided into two equal parts (counted *"one and two and"*). The presence of notes indicates the pitches *and rhythm*. The chorus of the song, used previously in example 2.16 to demonstrate how the rhythms do not always mirror the beats and their divisions, is shown below, now using notes within a time signature.

Example 2.24

Yes, Je - sus loves me, yes, Je - sus loves me,

yes, Je - sus loves me, the Bi - ble tells me so.

To become adept at rhythm reading, tap the *beat* with one hand (making sure to give more emphasis to the downbeat), tap the *division of the beat* with the other hand, and speak or sing the *rhythm*.

The song used in example 2.17 to illustrate duple-compound meter appears below in standard music notation.

Example 2.25

[Musical notation in 6/8 time with lyrics: "Oh, how I love Je-sus, oh, how I love Je-sus, oh, how I love Je-sus, be-cause He first loved me."]

In this case, duple-compound is represented by the $\frac{6}{8}$ time signature. In this meter, the dotted quarter note is prevalent since it is the unit and gets one beat. Also prevalent is the grouping of three eighth notes (grouped by *beams*), since they together form the duration of one unit. *The purpose for beaming notes together is to clarify the meter for the performer*, even though the meter is clearly identified by the time signature. Example 2.26 illustrates the same excerpt used in example 2.25, only this time, the notes are beamed *incorrectly*. Because of the misnotation, the music is very difficult to count accurately.

Example 2.26

[Musical notation in 6/8 time with measures numbered 1-8 and lyrics: "Oh, how I love Je-sus, oh, how I love Je-sus, oh, how I love Je-sus, be-cause he first loved me."]

The only measure that makes any notational sense in example 2.26 is measure six.

- Measures one and two are beamed as if the meter is $\frac{3}{4}$, which is inappropriate since $\frac{3}{4}$ denotes triple-simple. The feel then, for measures one and two, is notated as *strong, weak, weak* instead of *strong, weak*.
- Measure three would be fine if the three eighth notes were beamed together.
- The first two tied notes of measure four should be a dotted quarter note.
- In measure five, the final three eighth notes should be beamed together.
- The eighth notes in measure seven should be beamed together in groups of three.
- Measure eight is a complete disaster, even though all the note durations "add up" to the duration indicated by the time signature.

The song used in example 2.18 to illustrate beat subdivision in simple meter appears below in standard music notation. In $\frac{4}{4}$ time, the *unit* is a quarter note, the *division* is represented by eighth notes, and the *sub*division is represented by sixteenth notes.

Example 2.27

Hal - le - lu - jah! Hal - le - lu - jah! Hal - le - lu - jah! Hal - le - lu - jah! Hal - le - lu - jah!

Time signatures with a top digit *not evenly divisible by two, three, or four beats* indicate **asymmetrical meter** because symmetry, or equal balance, is not present. The most common examples of asymmetrical meter are time signatures with an upper number of five or seven.

Borrowed division occurs when, in simple time, a beat divides *unnaturally* into *three* equal parts (called a *triplet*); or when, in compound time, a beat divides *unnaturally* into *two* equal parts (called a *duplet*).

Example 2.28

O night___ di - vine,___ O___ night, O night di - vine!___

Example 2.28[4] above illustrates duplets that are *borrowed* from simple time into compound time. The *unit* in this example is a *dotted quarter note*. Natural division of the dotted quarter note is *three eighth notes*. In measure two above, beats three and four are divided evenly into *two* parts (duplets), thus the *division* of those beats is *borrowed* from simple time.

Sometimes a composer fits an unusual number of notes evenly within the space of a beat. The result is **irregular division** (or artificial grouping) of the beat. Example 2.29 shows various notes that may be used as the unit in simple and compound meters, plus their *natural divisions, borrowed divisions, irregular divisions,* and *natural subdivisions*.

---

[4] *Excerpt from* O Holy Night: *Lyrics by Placide Cappeau, 1847, translated by John Sullivan Dwight, 1855; music by Adolphe-Charles Adam, 1847. Public Domain. Tune name:* Cantique De Noel.

Example 2.29

	UNIT	DIVISION	BORROWED DIVISION	SUB-DIVISION	IRREGULAR DIVISIONS	NEXT NATURAL SUBDIVISION
SIMPLE	𝅝	𝅗𝅥 𝅗𝅥	3: 𝅗𝅥 𝅗𝅥 𝅗𝅥	♩ ♩ ♩ ♩	5: ♩♩♩♩♩ 6: ♩♩♩♩♩♩ 7: ♩♩♩♩♩♩♩	♫♫♫♫♫♫♫♫
	𝅗𝅥	♩ ♩	3: ♩ ♩ ♩	♫ ♫ ♫	5: ♫♫♫♫♫ 6: ♫♫♫♫♫♫ 7: ♫♫♫♫♫♫♫	♬♬♬♬♬♬♬♬
	♩	♫ ♫	3: ♫ ♫ ♫	♬ ♬ ♬ ♬	5 6 7	♬♬♬♬♬♬♬♬

	UNIT	BORROWED DIVISION	DIVISION	IRREGULAR DIVISIONS	SUBDIVISION
COMPOUND	𝅝.	2: ♩ ♩	♩ ♩ ♩	4: ♩♩♩♩ 5: ♩♩♩♩♩	♩♩♩♩♩♩
	𝅗𝅥.	2: ♫ ♫	♫ ♫ ♫	4: ♫♫♫♫ 5: ♫♫♫♫♫	♬♬♬♬♬♬
	♩.	2: ♬ ♬	♬ ♬ ♬	4: ♬♬♬♬ 5: ♬♬♬♬♬	♬♬♬♬♬♬

Notice that borrowed divisions and irregular divisions *require the use of a number* along the beam to indicate that *natural* division is *not* present.

In *any* meter, it is acceptable to use a *whole rest* to indicate silence for the *entire measure*. This applies only to *rests*.

Example 2.30

$\frac{2}{4}$ 𝄽 ‖ $\frac{3}{4}$ 𝄽 ‖ $\frac{4}{4}$ 𝄽 ‖ $\frac{5}{4}$ 𝄽 ‖ $\frac{6}{8}$ 𝄽 ‖

$\frac{9}{8}$ 𝄽 ‖ $\frac{12}{8}$ 𝄽 ‖ $\frac{3}{8}$ 𝄽 ‖ $\frac{6}{4}$ 𝄽 ‖ $\frac{12}{2}$ 𝄽 ‖

When two adjacent beats of rest are required in $\frac{3}{4}$ meter, two quarter rests are used instead of one half rest.

Example 2.31

$\frac{3}{4}$ ♩ 𝄽 𝄽 $\frac{3}{4}$ ♩ 𝄼 🚫

Because 4/4 is used so frequently, it has been assigned the designation *common meter*, which is abbreviated by the symbol 𝄴. 2/2 meter is typically used when a fast tempo is required for duple-simple, and is called *cut time*. The abbreviation symbol for cut time is 𝄵.

It is helpful to be aware of *rhythmic patterns* that occur within a beat. Example 2.32 demonstrates five possible rhythmic patterns with the quarter note as the unit. Each of these patterns makes use of partial subdivision of the beat.

Example 2.32

Sometimes music is composed in such a way that the piece does *not* begin on a *downbeat*. This is important to remember when determining the time classification of a piece by ear or when transcribing music by ear. *Not every composition begins on beat one*. The note or notes that precede the first downbeat are called the **anacrusis**, or **pick-up note(s)**.

Example 2.33

O come, let us a - dore Him, O come, let us a - dore Him, O come let us a - dore Him,___ Christ,_____ the Lord.

The musical notation in example 2.33[5] commences with the *anacrusis* (*not rests* prior to the pick-up note), thus causing the measure containing the anacrusis to contain fewer beats than indicated by the time signature. The *first measure of music*, when numbering the measures, is the first *full* measure. *Partial measures* of pick-up notes are *not* counted in measure numbering. Further, the *final measure of the composition will be an incomplete measure*, with the *remainder* of that measure constituted by the pick-up measure at the beginning of the composition. The first line of a composition is indented.

---

[5] O Come, Let Us Adore Him: *Traditional lyrics; music from Wade's* Cantus Diversi, *1751. Public Domain. Tune name:* Adeste Fideles (*refrain only*).

When determining the meter of music by ear, listen for strong and weak beats to determine whether the piece begins on a downbeat or anacrusis. A helpful device in discerning meter aurally is to attempt *conducting* the piece using various meter patterns to see which one "fits." The beat patterns for conducting duple, triple, and quadruple meters are shown below.

Example 2.34

Basic Conducting Patterns
(right-handed)

Duple   Triple   Quadruple

An advanced feature of *rhythm* is **syncopation**, which results when the natural emphasis of the meter is temporarily displaced. This happens when notes fall just before or just after strong beats, but not *on* those beats. This rhythmic activity *between* the beats (especially when notes are held over a beat) causes the steady pulse of the beat to seem disrupted until the syncopation ends.

Example 2.35

> "The pleasure we obtain from music comes from counting, but counting unconsciously."
> - philosopher and mathematician Gottfried Wilhelm Leibniz

In this type of syncopation, the notes fall between beats (on the "*and*" of each beat), and are *counter to the beat*. Some refer to this type of syncopation as *off-beat*. Tap the *beat* with one hand and the *rhythm* with the other hand. Then, tap only the *downbeat* of each measure with one hand, and tap the *rhythm* of the entire example with the other hand.

Notice how the second measure of example 2.35 has two eighth notes tied together (but not *beamed* together) in the middle of the measure. This is helpful notation for the performer. It is always important for the music reader to be able to *visually see* on the staff where each *strong beat* lies. Even without the numbers below the staff, at a glance, the reader can see where beat three (the second strong beat of the measure) falls.

Example 2.36 shows this measure with a quarter note replacing the two tied eighth notes.

Example 2.36

"If music be the food of love, play on."
- author William Shakespeare, Twelfth Night

The *rhythm* is exactly the same as the second measure of example 2.35, but the *notation* is not as clear since the reader cannot visually see where beat three falls.

Sometimes, syncopation is achieved simply by putting **accent marks** above or below the notes to be emphasized that counter the beat. Accent marks (>) instruct the performer to emphasize those notes, and are explained in greater detail in chapter six.

Example 2.37

Here, the emphases of each measure are on *beat one*, the *"and of two,"* and *beat four*. Tap the beat with one hand and the rhythm with the other, being careful to observe the accents. Recent composers have elected to show these accents by using deliberate *alternate beaming*. When syncopation is the desired effect in a recurring rhythmic pattern, the notation in example 2.38 *is* acceptable as an alternative to the notation in example 2.37.

Example 2.38

For the time being, it is not important to be concerned with such exceptions or attempt to write them. They are mentioned here solely as a matter of interest and awareness.

A unique type of syncopation is **hemiola**, in which the syncopation is not always obvious to the eye, but is easily heard. The aural effect of hemiola is that the meter has changed, when in fact, it has not. Hemiola is different from *borrowed division* in that borrowed division applies to how the beats are *divided* and hemiola applies to the perceived shifting of the *actual beats* themselves.

Example 2.39

Another example of hemiola is shown in example 6.18 in chapter six (page 163).

In this piano sonata[6] by Mozart, the aural affect (illustrated by the symbols for strong and weak beats) is that the meter changes in measures eight and nine from $\frac{3}{4}$ to $\frac{3}{2}$. It *sounds* as if *the beats have slowed down to half their original pace* even though the *rhythm* in the top staff is much "busier" than in previous measures. Mozart achieved this sensation by shifting the emphasis provided by the pianist's left hand (bottom staff), which was primarily providing the downbeat until measure eight.

Sometimes composers find it easier to write a piece in simple meter even when they want it performed in compound meter. To indicate that the music is to be performed in compound meter, the composer gives the instruction at the beginning of the piece that it has a *swing* or *shuffle* feel. The instruction that two even eighth notes are replaced with a quarter-eighth triplet is also provided, as illustrated in example 2.40.[7]

Example 2.40

This concludes the introduction to note duration and meter. Intervals will be covered in chapter three.

---

[6] Piano Sonata, K. 283, Movement I (Allegro): *Wolfgang Amadeus Mozart, 1774 (age eighteen). Public Domain.*
[7] Hail to the Chief: *Lyrics by Albert Gamse; music by James Sanderson, circa 1821. Public Domain.*

Assignments and Drills

Assignment 2.01

The objective of this assignment is legible and efficient note and rest writing.

1. Convert the note durations below as instructed by adding stems (and flags if necessary). Be careful to put the stems on the correct side of the note head, going the correct direction. REFER BACK TO EXAMPLES 1.18, 1.19, 2.01, AND 2.06 IF NECESSARY.

   half note   sixteenth note   quarter note   eighth note   thirty-second note   eighth note   dotted half note   thirty-second note

2. Write three whole rests, three half rests, three quarter rests, three eighth rests, and three sixteenth rests on the staff below. Be sure the rests appear on the proper spaces of the staff. REFER BACK TO EXAMPLE 2.02 IF NECESSARY.

3. Using *un-beamed dotted eighth notes* only, write the following notes on the staff in order:
   C4   G#4   E♭5   F4   F♭♭5   B×3   A5   D#5   D4   A♭4

   REFER BACK TO EXAMPLE 2.06 IF NECESSARY.

4. Copy the notes (and dots) from problem number 3 above to the staff below, but this time, beam the notes together in groups of two. REFER BACK TO EXAMPLE 2.08 IF NECESSARY.

Assignment 2.02

The objective of this assignment is to accurately notate rhythms in simple meter.

1. The chart below gives the rhythms for the first four measures of the song *My Country, Tis of Thee*.[8] Convert the rhythms to actual note values on space two of the staff below. The first measure is done for you. REFER BACK TO EXAMPLES 2.16 AND 2.23 IF NECESSARY.

My	coun-	try,	'tis———	of	thee,	sweet	land	of	lib=———	er-	ty,
▼	U	U	▼	U	U	▼	U	U	▼	U	U
1	+ 2	+ 3	+ 1	+ 2	+ 3	+ 1	+ 2	+ 3	+ 1	+ 2	+ 3 +

2. The meter in problem number one above is classified as triple-simple. Convert it from ¾ to 3/2 on the staff below. REFER BACK TO EXAMPLE 2.20 IF NECESSARY.

3. Convert the example again to 3/8 on the staff below. Do not use beams. REFER BACK TO EXAMPLE 2.20 IF NECESSARY.

---

[8] *My Country, 'Tis of Thee: Lyrics by Samuel Francis Smith, 1832. Music by anonymous, 1744. Public Domain. Tune name: America.*

Assignment 2.03

The objective of this assignment is to accurately notate rhythms in simple meter.

1. The chart below gives the rhythms for the first four measures (plus anacrusis) of the song *Polly Wolly Doodle*.[9] Convert the rhythms to actual note values on space two of the staff below. Beam notes according to their beats. The anacrusis and final measure are done for you. REFER BACK TO EXAMPLES 2.18 AND 2.27 IF NECESSARY.

2. The meter in problem number one above is classified as duple-simple. Convert it from $\frac{2}{4}$ to $\frac{2}{2}$ on the staff below. REFER BACK TO EXAMPLE 2.20 IF NECESSARY.

---

[9] Polly Wolly Doodle: *Traditional American Folk Song, circa 1880. Public Domain.*

Assignment 2.04

The objective of this assignment is to accurately notate rhythms in compound meter.

1. The chart below gives the rhythms for the first four measures (plus anacrusis) of the song *We're off to See the Wizard*[10] from the musical *The Wizard of Oz*. Convert the rhythms to actual note values on space two of the staff below. Beam notes according to their beats. The anacrusis and final measure are done for you. A tie is necessary to extend the duration of a note across the beat in measure two. REFER BACK TO EXAMPLES 2.17 AND 2.25 IF NECESSARY.

2. The meter in problem number one above is classified as duple-compound. Convert it from $\frac{6}{8}$ to $\frac{6}{16}$ on the staff below. REFER BACK TO EXAMPLE 2.21 IF NECESSARY.

---

[10] *We're off to See the Wizard:* Lyrics by E. Y. Harburg; Music by Harold Arlen. © 1938, 1939 (Renewed 1966, 1967) Metro-Goldwyn-Mayer, Inc. Administered by EMI. Worldwide print rights controlled by Warner Bros. Publications, Inc.

Assignment 2.05

The objective of this assignment is to accurately notate rhythms in compound meter.

1. The chart below gives the rhythms for the first four measures (plus anacrusis) of the hymn *Blessed Assurance, Jesus Is Mine.*[11] Convert the rhythms to actual note values on space two of the staff below. Beam notes according to their beats. The pick-up notes are done for you. REFER BACK TO EXAMPLES 2.17 AND 2.25 IF NECESSARY.

```
Bless-ed as- sur———— ance,——— Je-sus is mine! ———————— Oh, what a
  U      ▼            U    U    ▼         U    U
  3 + a  1 + a  2 + a  3 + a  1 + a  2 + a  3 + a

fore————taste——of glo-ry di-vine!————————
  ▼          U    U        ▼       U
  1 + a  2 + a  3 + a  1 + a  2 + a
```

[staff in 9/8 with pick-up notes for "Bless-ed as-" labeled measures 1, 2, 3, 4 with lyrics: Bless-ed as - sur - ance, Je-sus is mine! Oh, what a fore - taste of glo - ry di - vine!]

2. The meter in problem number one above is classified as triple-compound. Convert it from $^9_8$ to $^9_4$ on the staff below. REFER BACK TO EXAMPLE 2.21 IF NECESSARY.

[staff in 9/4 with pick-up notes labeled measures 1, 2, 3, 4 with lyrics: Bless-ed as - sur - ance, Je-sus is mine! Oh, what a fore - taste of glo - ry di - vine!]

---

[11] Blessed Assurance, Jesus Is Mine: *Lyrics by Fanny Crosby, 1873; Music by Phoebe Knapp, Public Domain.* Tune *name:* Assurance.

Assignment 2.06

The objective of this assignment is to interpret the meter and accurately identify missing time signatures in both simple and compound time.

Directions: The measures below are in a variety of time signatures. Insert the correct time signature for each. If you have trouble, remember that notes that are beamed together constitute the duration of a unit. REFER BACK TO EXAMPLES 2.20 AND 2.21 IF NECESSARY.

Note Duration and Meter

Assignment 2.07

The objective of this assignment is to effectively beam eighth notes and sixteenth notes according to the beat.

Directions: Re-notate the examples using beams to clarify the meter. REFER BACK TO EXAMPLES 2.25 AND 2.26 IF NECESSARY (EXAMPLE 2.25 SHOWS CORRECT BEAMING, EXAMPLE 2.26 SHOWS INCORRECT BEAMING).

Assignment 2.08

The objective of this assignment is to identify errors in rhythm notation and discover ways of clarifying the meter through thoughtful notation.

Directions: Re-notate each system below, correcting the errors in notation or clarifying the meter by re-beaming the notes and/or using alternate note durations. Make sure that your changes affect only the way note and rest durations are interpreted— the actual durations of note and rest values must not be altered. The first one is done for you. REFER BACK TO EXAMPLES 2.25, 2.26, AND 2.36 IF NECESSARY.

Assignment 2.09

The objective of this assignment is to identify and correct errors in pitch and rhythm notation.

Directions: Each measure below contains an error in notation. Write the correct notation in the space provided next to each measure. REFER BACK TO EXAMPLES 1.10, 1.18, 2.06, 2.08, 2.22, 2.25, 2.26, 2.31, AND 2.36 IF NECESSARY.

Questions for Review

1. How many thirty-second notes would it take to equal the duration of one quarter note?

2. What does a double dot do to the duration of a note?

3. Define the following terms: beat, meter, rhythm, syncopation.

4. Explain the difference between simple and compound meter.

5. How can a person deduce from the time signature whether the meter is simple or compound?

6. In simple time, what do the upper and lower digits of the time signature indicate?

7. In compound time, what do the upper and lower digits of the time signature indicate?

8. What is meant by the term *unit*?

9. Why must the unit always be a dotted note in compound meter?

10. What is meant by the term *borrowed division* and why is it named as such?

11. On a separate sheet of paper, illustrate the division, borrowed division, subdivision, irregular divisions, and further subdivision of a quarter note.

12. On a separate sheet of paper, illustrate the borrowed division, natural division, irregular divisions, and subdivision of a dotted half note.

13. What is the purpose of beaming notes that require flags?

14. What is meant by the term *anacrusis*?

15. In a composition, how is it determined which measure is considered *measure one*?

Assignments for Use with Anthology

A2.01 Identify the *time classification* (duple-simple, etc.) and the *unit* of each composition.

- Corelli: *Trio Sonata*, Opus 4, No. 11, Allemanda. Anthology page 67.
- Bach: *Invention No. 4 in D Minor*, BWV 775. Anthology page 106.
- Bach: *Invention No. 12 in A Major*, BWV 783. Anthology page 107.
- Bach: *Mass in B Minor*, BWV 232, Crucifixus. Anthology page 126.
- Haydn: *Piano Sonata in D Major*, Hob. XVI / 37, third movement (Finale). Anthology page 148.
- Beethoven: *Piano Sonata No. 8 in C Minor*, Opus 13, ("Pathétique"), third movement (Allegro). Anthology page 274.
- Zelter: *Volkstümliches Lied*, Der könig in Thule. Anthology page 311.
- Debussy: *Prelude to "Afternoon of a Faun."* Anthology page 432.
- Bartók: *Mikrokosmos*, Bulgarian Rhythm, No. 115, Vol. IV. Anthology page 479.
- Bartók: *Mikrokosmos*, Syncopation, No. 133, Vol. V. Anthology page 481.

A2.02 Identify the *time classification* and the *unit* of the following measures of Bartók: *Music for String Instruments, Percussion, and Celesta*, first movement (Andante). Anthology pages 484-489.

- Measure 4
- Measure 5
- Measure 6
- Measure 17
- Measure 21
- Measure 23
- Measure 24
- Measure 82

A2.03 Do the note values "add up" to the time signature in the final measure of the composition in A2.02? Why or why not?

A2.04 Explain the length of the note on the downbeat of the top staff on page 317, measure 11.

Chapter 3
Intervals

An *interval* is the distance between pitches. All intervals are classified numerically from 1 to 8, with the interval of 1 referred to as a *unison* and the interval of 8 known as an *octave*. Thus, the names of the intervals are unison (1), second (2), third (3), fourth (4), fifth (5), sixth (6), seventh (7), and octave (8). Intervals larger than an octave, called *compound intervals*, may be *reduced* by an octave to determine their *simple* classification. A 9th, when the octave is subtracted, becomes a 2nd, a 10th becomes a 3rd, an 11th becomes a 4th, etc.

The *numeric designation* of an interval is determined by calculating the number of lines and spaces used from the bottom note to the top note (including those two notes). In example 3.01, even though clefs are not present, the intervals are numerically identifiable since each line and space on the staff represents a different letter name.

Example 3.01

unison second third fourth fifth sixth seventh octave

Example 3.01 shows that if the bottom note of the interval is on a line, all odd-numbered intervals will also be on a line and if the bottom note is on a space, all odd-numbered intervals will also be on a space.

The intervals in example 3.01 are **harmonic intervals.** The term *harmonic* simply means that the notes are *simultaneous* with each other. The same intervals, shown in example 3.02 are *melodic intervals*, meaning that they are *not* simultaneous, but rather *in succession*.

Example 3.02

unison second third fourth fifth sixth seventh octave

Care must be taken when writing the *harmonic* interval of a *second*.

Example 3.03

"Music and rhythm find their way into the secret places of the soul."
- Greek philosopher Plato

The two notes comprising a harmonic second must be written on *adjacent* lines and spaces. The *higher* of the two notes is *always* written to the *right*. Even if a stem is involved, the higher note always goes to the right, regardless of stem direction.

When writing harmonic seconds, if the notes are dotted and the lower of the two notes is on a line, the dot for that note goes *below* the line. This is the exception to the principle explained in example 2.06. If this exception is not followed, the result appears to be a double-dotted note on the higher of the two notes and no dot on the lower note.

Example 3.04

"Inspiration is enough to give expression to the tone in singing, especially when the song is without words."
- composer Franz Liszt

While the process for identifying the numeric classification of intervals requires painstaking *counting* of lines and spaces at first, potential music theorists must practice *recognizing* intervals by sight so that they may quickly and accurately identify them. The ability to *see* an interval and immediately *know* what it is will prove to be necessary and invaluable in the continued study of music theory because *all further study of harmony depends on this skill*.

Intervals are classified by number *and* by quality. **Quality** is the term for the specific *type* of interval *within* the numeric classification. For example, if a treble clef had been present in example 3.04, the interval would have been a *minor* second (half step), because the notes would have been E - F. If a bass clef had been present in example 3.04, the notes would have been G - A, making the *quality* of the interval a *major* second (whole step).

Intervals fall into two categories by quality: Those that are *perfect* and those that are *major or minor*.

Perfect intervals are intervals of a *unison, fourth, fifth,* and *octave*.

The intervals of a *second, third, sixth,* and *seventh* may be **major** or **minor**.

If a *perfect* interval (P) is *increased* in size by a half step, its *quality* becomes **augmented** (A).

If a *perfect* interval (P) is *decreased* in size by a half step, its *quality* becomes **diminished** (d).

All *unaltered*[1] unisons and octaves are *perfect*. A *perfect unison* is also called a **prime unison**.

All *unaltered* fourths are *perfect* EXCEPT FOR F - B, which is *augmented*. This is illustrated in example 3.05.

Example 3.05

P4   P4   P4   A4   P4   P4   P4

The interval F - B *sounds* different than all the other fourths above because it is *larger*. All the other fourths in example 3.05 are *perfect* fourths because they are exactly *five* half steps from bottom to top. The interval F - B, however, is *six* half steps from bottom to top. Therefore, it is *augmented*.

Example 3.06

Five half steps between A and D (P4)

Six half steps between F and B (A4)

To convert F - B from an *augmented fourth* to a *perfect fourth*, the F may be raised *or* the B may be lowered.

Example 3.07

P4   P4

"Though everything else may appear shallow and repulsive, even the smallest task in music is so absorbing, and carries us so far away from town, country, earth, and all worldly things, that it is truly a blessed gift of God."
- composer Felix Mendelssohn

---

[1] The term *unaltered* means *not affected by accidentals*.

Anything that applies to an *unaltered* interval is also true of intervals where both notes are affected by the *same* accidentals.

Example 3.08

P4   P4   P4   A4   A4   A4

In the first measure of example 3.08, E - A is a perfect fourth. When both notes are raised a half step in the next measure, the interval remains a perfect fourth. When both notes are lowered a half step in the third measure, the *interval* remains unchanged. The same principle applies to the augmented fourth (F - B) that follows in measures four through six.

All *unaltered* fifths are *perfect* EXCEPT FOR B - F, which is *diminished*.

Example 3.09

P5   P5   P5   P5   P5   P5   d5

The interval B - F *sounds* different than all the other fifths in example 3.09 because it is *smaller*. All the other fifths are *perfect* fifths because they are exactly *seven* half steps from bottom to top. The interval B - F, however, is *six* half steps from bottom to top. Therefore, it is *diminished*. To convert B - F from a *diminished fifth* to a *perfect fifth*, the F may be raised *or* the B may be lowered.

Seconds, thirds, sixths, and sevenths may be classified as major or minor, but *not* perfect.

If a *major* interval (M) is *increased* in size by a half step, its *quality* becomes *augmented* (A).

If a *major* interval (M) is *decreased* in size by a half step, its *quality* becomes *minor* (m).

If a *minor* interval (m) is *increased* in size by a half step, its *quality* becomes *major* (M).

If a *minor* interval (m) is *decreased* in size by a half step, its *quality* becomes *diminished* (d).

All *unaltered* seconds are *major* EXCEPT FOR B - C and E - F, which are *minor*.

Example 3.10

M2   M2   m2   M2   M2   M2   m2

Refer back to examples 1.12 and 1.13 in chapter one, where this concept was introduced using the terms *whole step* and *half step* instead of *major second* and *minor second*.

***Unaltered* thirds constructed on C, F, and G are *major*. All others are *minor*.**

Example 3.11

M3   m3   m3   M3   M3   m3   m3

The thirds built on C, F, and G are four half steps apart. The thirds built on D, E, A, and B are only three half steps apart.

Inversion is the process of rearranging the order of notes within an interval so that the note that was on top is now on the bottom and the note that was on the bottom is now on the top. This is accomplished by keeping one note in the same location (fixed) and raising or lowering the other note *one octave* to the *other side* of the fixed note. Example 3.12 demonstrates the *inversions* of the seconds in example 3.10.

Example 3.12

original interval: M2   M2   m2   M2   M2   M2   m2

inversion: m7   m7   M7   m7   m7   m7   M7

When the *seconds* were inverted, they became *sevenths*. When the *major* intervals were inverted, they became *minor*, and when the *minor* intervals were inverted, they became *major*.

The same principle applies to thirds and sixths. When *thirds* are inverted, they become *sixths*; *major* inverts to *minor* and *minor* inverts to *major*.

Example 3.13

original interval: M3, m3, m3, M3, M3, m3, m3
inversion: m6, M6, M6, m6, m6, M6, M6

A helpful way to quickly determine the quality of larger intervals (such as sixths and sevenths) is to *invert* them (to thirds and seconds), knowing that *major* intervals invert to *minor*.

Fourths and fifths invert to each other. *Perfect* intervals invert to *perfect* intervals, *augmented* invert to *diminished*, and *diminished* invert to *augmented*.

Example 3.14

P4, P4, P4, A4, P4, P4, P4
P5, P5, P5, d5, P5, P5, P5

Two intervals that sound the same but are spelled differently are **enharmonic intervals**. A few such intervals are shown in example 3.15.

Example 3.15

P4, A3, m3, A2, A4, d5, M6, d7, M7, d8, M2, d3, M3, d4

The interval of the A4/d5 shown in the third measure of example 3.15 is referred to as a **tritone** (made of three whole steps). The *tritone* is the most commonly-encountered enharmonic interval in actual music.

If an augmented fourth is increased in size by a half step, it becomes a *doubly-augmented (AA)* fourth. If a diminished fifths is decreased in size, it becomes a *doubly-diminished (dd)* fifth. Such intervals do occur in music, but rarely.

Example 3.16

AA4   dd5

> "Music is God's gift to man, the only art of Heaven given to earth, the only art of earth we take to Heaven."
> - poet Walter Savage Landor

The AA4 in example 3.16 is *enharmonic* with a P5, and the dd5 is *enharmonic* with a P4. See example 3.17 for the enharmonic spellings of the intervals in example 3.16

Example 3.17

P5   P4

When inverting octaves, they become unisons, and when inverting unisons, they become octaves. Example 3.14 showed that *perfect* intervals invert to *perfect* intervals, *augmented* invert to *diminished*, and *diminished* invert to *augmented*, using fourths and fifths as examples. This same principle applies to octaves and unisons with one exception. An *augmented octave* will *not* invert.

Example 3.18

1   2   3   4   5
P8 P1   A1 d8   P1 P8   d8 A1   A8 A1
                                            d8

- In measure one above, the P8 inverts to a P1.
- In measure two, the A1 inverts to a d8.
- In measure three, the P1 inverts to a P8.
- In measure four, the d8 inverts to an A1.
- Measure five shows what happens when attempts are made to invert the A8. It *reduces* to an A1, which in turn inverts to a d8.

A perfect unison (P1) *cannot* be altered to become *diminished* (d1 does not exist).

This concludes the introduction to intervals. Scales and keys will be covered in chapter four.

INTERVALS

Assignments and Drills

Assignment 3.01

The objective of this assignment is efficient numeric classification of intervals.

Instructions: Write the *numeric classification* of each harmonic interval in the space provided. Measure one is done for you. Try to complete the assignment in less than five minutes. REFER BACK TO EXAMPLE 3.01 IF NECESSARY.

Assignment 3.02

The objective of this assignment is efficient quality designation of intervals.

Instructions: Go back through assignment 3.01 and indicate the *quality* of each interval. For example, the answer to measure one is m3, measure two is P4, etc. Try to complete the assignment in less than ten minutes. REFER BACK TO EXAMPLES 3.05—3.14 IF NECESSARY.

Assignment 3.03

The objective of this assignment is efficient numeric classification of intervals.

Instructions: Write the *numeric classification* of each harmonic interval in the space provided. Measure one is done for you. Try to complete the assignment in less than four minutes. REFER BACK TO EXAMPLE 3.01 IF NECESSARY.

7

Assignment 3.04

The objective of this assignment is efficient quality designation of intervals.

Instructions: Go back through assignment 3.03 and indicate the *quality* of each interval. For example, the answer to measure one is M7, etc. Try to complete the assignment in less than ten minutes. REFER BACK TO EXAMPLES 3.05—3.14 IF NECESSARY.

Assignment 3.05

The objective of this assignment is efficient identification of interval qualities.

Instructions: Each system contains a different numeric classification of intervals. The first system has thirds, the second system has fourths, the third system has fifths, the fourth system has sixths, and the final system has sevenths. Write the *quality* of each harmonic interval in the space provided. Measure one is done for you. Try to complete the assignment in less than ten minutes. REFER BACK TO EXAMPLES 3.01, 3.05—3.14, AND 3.16 IF NECESSARY.

Assignment 3.06

The objective of this assignment is creation and identification of enharmonic intervals.

Instructions: To the right of each interval in assignment 3.05, write an enharmonic interval and label it below. For example, in the space next to the A3 in measure one, write the notes G (second line) and C (third space), and label the interval P4. When writing an enharmonic interval, one note stays the same as in the original interval, but the other note will be respelled. REFER BACK TO EXAMPLES 3.15, 3.16, AND 3.17 IF NECESSARY.

Assignment 3.07

The objective of this assignment is efficient inversion of intervals.

1. In the extra space in measures 1 through 15, invert each second to a seventh.
2. In the extra space in measures 16 through 30, invert each third to a sixth.

Try to complete the assignment in less than six minutes.
REFER BACK TO EXAMPLES 3.12 AND 3.13 IF NECESSARY.

Assignment 3.08

The objective of this assignment is efficient identification of intervals.

Instructions: Go back through assignment 3.07 and label each interval. For example, measure one will be M2, m7; measure two will be m2, M7. Try to complete the assignment in less than fifteen minutes. REFER BACK TO THE BOTTOM OF PAGE 60 AND EXAMPLES 3.10—3.14 IF NECESSARY.

INTERVALS

Assignment 3.09

The objective of this assignment is efficient inversion of intervals.

1. In the extra space in measures 1 through 15, invert each sixth.
2. In the extra space in measures 16 through 30, invert each seventh.

Try to complete the assignment in less than five minutes.
REFER BACK TO EXAMPLES 3.12 AND 3.13 IF NECESSARY.

Assignment 3.10

The objective of this assignment is efficient identification of intervals.

Instructions: Go back through assignment 3.09 and label each interval. Try to complete the assignment in less than fifteen minutes.

REFER BACK TO THE BOTTOM OF PAGE 60 AND EXAMPLES 3.10—3.14 IF NECESSARY.

Assignment 3.11

The objective of this assignment is efficient identification of intervals.

Instructions: Identify each interval by numeric classification *and* quality. Measures 1 through 15 are harmonic; measures 16 through 30 are melodic. Measures 1 and 16 are done for you. Try to complete the assignment in less than ten minutes. REFER BACK TO EXAMPLES 3.01, 3.02, AND 3.05—3.14 IF NECESSARY.

Measure 1 is labeled: d5

Measure 16 is labeled: m3

Assignment 3.12

The objective of this assignment is efficient identification of intervals.

Instructions: Identify each interval by numeric classification *and* quality. Measures 1 through 15 are harmonic; measures 16 through 30 are melodic. Try to complete the assignment in less than ten minutes. REFER BACK TO EXAMPLES 3.01, 3.02, 3.05—3.14, AND 3.16 IF NECESSARY.

Assignment 3.13

The objective of this assignment is creation and identification of enharmonic intervals.

Instructions: To the right of each *harmonic* interval (measures 1 through 15 only), write an enharmonic interval and label it below. For example, in the space next to the d2 in measure one, write the notes A# (second space) twice, and label the interval P1, or write the notes B♭ (third line) twice, and label it P1. REFER BACK TO EXAMPLE 3.15, 3.16, AND 3.17 IF NECESSARY.

Assignment 3.14

The objective of this assignment is efficient creation of intervals.

Instructions: Create the requested harmonic interval *above* the note provided without altering the note that is given. Try to complete the assignment in less than fifteen minutes.
REFER BACK TO EXAMPLES 3.01—3.16 IF NECESSARY.

1. M2
2. m3
3. m6
4. M6
5. P5
6. m2
7. M3
8. P4
9. m7
10. M7
11. P4
12. A5
13. m3
14. m7
15. P5
16. m2
17. m2
18. m3
19. M3
20. A8
21. M2
22. M3
23. d3
24. m2
25. M6
26. A1
27. P4
28. P5
29. m2
30. M3

Intervals

Assignment 3.15

The objective of this assignment is efficient creation of intervals.

Instructions: Create the requested harmonic interval *above* the note provided without altering the note that is given. Try to complete the assignment in less than fifteen minutes.
REFER BACK TO EXAMPLES 3.01—3.16 IF NECESSARY.

1. M6
2. m6
3. M3
4. M3
5. P5
6. M6
7. m3
8. M3
9. m7
10. A2
11. d3
12. P5
13. M3
14. M2
15. A3
16. M2
17. d2
18. d4
19. M3
20. d3
21. M2
22. m3
23. m7
24. AA4
25. m6
26. m2
27. d8
28. dd5
29. A4
30. P4

Assignment 3.16

The objective of this assignment is efficient creation of intervals.

Instructions: Create the requested harmonic interval *below* the note provided without altering the note that is given. Try to complete the assignment in less than fifteen minutes.
REFER BACK TO EXAMPLES 3.01—3.16 IF NECESSARY.

1. M2
2. m3
3. P4
4. P5
5. m6
6. M7
7. m3
8. M3
9. m3
10. m7
11. M6
12. P5
13. M7
14. m3
15. P4
16. m2
17. m2
18. m3
19. M2
20. A7
21. m2
22. A2
23. M2
24. M7
25. A8
26. d5
27. A4
28. M3
29. P4
30. M3

Assignment 3.17

The objective of this assignment is efficient creation of intervals.

Instructions: Create the requested harmonic interval *below* the note provided without altering the note that is given. Try to complete the assignment in less than fifteen minutes.
REFER BACK TO EXAMPLES 3.01—3.16 IF NECESSARY.

#	Interval	#	Interval	#	Interval	#	Interval	#	Interval
1	A5	2	M3	3	P4	4	d5	5	m6
6	M7	7	M6	8	P5	9	P4	10	m3
11	M6	12	A3	13	d2	14	M3	15	P4
16	P4	17	P5	18	d4	19	M2	20	P4
21	m2	22	m2	23	m7	24	M6	25	m3
26	M3	27	m7	28	M7	29	P5	30	A8

Assignment 3.18

The objective of this assignment is efficient identification of compound intervals.

Instructions: Identify each *compound interval* on the grand staff below. In the second blank, write the *reduction* of the interval. Try to complete the assignment in less than ten minutes. Measure one is done for you. Refer back to the first paragraph of chapter three if necessary.

m10 m3

Questions for Review

1. What is the difference between *melodic* and *harmonic* intervals?

2. What is the difference between the terms *harmonic* and *enharmonic*?

3. What is meant by *numeric classification* of intervals?

4. What is meant by the *quality* of the interval?

5. Why is the interval of F - B an *augmented* fourth when all other unaltered fourths are *perfect*?

6. Explain the process of inversion.

7. What is meant by the term *tritone*?

Assignments for Use with Anthology

A3.01 Identify the numeric classification of each harmonic interval in <u>measures 1-10</u> of D. Scarlatti: *Sonata in D Major*, Allegrissimo. Anthology page 137. For example, in measure one, the first interval is a third, the second interval is a third, and the third interval is a fifth.

A3.02 Identify the harmonic interval (including quality) between the notes on each *downbeat* of <u>measures 2-31</u> of the minuet on page 77 of the anthology. For example, measure two is **m3** (B to D), measure 3 is **M3** (C to E). NOTE: THE **F** NOTES IN MEASURES 7, 18, AND 23 ARE ACTUALLY **F#**. DISREGARD THE MINATURE NOTE (CALLED A GRACE NOTE) FOR THE TIME BEING.

A3.03 Identify the harmonic interval between the notes on each *downbeat* of the march on page 76 of the anthology. NOTE: ALL OF THE NOTES ON **F** AND **C** ARE ACTUALLY **F#** AND **C#**.

A3.04 Identify each of the harmonic intervals between the lowest two parts (*bass* and *tenor*) of Gervaise: *Pavane Passamaize*. Anthology page 38. NOTE: ALL OF THE NOTES ON **B** ARE ACTUALLY **B-FLAT**. THE TWO E NOTES WITH THE FLAT SYMBOL ABOVE THEM ARE TO BE FLATTED. (IN THE RENAISSANCE, PERFORMERS OFTEN KNEW WHEN TO ADD ACCIDENTALS SO THEY WERE NOT ALWAYS WRITTEN INTO THE SCORE. THIS IS CALLED *MUSICA FICTA*. THE EDITOR HAS ADDED THEM HERE ABOVE THE STAVES.)

A3.05 Identify the following intervals in Beethoven: *Piano Sonata No. 8 in C Minor*, Opus 13, ("Pathétique"), first movement (Allegro). Anthology pages 265-266.

Be sure to check the entire measure for accidentals in each instance. All of the following are in the right hand of the piano:

- Measure 35, beat 4. _____
- Measure 36, beat 2. _____
- Measure 36, beat 4. _____
- Measure 39, beat 4. _____
- Measure 40, beat 2. _____
- Measure 121, beat 4. _____

Chapter 4
Scales and Keys

The word *scale* comes from the Latin word for *ladder* (scala). A **scale** is a succession of ascending and/or descending pitches within the range of an octave. Western music utilizes two *types* of scales: *diatonic* and *non-diatonic*. This chapter focuses primarily on *diatonic* scales and the keys they produce.

Diatonic scales establish *keys* or *modes*. A **key** is based on a specific *scale*, with the starting note referred to as the **tonic** (the *foundational* tone for each scale/key). Thus, the **tonality** (tonal center) of a key is based on the starting note of the scale to which the key belongs.

As scales took shape in the history of Western music, seven **modes** (*types* of keys) emerged, each based on a different unaltered note, and each using all the remaining unaltered notes in succession. Each mode and its respective name is shown in ascending fashion in example 4.01 below.

Example 4.01

1. Aeolian mode (tonic is A)
2. Locrian mode (tonic is B)
3. Ionian mode (tonic is C)
4. Dorian mode (tonic is D)
5. Phrygian mode (tonic is E)
6. Lydian mode (tonic is F)
7. Mixolydian mode (tonic is G)

As music composition evolved, *two* of these modes usurped prominence: the *Aeolian* mode, now called *minor* because it is used with less frequency, and the *Ionian* mode, now called *major* because it is used more frequently. In recent years, the other ancient modes have resurfaced in the works of innovative composers who have sought to rediscover and utilize these alternate scale systems, but because of the popularity of the major/minor system, they remain obscure to many.

The distinguishing factor of each mode is its order of whole steps and half steps. The half steps occur in different places in each mode, giving each one a distinctive, unique sound.

Example 1.12 showed that the half steps of the major scale (*Ionian* mode) *always* occur between scale degrees *three and four* (E to F) and *seven and eight* (B to C). As an exercise, identify where the half steps are in *each* mode in example 4.01.

Memorizing the modes is a necessity for the music theorist, who should be readily familiar with them at all times. Example 4.02 below illustrates a helpful tool for memorizing the modes in order from A - G.[1]

Example 4.02

AFTER	AEOLIAN	(A)
LEARNING	LOCRIAN	(B)
INTERVALS FROM	IONIAN	(C)
DUNBAR,	DORIAN	(D)
PEOPLE	PHRYGIAN	(E)
LEARN	LYDIAN	(F)
MODES.	MIXOLYDIAN	(G)

"Music is the mediator between the spiritual and the sensual life."

- composer Ludwig Van Beethoven

In all diatonic scales, the scale degrees are *named* according to their *function* within the key.

Example 4.03

SCALE DEGREE	NAME
1	TONIC
2	SUPERTONIC
3	MEDIANT
4	SUBDOMINANT
5	DOMINANT
6	SUBMEDIANT
7	SUBTONIC or LEADING TONE
8	TONIC

- Aside from the *tonic*, the *fifth* scale degree is the most important tone in the key, thus it is called the **dominant**.
- Scale degree *four* is the **subdominant** (a *dominant*, or fifth, *below* tonic).
- Scale degree *two* is the **supertonic** since it is one step *above* tonic.
- The *seventh* scale degree is called the **subtonic** (one step *below* tonic) *if* it is a *whole step* below the tonic. If the seventh scale degree is a *half step* below tonic, it is called the **leading tone** because it *functions* toward the tonic.
- The *third* scaled degree is known as the **mediant** (midway to the *dominant*).
- Degree *six* of the scale is the **submediant** (midway to the *subdominant* if going *down*). It is the same distance *below* tonic as the mediant, or third, is *above* tonic.
- Scale degree *eight* is the return of the **tonic**, an octave above the starting point.

---

[1] mnemonic device developed by Polly Blanshan in 2006.

Example 4.04

Aeolian mode

tonic — supertonic — mediant — subdominant — dominant — submediant — subtonic — tonic

Ionian mode

tonic — supertonic — mediant — subdominant — dominant — submediant — leading tone — tonic

Example 4.04 above shows ascending minor and major scales, with the names of their scale degrees below each note. The seventh degree of the *minor* scale is the *subtonic* because it is a *whole step* below tonic. The seventh degree of the *major* scale is the *leading tone* because it is a *half step* below tonic.

As an aural illustration of the *function* of the *leading tone*, listen to only the first seven tones of the major scale. Legend has it that Mozart was a lazy child and his mother would play those notes to get him out of bed. He could not stand hearing the leading tone *unresolved*, so he would leap up and dash to the keyboard to play the tonic note at the end of the scale.

In each scale except for Locrian, the distance from tonic to dominant is a *perfect fifth*. Because the interval from *tonic* to *dominant* (the two most important notes in the scale) in Locrian mode is a *diminished* fifth (a tritone), the Locrian mode was *not* used as a functional mode for composition. The *tritone* has historically been considered a **dissonant interval** (unpleasant, harsh, nasty, not tasty[2]), and, because of this, was nicknamed the *diabolus in musica* ("the devil in music").

A comparison of modes is helpful for those familiar with the sounds of major and minor scales. Note the similarities between Aeolian, Dorian, and Phrygian modes in example 4.05.

Example 4.05

Aeolian mode

tonic — supertonic — mediant — subdominant — dominant — submediant — subtonic — tonic

Dorian mode

tonic — supertonic — mediant — subdominant — dominant — submediant — subtonic — tonic

Phrygian mode

tonic — supertonic — mediant — subdominant — dominant — submediant — subtonic — tonic

---

[2] *Theorist Kevon Lyle refers to* **consonances** *and aurally satisfying moments in music as "tasty."*

All the scales in example 4.05 have these common characteristics:

- The interval of a *minor* third between *tonic* and *mediant*.
- The interval of a *perfect* fourth between *tonic* and *subdominant*.
- The interval of a *perfect* fifth between *tonic* and *dominant*.
- The presence of *subtonic* instead of *leading tone*.

Because of this, it can be said that *Dorian* and *Phrygian* are *like* minor.

The difference in sound between *Dorian* and *minor* has to do with the *sixth scale degree*. In the minor scale, the distance from *tonic to submediant* is a *minor* sixth. In Dorian, the distance from tonic to submediant is a *major* sixth. Therefore, **Dorian is like minor with a raised submediant**.

The difference in sound between *Phrygian* and *minor* has to do with the *second scale degree*. In the minor scale, the distance from *tonic to supertonic* is a *major* second. In Phrygian, the distance from tonic to supertonic is a *minor* second. Therefore, **Phrygian is like minor with a lowered supertonic**.

Note the similarities between Ionian, Lydian, and Mixolydian modes in example 4.06.

Example 4.06

Ionian mode

tonic   supertonic   mediant   subdominant   dominant   submediant   leading tone   tonic

Lydian mode

tonic   supertonic   mediant   subdominant   dominant   submediant   leading tone   tonic

Mixolydian mode

tonic   supertonic   mediant   subdominant   dominant   submediant   subtonic   tonic

Each scale in example 4.06 has the following characteristics in common:

- The interval of a *major* second between *tonic* and *supertonic*.
- The interval of a *major* third between *tonic* and *mediant*.
- The interval of a *perfect* fifth between *tonic* and *dominant*.
- The presence of a *major* sixth between *tonic* and *submediant*.

Because of this, it can be said that *Lydian* and *Mixolydian* are *like* major.

The difference in sound between *Lydian* and *major* has to do with the *fourth scale degree*. In the major scale, the distance from *tonic to subdominant* is a *perfect* fourth. In Lydian, the distance from *tonic to subdominant* is an *augmented* fourth. Therefore, **Lydian is like major with a raised subdominant**.

The difference in sound between *Mixolydian* and *major* has to do with the *seventh scale degree*. In the major scale, the seventh degree is the *leading tone*, since it is a *half step below tonic*. In Mixolydian, however, the distance from scale degree seven to tonic is a *whole step*, thus rendering it the *subtonic*. Therefore, **Mixolydian is like major with a lowered seventh**.

Of interesting note is the *interval relationships* between each scale degree and tonic in a *major* scale. The second, third, sixth, and seventh from the tonic are all *major* and the fourth and fifth are *perfect*.[3]

Transposition is the process of *restating music at a higher or lower pitch*. A major scale (or *any* mode for that matter) can occur on any note (not just *C*). The important factor in transposition is that *all intervals* from the original starting note are *exactly the same* in the transposed version.

Example 4.07 shows a major scale on *C*, followed by its exact transposition up a whole step.

Example 4.07

If the first scale had simply been moved up a step to start on *D without any accidentals*, the result *would have been* the *Dorian* mode. However, since it was transposed *exactly* so that each interval maintained its identical *quality* and exact distance from tonic, the result is a replication of *Ionian*, but on *D* instead of *C*.

Since this type of transposition can be a tedious process, it is helpful to memorize the sequence of whole steps and half steps for the major scale so that it can be constructed on any note. Diatonic eight-note scales are comprised of two **tetrachords** (groups of four, like the boxes in the video game *Tetris®*). The first four notes of a scale comprise the *lower tetrachord*, and the final four notes of the scale comprise the *upper tetrachord*. In a major scale, the interval *between* tetrachords is a major second (whole step).

---

[3] *Once key signatures are memorized, this is helpful information when deducing the interval quality of sixths and sevenths. Considering the lower of the two notes of an interval as tonic of a major key, if the upper note would fit into the key signature of the tonic note, the interval is major.*

Example 4.08

[Musical notation showing lower tetrachord and upper tetrachord on treble staff]

Example 4.09 highlights the intervals between adjacent scale degrees of each tetrachord using W for *whole step* and H for *half step*.

Example 4.09

[Musical notation showing lower tetrachord and upper tetrachord with W and H markings between notes: W W H (W) W W H]

A *major* scale, regardless of the tonic note, *always* follows the pattern of WWH (W) WWH.

As an exercise, identify the quality of seconds in and between the tetrachords for *all* modes back in example 4.01.

Example 4.10

[Musical notation of B major scale with five sharps as accidentals]

Example 4.10 is a *major scale* (like the one in example 4.09 on **C**) constructed on **B**. The intervals between adjacent scale degrees are WWH (W) WWH. There is an abundance of accidentals in this scale (five sharps). To simplify the process of composition and music reading, *key signatures* are employed. **Key signatures** are placed at the beginning of each staff, just to the right of the clef, instructing the performer to apply the accidentals there to *every* instance (in *every octave* and *every measure*) of notes that appear on the lines and spaces bearing the accidentals. Unlike *time signatures*, which appear only at the beginning of a composition unless the meter changes, *key signatures* always appear on *each system*.

Example 4.11 produces exactly the same musical result as example 4.10. The use of *key signatures* conveniently assists performers and composers alike by limiting the accidentals they must read and write throughout the composition.

Example 4.11

[Musical notation of B major scale with five-sharp key signature]

There are three types of key signatures:

- Those without any accidentals
- Those containing sharps (called *sharp keys*)
- Those containing flats (called *flat keys*)

> "There are still so many beautiful things to be said in C major."
> *- composer Sergei Prokofiev*

Key signatures *do not* contain both sharps and flats simultaneously.

In sharp key signatures, the sharps *always* appear in the following order:

F#   C#   G#   D#   A#   E#   B#

This order must be memorized so that it can be repeated quickly without requiring memorization tricks.

If a key signature has only one sharp, that sharp will always be **F#**. If a key signature has only two sharps, those sharps will always be **F#** and **C#**. If three sharps are in the key signature, they will always be **F#**, **C#,** and **G#**.

Example 4.12 shows all of the sharps in order on the grand staff as well as on the alto and tenor clefs.

Example 4.12

For *major* keys, the *last sharp* in the key signature is the *leading tone* of the key, meaning that the *tonic* is one half step above the last sharp.

For example, if a key signature has four sharps, those four sharps must be **F#**, **C#**, **G#,** and **D#** in that order. **D#** is the leading tone of the key, so it can be deduced that the *major key with four sharps* is E major.

Example 4.13 identifies all major sharp keys by key signature in treble clef.

Example 4.13

G major   D major   A major   E major   B major   F# major   C# major

Notice the intervallic relationships between the keys. The *tonic* of each key is a *perfect fifth above* its predecessor. As each sharp is added to the key signature, the tonic moves up a perfect fifth (or down a perfect fourth).

In flat key signatures, the flats *always* appear in the following order:

B♭   E♭   A♭   D♭   G♭   C♭   F♭

This order must be memorized so that it can be repeated quickly without requiring memorization tricks.

If a key signature has only one flat, that flat will always be **B♭**. If a key signature has only two flats, those flats will always be **B♭** and **E♭**. If three flats are in the key signature, they will always be **B♭, E♭,** and **A♭**.

Example 4.14 shows all of the flats in order on the grand staff as well as on the alto and tenor clefs.

Example 4.14

For *major* flat keys, the word *flat* is part of the *name of the key*, with one exception: the key of F major, which has one flat (**B♭**). In all others, the *second-to-last flat* in the key signature represents the *tonic* of the key.

For example, if a key signature has five flats, those five flats must be **B♭, E♭, A♭, D♭,** and **G♭** in that order. **D♭** is the second-to-last flat, so it can be deduced that the *major key with five flats is D-flat major*.

It is important to include the word *flat* in the *name* of the key when identifying flat keys in major.

Example 4.15 identifies all major flat keys by key signature in treble clef.

Example 4.15

F major, B♭ major, E♭ major, A♭ major, D♭ major, G♭ major, C♭ major

Again, notice the intervallic relationships between the keys. The *tonic* of each key is a *perfect fifth below* its predecessor. As each flat is added to the key signature, the tonic moves down a perfect fifth (or up a perfect fourth).

Because of the interval of a perfect fifth between major keys that differ by only one accidental, all major keys can be put on a chart indicating their relationships to one another. This chart is known as the ***circle of fifths***, and begins at the top with the key of C major, which has *no* sharps or flats.

Example 4.16

Flat Keys ← | Sharp Keys →

- C (0)
- (1) F
- G (1)
- (2) B♭
- D (2)
- (3) E♭
- A (3)
- A♭ (4)
- E (4)
- C♯ (7)
- B (5)
- D♭ (5)
- C♭ (7)
- F♯ (6)
- G♭ (6)

The circle begins with **C** (no sharps or flats) and continues clockwise through the sharps, *up* by perfect fifths, until **C-sharp** is reached.

The circle begins with **C** (no sharps or flats) and continues counter-clockwise through the flats, *down* by perfect fifths, until **C-flat** is reached.

Note that the letter name **C** is the beginning point *and* ending point in both directions.

The three sharp keys at the bottom of the circle (**C#, F#,** and **B**) *overlap* with three flat keys (**D♭, G♭,** and **C♭**) because the *pairs* of keys are *enharmonic keys*.

Just as the *notes* C-sharp and D-flat are *enharmonic,* so are the *keys* C-sharp and D-flat. The same is true for the key pairings of F-sharp/G-flat and B/C-flat.

Every *major* key has a *minor* key that is considered a *relative*. **Relative keys** are those that share the *same key signature,* but have a *different tonic* and *mode*.

Refer back to example 4.01 and note that the Aeolian mode (*minor* scale with **A** as tonic) shares the *same key signature* (no sharps or flats) as the Ionian mode (*major* scale with **C** as tonic). The keys of A minor and C major have *identical key signatures*, but *different tonics*. Thus, it is said that the *relative minor key* of C major is A minor and the *relative major key* of A minor is C major.

The interval separating relative keys is *always a minor third*. **C** (major) is a minor third above **A** (minor), so the *relative minor key* is always a minor third *below* its relative major key.

Example 4.17 shows the circle of fifths with each minor key on the inside of the circle adjacent to its relative major counterpart. Minor keys are indicated here in lowercase.

Example 4.17

For minor keys, the circle begins with "*a*" (no sharps or flats) and continues clockwise through the sharps, *up* by perfect fifths, until *a-sharp* is reached.

The circle begins with "*a*" (no sharps or flats) and continues counter-clockwise through the flats, *down* by perfect fifths, until *a-flat* is reached.

Note that the letter name "*a*" is the beginning point *and* ending point in both directions.

Observe the relationship between the major and minor keys that share the same key signature. *The relative minor key is always a minor third* below *the relative major key*. Also notice the continued perfect fifth relationship between the tonics of each minor key around the inner circle.

Example 4.18 shows key signatures for all sharp keys and all flat keys in treble clef with the major keys listed above their *relative* minors. Sharp keys are on the first system and flat keys are on the second system.

Example 4.18   relative keys

| G major | D major | A major | E major | B major | F# major | C# major |
| E minor | B minor | F# minor | C# minor | G# minor | D# minor | A# minor |

| F major | B♭ major | E♭ major | A♭ major | D♭ major | G♭ major | C♭ major |
| D minor | G minor | C minor | F minor | B♭ minor | E♭ minor | A♭ minor |

Every *major* key also has a *minor* key that is considered a *parallel key*. **Parallel keys** are those that share the *same tonic,* but have *different key signatures*. The *parallel* minor key of *C major*, for instance, is *C minor*. In *parallel* keys, the *tonic* remains the same, but the *mode* changes. Example 4.19 is a diagram of *parallel keys*.

Example 4.19   parallel keys

MAJOR: A major, B♭ major, B major, C major, C# major, D major
PARALLEL
MINOR: A minor, B♭ minor, B minor, C minor, C# minor, D minor

MAJOR: E♭ major, E major, F major, F# major, G major, A♭ major
PARALLEL
MINOR: E♭ minor, E minor, F minor, F# minor, G minor, A♭ minor

Note: The keys of D-flat major, G-flat major, and C-flat major do not have *parallel* minor keys. Their enharmonic keys (**C#, F#,** and **B**) are on the chart in example 4.19. The keys of G# minor, D# minor, and A# minor do not have *parallel* major keys. Their enharmonic keys (A-flat minor, E-flat minor, and B-flat minor) are on the chart in example 4.19.

When writing in *minor* mode, composers of the common practice era often made adjustments to the minor scale that affected the upper tetrachord. These scale alterations resulted in *three functional forms* of the minor scale, known as *natural minor, harmonic minor,* and *melodic minor.*

The **natural minor** scale is simply the Aeolian mode in its unaltered form (as shown in examples 4.01, 4.04, and 4.05). Example 4.20 shows the *tetrachords* of the *natural minor* scale.

Example 4.20 natural minor scale

"Music is the universal language of mankind."
- poet Henry Wadsworth Longfellow

The primary feature of the *minor* mode that distinguishes it from *major* is the interval of a *minor third* from the *tonic to the mediant*. While leaving the lower tetrachord unaffected by accidentals, composers found the absence of the leading tone to be musically unsatisfying at times, so they raised the seventh scale degree by a half step, making the scale *harmonic*.

The **harmonic minor scale** is the Aeolian mode with a *raised seventh*. Example 4.21 shows the *tetrachords* of the *harmonic minor* scale.

Example 4.21 harmonic minor scale

"When I don't like a piece of music, I make a point of listening to it more closely."
– composer Florent Schmitt

When the seventh scale degree of the Aeolian mode is raised by a half step, converting it from *subtonic* to *leading tone*, the melodic interval of an *augmented second* is created between the *sixth* and *seventh* scale degrees.

Despite the intervallic anomalies in the upper tetrachord, the *harmonic minor* scale has remained the preferred form of the minor scale for composers since the common practice era.

While *key signatures* do not include sharps and flats simultaneously, the D and G harmonic minor *scales* require both. In these cases, the key *signatures* include only flats; the sharps are applied individually to the notes they affect.

The ***melodic minor*** scale is the most diverse and interesting of the three forms, incorporating a *raised sixth and raised seventh* while ascending, and reverting to unaltered Aeolian mode while descending.

In its *ascending* form, the *melodic minor* scale has the *lower tetrachord* of the *Aeolian* mode (*natural minor*) and the *upper* tetrachord of *Ionian* (*major*). Its *descending* form reverts to the upper *and* lower tetrachords of the *natural minor* scale.

Example 4.22   melodic minor scale — ascending and descending forms

Example 4.23   melodic minor scale — ascending and descending forms

"A song has a few rights the same as ordinary citizens... if it happens to feel like flying where humans cannot fly... to scale mountains that are not there, who shall stop it?"
  — *composer Charles Ives*

Alterations to the minor scale indicating harmonic or melodic forms are *always* in the form of *accidentals* and are *never added to the key signature*. Some compositions are purely in one form of the minor scale, but many vacillate between these forms throughout.

Use of the melodic minor scale in music is shown in an excerpt from *You Are My Hiding Place*[4] in example 4.24.

Example 4.24

I will trust in You, _____ I will trust in You, _____

---

[4] You Are My Hiding Place: *Lyrics and music by Michael Ledner.* © 1981 Maranatha! Music.

In example 4.24, the key is *A minor* (no sharps or flats), and as the melody *ascends*, the sixth and seventh scale degrees (F and G) are *raised* (F# and G#). Then, as the melody *descends*, the sixth and seventh scale degrees are returned to their *natural* form.

When a composition is in one of the *original modes*, it may also use a *key signature*. Modal key signatures are determined as follows:

> The key signature for *Dorian* is always a *major second below* the *tonic* note.
> The key signature for *Phrygian* is always a *major third below* the *tonic* note.
> The key signature for *Lydian* is always a *perfect fourth below* the *tonic* note.
> The key signature for *Mixolydian* is always a *perfect fifth below* the *tonic* note.

This works because the all modes in their unaltered form use the key signature for C major (no sharps or flats). The *tonic* note of *Dorian* is a *major second above* **C**, the *tonic* note of *Phrygian* is a *major third above* **C**, and so on. So, if the *tonality* for a piece is **E**, but the *key signature* suggests A major, it can be deduced that the piece is in *E Mixolydian* (or Mixolydian *on* **E**).

Example 4.25

[Musical notation: "What Wondrous Love Is This" with lyrics:]
What won-drous love is this, O my soul, O my soul, what won-drous love is this, O my soul! What won-drous love is this that caused the Lord of bliss to bear the dread-ful curse for my soul, for my soul, to bear the dread-ful curse for my soul!

The **tonal center** (tonic) of example 4.25[5] is **E**, but the key signature suggests D major. The mode, then, is *Dorian* because the *tonic* note is a *major second above* the *key signature*.

---

[5] What Wondrous Love Is This: *Appalachian folk hymn, circa 1835. Public Domain. Tune name:* Wondrous Love.

Analyze example 4.26 below[6] and deduce the mode from the relationship of the tonic note to the key signature.

Example 4.26

Sing we now of Christ - mas, No - el,   sing we here!

Sing our grate - ful prais - es to the   Babe so dear.

Sing we No - el! The King is born, No - el!

Sing we now of Christ - mas, sing we   all, No - el!

In addition to the scales that produce keys (*diatonic* scales), various *non-diatonic* scales are used in Western music. The **chromatic scale** uses *all* the tones within the range of an octave, and is thus comprised of only *half steps*. The ascending form uses sharps and the descending form uses flats. This is shown in example 4.27 in the bass clef.

Example 4.27

Just as the *chromatic scale* uses all *half steps*, the **whole-tone scale** uses all *whole steps*.

Example 4.28

Unlike diatonic scales, the whole-tone scale uses only *six pitch classes* (instead of seven) and therefore does not use every letter name. The term **pitch class** refers to *all notes of identical sound in any octave*. In example 4.28, there are six pitch classes: **A**, **B**, **C#**, **D#**, **F**, and **G**. The **A** at the top of the scale is *not* another pitch class because **A** was already counted at the beginning of the scale. *Enharmonic notes* also share a *pitch class*. D-sharp and E-flat, for example, are a single *pitch class*.

---

[6] Sing We Now of Christmas: *Anonymous French carol, circa 1450. Public Domain. Tune name:* Noel Nouvelet.

Example 4.29 is another example of the *whole-tone scale*.

Example 4.29

The *whole-tone* scales in example 4.28 and 4.29 are the only two existent whole-tone scales. Because these scales are *non-diatonic* (without a tonic) all others are merely *duplicates* of these scales, starting on a different scale degree. Example 4.30 *appears* to be a completely different scale than either of the whole-tone scales in examples 4.28 and 4.29, but it shares exactly the same *pitch classes* as example 4.29, and each note is still a *whole step* apart.

Example 4.30

"Love cannot express the idea of music, while music may give an idea about love."

- composer Hector Berlioz

This is considered a *transposition* of example 4.29.

Notice that although the *whole-tone scale* only uses *whole steps*, the *interval* of a *diminished third* is always present in addition to the *major seconds*.

The **octatonic scale** alternates between half steps and whole steps.

Example 4.31

The octatonic scale in example 4.31 begins with a half step and ends with a whole step. The alternate form begins with a whole step and ends with a half step. This scale is called *octatonic* because it uses *eight* different pitch classes.

The **blues scale** is a hybrid between a *diatonic* scale and a *non-diatonic* scale. It is a *major scale* with the chromatic *addition* of a lowered third and a lowered seventh. It is primarily *diatonic* because it conforms to a major key, but it does *add* chromaticism.[7]

Example 4.32

---

[7] *The whole-tone scale, the octatonic scale, and the blues scale gained prominence* after *the common practice era.*

The **pentatonic scale** is a *diatonic* scale that uses only five notes. It is sometimes referred to as a *gap scale* because it is a major scale with the fourth and seventh scale degrees missing. The black keys of the piano comprise the pitches of the pentatonic scale, although the scale may be transposed to all white keys or a combination of white and black keys. This scale contains *no half steps* and is comprised of *major seconds* and *minor thirds* only.

Example 4.33

Example 4.33 is one of many transpositions of the *pentatonic scale*.

The entire melody of the music back in examples 2.23 and 2.24 is pentatonic.

This concludes the introduction to scales and keys. Triads and harmonic analysis will be covered in chapter five.

Q: What was the musician's excuse for his weight gain?

A: The Phrygian scale was broke.

- music theorist Crystal Swan

Assignments and Drills

Assignment 4.01

The objective of this assignment is familiarity with the modes.

Instructions: Identify the name of each *mode* below. Number one is done for you. REFER BACK TO EXAMPLES 4.01, 4.02, 4.05, 4.06, AND 4.07 IF NECESSARY.

1. Phrygian

2.

3.

4.

5.

6.

7.

8.

Assignment 4.02

The objective of this assignment is familiarity with major and minor scales.

Instructions: Go back through assignment 4.01 and convert numbers two, seven, and eight to *major scales* using accidentals; convert number six to a *natural minor scale* using accidentals. REFER BACK TO EXAMPLES 4.09 AND 4.20 IF NECESSARY.

Assignment 4.03

The objective of this assignment is mode construction.

Instructions: Create ascending *Dorian* modes on each note provided below. REFER BACK TO EXAMPLES 4.01 AND 4.05 IF NECESSARY.

1.

2.

3.

4.

Assignment 4.04

The objective of this assignment is mode construction.

Instructions: Create ascending *Phrygian* modes on each note provided below. REFER BACK TO EXAMPLES 4.01 AND 4.05 IF NECESSARY.

1.

2.

3.

4.

Assignment 4.05

The objective of this assignment is mode construction.

Instructions: Create ascending *Lydian* modes on each note provided below. REFER BACK TO EXAMPLES 4.01 AND 4.06 IF NECESSARY.

Assignment 4.06

The objective of this assignment is mode construction.

Instructions: Create ascending *Mixolydian* modes on each note provided below. REFER BACK TO EXAMPLES 4.01 AND 4.06 IF NECESSARY.

Assignment 4.07

The objective of this assignment is major scale construction.

Instructions: Create ascending *major scales* on each note provided below. Refer back to examples 4.07–4.10 if necessary.

Assignment 4.08

The objective of this assignment is minor scale construction.

Instructions: Create ascending *natural minor* scales on each note provided below. Refer back to example 4.20 if necessary.

1.
2.
3.
4.
5.
6.
7.
8.

Assignment 4.09

The objective of this assignment is minor scale construction.

Instructions: Create ascending *harmonic minor* scales on each note provided below. REFER BACK TO EXAMPLE 4.21 IF NECESSARY.

Assignment 4.10

The objective of this assignment is minor scale construction.

Instructions: Create complete *melodic minor* scales (ascending and descending) on each note provided below. REFER BACK TO EXAMPLES 4.22 AND 4.23 IF NECESSARY.

Assignment 4.11

The objective of this assignment is fluent notation of sharp key signatures in various clefs.

Instructions: Practice writing the order of sharps on each staff below (five times). ONLY REFER BACK TO EXAMPLE 4.12 ONCE FOR EACH CLEF.

Assignment 4.12

The objective of this assignment is fluent notation of flat key signatures in various clefs.

Instructions: Practice writing the order of flats on each staff below (five times). ONLY REFER BACK TO EXAMPLE 4.14 ONCE FOR EACH CLEF.

Assignment 4.13

The objective of this assignment is fluent replication of the circle of fifths.

Instructions: Complete the circle of fifths by filling in the blanks below. Try *not* to refer back to examples 4.16 and 4.17. Start with **C** at the top of the circle and go clockwise around the circle using ascending perfect fifths until you get to C-sharp. Then go counter-clockwise around the circle using descending fifths until you get to C-flat. In the case of enharmonic keys near the bottom, keep the *sharp* keys closest to the rim of the circle on both sides.

← Flat Keys   Sharp Keys →

C
a

Assignment 4.14

The objective of this assignment is fluent replication of the circle of fifths.

Instructions: Complete the circle of fifths below. Try to do the entire circle from memory.

Assignment 4.15

The objective of this assignment is key signature recognition for major keys.

Instructions: Identify each *major* key below by writing the name of the key above each measure. Try to complete the assignment *without* referring back to any examples in chapter four. Remember that the *last sharp* in the key signature is the *leading tone* of the key (tonic is just a half step up) and that the *second-to-last flat in* the key signature *equals the name of the key*.

Assignment 4.16

The objective of this assignment is key signature recognition for minor keys.

Instructions: Go back through assignment 4.15 and write the name of the *minor* key below each measure. Try to complete the assignment *without* referring back to any examples in chapter four. Remember that the *relative minor* key is always a *minor third below* the relative major key.

Assignment 4.17

The objective of this assignment is fluent notation of major key signatures in various clefs.

Instructions: Write each key signature on the staff as indicated below. Number one is completed for you. Try to complete the assignment *without* referring back to any examples in chapter four. Remember that the note that is a half step below tonic will be the *last sharp* in the key signature and that the name of the flat key will equal the *second-to-last flat in* the key signature.

| A major | B-flat major | D-flat major | D major | F major |

| B major | E major | E-flat major | C-flat major | F-sharp major |

| C major | G major | G-flat major | A-flat major | C-sharp major |

Assignment 4.18

The objective of this assignment is fluent notation of minor key signatures in various clefs.

Instructions: Write each key signature on the staff as indicated below. Number one is completed for you. Try to complete the assignment *without* referring back to any examples in chapter four. Remember that each minor key is a minor third below its relative major key. Figure out the major key that shares the same key signature and write that key signature on the staff.

| C minor | G minor | A-flat minor | C-sharp minor | E minor |

| E-flat minor | F-sharp minor | B minor | D minor | A-sharp minor |

| D-sharp minor | F minor | A minor | G-sharp minor | B-flat minor |

Assignment 4.19

The objective of this assignment is fluent notation of parallel key signatures in various clefs.

1. Write the key signature indicated on the upper staff.
2. Write the key signature for *the parallel* key on the lower staff and label it.

The first two are done for you. Try to complete the assignment without referring back to any examples in chapter four.

E major   D minor   C minor   B-flat major   G major   C-sharp major

E minor   D major

F minor   B major   A-flat minor   A major   F-sharp minor   E-flat major

Assignment 4.20

The objective of this assignment is identification of scale degrees by name.

Instructions: Write the name of each scale degree in the blanks provided.
REFER BACK TO EXAMPLES 4.03 AND 4.04 IF NECESSARY.

Scale degree one: __Tonic__

Scale degree two: _____

Scale degree three: _____

Scale degree four: _____

Scale degree five: _____

Scale degree six: _____

Scale degree seven (major): _____

Scale degree seven (nat. minor): _____

Assignment 4.21

The objective of this assignment is identification of scale degrees in major keys.

Instructions: Identify the name of the note requested. Number one is done for you.

REFER BACK TO EXAMPLES 4.03, 4.04, 4.18, AND 4.19 IF NECESSARY.

1. Mediant in the key of D major. ___F#___

2. Supertonic in the key of B major. _____

3. Dominant in the key of A major. _____

4. Leading tone in the key of E major. _____

5. Subdominant in the key of F major. _____

6. Tonic in the key of C-sharp major. _____

7. Mediant in the key of E-flat major. _____

8. Submediant in the key of A-flat major. _____

9. Dominant in the key of D-flat major. _____

10. Supertonic in the key of G-flat major. _____

11. Subdominant in the key of B major. _____

12. Mediant in the key of B major. _____

13. Subdominant in the key of E-flat major. _____

14. Leading tone in the key of B-flat major. _____

15. Leading tone in the key of D major. _____

16. Dominant in the key of B major. _____

17. Tonic in the key of A major. _____

18. Submediant in the key of A major. _____

19. Submediant in the key of G major. _____

20. Mediant in the key of C-sharp major. _____

Assignment 4.22

The objective of this assignment is identification of scale degrees in minor keys.

Instructions: Identify the name of the note requested. For all keys, supply the answer in *harmonic* minor. Number one is done for you.

REFER BACK TO EXAMPLES 4.03, 4.04, 4.18, AND 4.19 IF NECESSARY.

1. Mediant in the key of F minor. ___Ab___

2. Supertonic in the key of C-sharp minor. _____

3. Dominant in the key of B minor. _____

4. Leading tone in the key of A minor. _____

5. Subdominant in the key of B-flat minor. _____

6. Tonic in the key of G-sharp minor. _____

7. Mediant in the key of C minor. _____

8. Submediant in the key of D minor. _____

9. Dominant in the key of E minor. _____

10. Supertonic in the key of F-sharp minor. _____

11. Subdominant in the key of G minor. _____

12. Mediant in the key of F-sharp minor. _____

13. Subdominant in the key of D-sharp minor. _____

14. Leading tone in the key of A-flat minor. _____

15. Leading tone in the key of G-sharp minor. _____

16. Dominant in the key of F minor. _____

17. Tonic in the key of F minor. _____

18. Submediant in the key of C minor. _____

19. Submediant in the key of E minor. _____

20. Mediant in the key of B minor. _____

Assignment 4.23

The objective of this assignment is identification of major and minor keys by their specific scale degrees.

Instructions: Identify the name of the key requested. Numbers one and two are done for you.

REFER BACK TO EXAMPLES 4.03, 4.04, 4.18, AND 4.19 IF NECESSARY.

1. B is the mediant of what minor key? _G-sharp minor_
2. B-flat is the supertonic of what major key? _A-flat major_
3. C is the submediant of what major key? _____
4. C-sharp is the submediant of what major key? _____
5. G is the subdominant of what minor key? _____
6. F is the dominant of what minor key? _____
7. A-flat is the mediant of what minor key? _____
8. F-sharp is the leading tone of what major or minor key? _____
9. F-sharp is the mediant of what major key? _____
10. D is the leading tone of what major or minor key? _____
11. E is the submediant of what major key? _____
12. E is the submediant of what minor key? _____
13. B is the leading tone of what major or minor key? _____
14. D-flat is the supertonic of what major key? _____
15. E-flat is the subdominant of what minor key? _____
16. F-sharp is the dominant of what major key? _____
17. B-flat is the dominant of what minor key? _____
18. B-flat is the submediant of what minor key? _____
19. G is the leading tone of what major or minor key? _____
20. D is the mediant of what major key? _____

Assignment 4.24

The objective of this assignment is key signature identification.

Instructions: Identify the number of sharps or flats in each key. Numbers one and two are done for you. Try to complete the assignment without referring back to any examples in chapter four.

1. B major: _five sharps_
2. G minor: _two flats_
3. E-flat major: _____
4. B minor: _____
5. F-sharp major: _____
6. A minor: _____
7. D-flat major: _____
8. C minor: _____
9. E major: _____
10. D-sharp minor: _____
11. G major: _____
12. F minor: _____
13. C-sharp major: _____
14. C-sharp minor: _____
15. A-sharp minor: _____
16. A major: _____
17. D major: _____
18. F major: _____
19. F-sharp minor: _____
20. B-flat major: _____

Assignment 4.25

The objective of this assignment is key signature identification.

Instructions: Identify the keys requested. Numbers one and two are done for you. Try to complete the assignment without referring back to any examples in chapter four.

1. The minor key with two sharps: __B minor__
2. The major key with four flats: __A-flat major__
3. The minor key with one flat: _____
4. The major key with four sharps: _____
5. The minor key with two flats: _____
6. The major key with six flats: _____
7. The minor key with three sharps: _____
8. The major key with seven sharps: _____
9. The minor key with five flats: _____
10. The major key with five flats: _____
11. The minor key with one sharp: _____
12. The major key with seven flats: _____
13. The minor key with three flats: _____
14. The major key with three sharps: _____
15. The minor key with six flats: _____
16. The major key with three flats: _____
17. The minor key with five sharps: _____
18. The minor key with seven flats: _____
19. The major key with one flat: _____
20. The minor key with no flats or sharps: _____

Questions for Review

1. Define the term *pitch class*.

2. Why do no two modes sound alike even though they all utilize identical pitch classes?

3. Which mode sounds like major with a lowered seventh?

4. Which mode sounds like major with a raised fourth?

5. True or false: the lower tetrachord of a major scale is identical to the upper tetrachord of another major scale.

6. How do you determine the key signature for a major sharp key?

7. How do you determine the key signature for a major flat key?

8. How do you determine the key signature for a minor key?

9. What is the difference between the subtonic and leading tone?

10. Why is there no such key as G-sharp major?

11. What is the difference between parallel keys and relative keys?

Assignments for Use with Anthology

For each assignment below, identify the key of the referenced excerpt. Note that the key of the composition, often indicated in the title, represents the tonic at the *beginning* of the piece. The excerpts below are taken from various movements or sections within the composition that are not necessarily still in the same key as at the beginning of the work.

A4.01 Bach: *Mass in B Minor*, BWV 232, Crucifixus. Anthology page 126.

A4.02 Mozart: *Piano Sonata in D Major*, K. 284, variation VII. Anthology page 175.

A4.03 Mozart: *Piano Sonata in B-flat Major*, K. 333, second movement (Andante). Anthology page 187.

A4.04 Mozart: *Fantasia in C Minor*, K. 475, Andantino. Anthology page 213.

A4.05 Mozart: *The Bird Catcher's Song* (from the opera *The Magic Flute*). Anthology page 224.

A4.06 Beethoven: *Piano Sonata No. 1 in F Minor*, Opus 2, No. 1, third movement (Trio). Anthology page 255.

A4.07 Schubert: *Erlkönig*, D. 328. Anthology page 320.

A4.08 Beach: *Three Songs*, Opus 11, Dark is the Night. Anthology page 424.

Chapter 5
Triads and Harmonic Analysis

Harmony in common practice Western music is based on *chords*. **Chords** are the result of *three or more simultaneous pitches*. In a *harmonic interval*, *two* simultaneous pitches are present; a *chord* has *more than two* simultaneous pitches.

The foundational and most common types of chords are *three-note* chords called *triads*. **Triads** are *tertian*, meaning that they are constructed with *thirds*.

Example 5.01 illustrates the triads that are created when constructed on each degree of a major scale.

Example 5.01

The *lowest note* (foundation) of each triad is called the **root**. The middle note of each triad is called the **third**. The highest note of each triad is called the **fifth**.

A triad is identified by its *root* and its *quality*. In the C major scale in example 5.01, the *tonic* triad is a *C major* triad. This is because the root of the chord is **C** and the quality of the chord is major.

Triad qualities are determined as follows:
- **Major** triads:
    The interval from the root to the third is a *major* third.
    The interval from the third to the fifth is a *minor* third.
    The interval from the root to the fifth is a perfect fifth.
- **Minor** triads:
    The interval from the root to the third is a *minor* third.
    The interval from the third to the fifth is a *major* third.
    The interval from the root to the fifth is a perfect fifth.
- **Diminished** triads:
    The interval from the root to the third is a *minor* third.
    The interval from the third to the fifth is a *minor* third.
    The interval from the root to the fifth is a *diminished* fifth.
- **Augmented** triads:
    The interval from the root to the third is a *major* third.
    The interval from the third to the fifth is a *major* third.
    The interval from the root to the fifth is an *augmented* fifth.

Example 5.02 illustrates the triads that are created on every degree of a major scale. The *quality* of each triad is labeled below.

Example 5.02

M   m   m   M   M   m   d   M

The *tonic* triad is *C major* because **C** is the root and the distance from the *root to the third* is a *major* third, while the distance from the *third to the fifth* is a *minor* third.

The *supertonic* triad is *D minor* because **D** is the root and the distance from the *root to the third* is a *minor* third, while the distance from the *third to the fifth* is a *major* third.

The *leading tone* triad is *B diminished* because **B** is the root and the distance from the *root to the third* is a *minor* third, while the distance from the *third to the fifth* is also a *minor* third. The distance from the *root to the fifth* is a *diminished* fifth.

In **harmonic analysis,** *roman numerals* are used to quickly identify the *function* of chords within the key.[1] The *number* indicated by the roman numeral identifies the *scale degree* (tonic, supertonic, mediant, etc.) and the *case* (uppercase/lowercase) identifies the *quality*.

- *Major* triads are indicated *by uppercase* roman numerals.
- *Minor* triads are indicated by *lowercase* roman numerals.
- *Diminished* triads are *lowercase* followed by °.[2]
- *Augmented* triads are *uppercase* followed by ⁺.

Example 5.03 illustrates the triads that are created on every degree of a major scale along with the *harmonic analysis* of each triad labeled below.

Example 5.03

C: I   ii   iii   IV   V   vi   vii°   I

---

[1] *Chord* functions *will be explained in greater detail in chapter nine on harmonic progression.*
[2] *The symbol* ° *is affectionately referred to as a Cheerio®, although that is not its technical term.*

Example 5.04 illustrates the triads that are created on every degree of a *natural minor scale* along with the *harmonic analysis* of each triad labeled below.

Example 5.04

Cm   i   ii°   III   iv   v   VI   VII   i

The *tonic* triad is *C minor* because **C** *is the root* and the distance from the *root to the third* is a *minor* third, while the distance from the *third to the fifth* is a *major* third.

When the *seventh scale degree is raised* to convert the scale to *harmonic minor,* that scale degree is raised in *all* the triads in which it appears. For instance, if the scale in example 5.04 were to be converted to *harmonic* minor, the seventh scale degree (B-flat) would be raised a half step (B-natural). That would affect not only the *root of the subtonic*, making it the *leading tone*, but it would also affect the *third* of the *dominant triad*, changing the *quality* of the G minor triad to G *major* (B-flat, the third, becomes B-natural) Further, it would affect the fifth of the mediant triad (B-flat becomes B-natural, making the E-flat chord *augmented*).

Example 5.05 demonstrates how converting a natural minor scale to *harmonic* minor affects the *quality* of the triads built on the third, fifth, and seventh scale degrees.

Example 5.05

Cm   i   ii°   III+   iv   V   VI   vii°   i

The chart in example 5.06 shows the *qualities* of triads built on each scale degree in major, natural minor and harmonic minor.

Example 5.07 shows these triads in relation to the specific notes of corresponding major and minor scales constructed on C, with all twelve pitch classes represented on the chart.

The triad *qualities* matching each scale degree on these charts are *consistent* from key to key. For instance, in a *major* key, the *supertonic* is *always* a *minor* triad and is *always* constructed on the note a *major* second above tonic. This means that in *major*, supertonic is *always* represented by ii and *never* by II.

It is important for theorists to be able to replicate the charts in examples 5.06 and 5.07 from memory.

Example 5.06

SCALE DEGREE	MAJOR	natural minor	harmonic minor
TONIC	I	i	i
SUPERTONIC	ii	ii°	ii°
MEDIANT	iii	III	III⁺
SUBDOMINANT	IV	iv	iv
DOMINANT	V	v	V
SUBMEDIANT	vi	VI	VI
SUBTONIC		VII	
LEADING TONE	vii°		vii°
TONIC	I	i	i

Example 5.07

Key of C	C	C#/D♭	D	D#/E♭	E	F	F#/G♭	G	G#/A♭	A	A#/B♭	B
DIATONIC TRIADS in major	I		ii		iii	IV		V		vi		vii°
DIATONIC TRIADS in natural minor	i		ii°	III		iv		v		VI	VII	
DIATONIC TRIADS in harmonic minor	i		ii°	III+		iv		V		VI		vii°

Triads seldom appear in an actual musical score in their most basic forms. Often they are spread between instruments or voices, or written in a form that requires some investigating on the part of the theorist to discover and analyze.

Although there are *four* notes on the grand staff in example 5.08, the result is still a *triad* because one of the notes is *doubled*. Only *three separate pitch classes* are present: B, D-sharp, and F-sharp. Thus, the chord in example 5.08 is a *B major triad*. If the *key* is E major, as the signature suggests, the chord represented here is a *dominant* triad (V).

Example 5.08

The style of composition in example 5.08 is known as *chorale style*. **Chorale style** means that the music is written for four vocal parts, simply called *voices*, represented by the vocal ranges of soprano, alto, tenor, and bass (SATB). The grand staff is *bracketed* by a *straight* line, and the bar lines *do not* connect the staves. The soprano and alto parts share the *treble clef*, with *soprano* stems *always* going *up* and alto stems *always* going *down* regardless of their relation to the third line of the staff. Likewise, the tenor and bass *voices* share the *bass clef* with the *tenor* stems going *up* and the *bass* stems going *down*. The term *chorale style*, sometimes called *hymn style*, gets its name from the Baroque era of music history when J.S. Bach (among others) *harmonized* many Renaissance hymn (*chorale*) melodies.

The music in example 5.09[3] is written for *string quartet* (two violins, one viola, one violoncello). The staves are bracketed together, signifying that the instruments all belong to the same instrument "family" (strings), and the bar lines connect the staves. The second violins, violas, and celli provide the **accompaniment** (chords) for the **melody**, which is played by the first violins.

Example 5.09

The music theorist can discern a great deal about tonality and **harmonic progression** (chord progressions) through careful analysis of each chord.

- In example 5.09, the first triad (beat one of measure one) is a D minor triad.
- The second triad (measure one, beat two) is also a D minor triad (inverted).
- The third triad (measure one, beat three) is an inverted C-sharp diminished triad.
- Measures two and three repeat the same chords as measure one, except for the final chord in measure three, which is an A major triad.

Clearly the *tonality* is *D minor* (harmonic). The *harmonic progression* is i - vii° - i - vii° - i - V.

The Mozart piano sonata used back in example 2.39 appears again in example 5.10. The circled notes in measures five through seven are *nonharmonic* (not part of the harmony), and are not to be included in analysis at this point.

---

[3] String Quartet, Opus 18, No. 1. Second movement (Adagio), measures 1-3: *Ludwig Van Beethoven, circa 1798. Public Domain.*

Example 5.10

- The chord in measure five of example 5.10 is a C major triad.
- The chord in measure six is an inverted G major triad.
- The chord in measure seven, beat one, is an incomplete A minor triad (the fifth is missing).
- The chord in measure seven, beat two, is a G major triad.
- The chord in measure seven, beat three, is an inverted D major triad.
- The chord highlighted in measure eight, beat one, is a G major triad.
- The chord highlighted in measure eight, beat three, is an inverted C major triad.
- The chord highlighted in measure nine is an inverted G major triad.

The *key* in example 5.10 is G major and the *harmonic progression* through measure nine, beat two, is IV - I - ii - I - V - I - IV - I.

Example 5.11, drawn from the same Mozart sonata, illustrates *arpeggiated chords* (also called *broken chords*). An **arpeggio** is a "spreading out" of the chord so that all the tones sound in succession instead of simultaneously. As the notes are played, they are *sustained* (held out) by the pedal on the piano so that ultimately, all the notes *are* heard together.

Example 5.11

The sonata has *modulated* (changed keys) by this point to the key of D. When modulating for a brief period, composers often use accidentals instead of inserting the new key signature. The chords in measure 50 are E minor (inverted), D major (inverted), and A major. In the key of D, the harmonic progression is ii - I - V.

When the *bass* note (lowest-sounding tone) of a triad is either the *third* or the *fifth*, the triad is in an inversion. When the *bass* note of a triad is the *root*, the chord is *not* inverted (regardless of the order of the third and fifth). This is called **root position**.

Example 5.12 root position triads

Each of the C major triads in example 5.12 is in *root position* because the *lowest-sounding* tone is the *root*. Measures three through seven are in *chorale style*.

The triads in measures three and four are in **close spacing** because the distance between the *soprano and tenor* is *less than an octave*. When the distance between the *soprano and tenor* is *an octave or more*, the voice spacing is referred to as **open spacing**.

Example 5.13 first inversion triads

Each of the C major chords in example 5.13 is in **first inversion** because the *lowest-sounding note* is the *third*. Each triad in measures three through seven is in *open spacing*.

Each C major triad in example 5.14 below is in **second inversion** because the *lowest-sounding* pitch is the *fifth*. They are all in *close spacing* except for the chords in measures six and eight which are in *open spacing*.

Example 5.14 second inversion triads

"There is nothing in the world so much like prayer as music is."
- *theologian and hymnist William P. Merrill*

When analyzing music that encompasses multiple staves, such as in examples 5.09 and 5.11, it is helpful to reduce the chords to *simple position*, either mentally or on paper. **Simple position** is the placement of all present *pitch classes* from multiple staves *on a single staff* in their *closest spacing, maintaining the inversion* that is present (disregarding actual octave placement). Example 5.15 is a reproduction of example 5.09 with the addition of *simple position* reduction.

129

Example 5.15

Example 5.16 below is a reproduction of example 5.11 with the addition of *simple position reduction* below the grand staff. In this example, a bass clef is used for the chord reduction.

Example 5.16

"Art is dangerous. It is one of the attractions: when it ceases to be dangerous you don't want it."

-jazz musician Duke Ellington

Chord *inversions* are indicated in the *harmonic analysis* by numeric symbols. The symbol for a *first inversion* triad is ^{6} and the symbol for a *second inversion* triad is $^6_4$. The rationale for these symbols will be explained in chapter seven.

When providing *harmonic analysis* for a piece of music, *the first step is always identification of the key.* A *major* key is indicated by the *uppercase letter name* of the key followed by a colon, and a *minor* key is indicated by the *uppercase letter name* of the key *followed by a lowercase m* (for minor) and a colon.

The Beethoven string quartet used in examples 5.09 and 5.15 is presented again in example 5.17, complete with harmonic analysis.

Example 5.17

Dm: i i⁶ vii°⁶ i i⁶ vii°⁶ i i⁶ V

Example 5.18 below is a reproduction of example 5.10 with the addition of *harmonic analysis*.

Example 5.18

G: IV   I⁶   ii I V⁶

I   IV⁶   I⁶₄

Example 5.19 below is a reproduction of example 5.11 with the addition of *harmonic analysis*.

Example 5.19

D: ii⁶   I⁶₄   V

"Inspiration usually comes during work, rather than before it."

—author *Madeleine L'Engle*

Harmonic analysis is a valuable tool, primarily because it helps the theorist quickly understand chord *relationships* within the key.

Modern devices such as *pop-chord symbols* (also called *guitar chord symbols*) are also useful to the musician in a variety of applications, most notably as a time-saving device for music composition. Many people who cannot even read musical notation have learned to play chords on guitar or piano by learning *pop-chord* notation. **Pop-chord symbols** are English alphabet characters that are placed *above* the staff, indicating the chords and inversions to be played.

Example 5.20 explains *pop-chord symbols* using **C** as the root of each triad. The *principles* derived from this example apply to chords with *any* root.

Example 5.20

triad	major	minor	diminished	augmented
root position	C	Cm	C°	C+
first inversion	C/E	Cm/E♭	C°/E♭	C+/E
second inversion	C/G	Cm/G	C°/G♭	C+/G#

Note: C+/E is enharmonic with a root position E augmented triad (E+), and C+/G# is enharmonic with a root position A-flat augmented triad (Ab+).

Some musicians prefer to use the abbreviation *dim* instead of ° for diminished triads. This is acceptable and common.

The slash (/) in *pop-chord* notation simply *means above*, and is referred to as "over." A first inversion C major triad is *C over E* (C/E). The letter *before* the slash is the *chord* and the letter *after* the slash is the *bass note*.

The Beethoven string quartet examples used in this chapter are presented again in example 5.21 using *pop-chord symbols* instead of *harmonic analysis*.

Example 5.21

"If I were not a physicist, I would probably be a musician. I often think in music. I live my daydreams in music. I see my life in terms of music."

- Albert Einstein

The excerpts from the Mozart piano sonata used in this chapter are presented again in examples 5.22 and 5.23 using *pop-chord symbols* instead of *harmonic analysis*.

Example 5.22

"Let us not get so busy or live so fast that we can't listen to the music of the meadow or the symphony that glorifies the forest. Some things in the world are far more important than wealth; one of them is the ability to enjoy simple things."
- writer Dale Carnegie

Example 5.23

Use of *pop-chord symbols*, although shown here for instructional purposes, is *not* encouraged in musical analysis of music from the common practice era. Pop-chord notation identifies chords with no regard for their relationship to each other within the key. Informal use of pop-chord symbols, however, for those already familiar with them, may be helpful when learning harmonic analysis.

Pop-chord symbols are most frequently used in **lead sheets**, which provide a melody line in treble clef, lyrics, and chord symbols, as shown in example 5.24.[4]

"Music is spiritual.
The music business is not."
- singer/songwriter Van Morrison

---

[4] When I Survey the Wondrous Cross: *Lyrics by Isaac Watts, 1707; music attributed to Lowell Mason, 1824, based on Gregorian chant. Public Domain. Tune name:* Hamburg.

Example 5.24

[Musical notation: "When I survey the wondrous cross, on which the Prince of Glory died, my richest gain I count but loss, and pour contempt on all my pride."]

Chord symbols: F | Dm | Gm C | F | F | B♭/F | F C/E | Dm Dm/C | E°/B♭ F/A | C | F | Dm | Gm C | F | F | C | Dm | Gm/B♭ C | F

The pop-chord symbol on beat two of measure seven in example 5.24 indicates a D minor triad over **C**, even though **C** is not part of the D minor triad. **C** is *nonharmonic* (not part of the chord); instances such as this where the note indicated after the slash is not part of the chord are common in both popular music and music of the common practice era.

Example 5.25 on the following page is a reproduction of example 5.24 with *harmonic analysis* in addition to *pop-chord symbols*.

> "The whole problem can be stated quite simply by asking, 'Is there a meaning to music?' My answer would be, 'Yes.' And 'Can you state in so many words what the meaning is?' My answer to that would be, 'No.'"
>
> *— composer Aaron Copland*

Example 5.25

(Musical score with lyrics and harmonic analysis in F major)

Measures 1–4:
Chords: F | Dm | Gm C | F
Lyrics: When I sur-vey the won-drous cross
Analysis: F: I | vi | ii V | I

Measures 5–8:
Chords: F | B♭/F F C/E | Dm Dm/C E°/B♭ F/A | C
Lyrics: on which the Prince of Glo-ry died,
Analysis: I | IV$^6_4$ I V^6 | vi vii°$^6_4$ I^6 | V

Measures 9–12:
Chords: F | Dm | Gm C | F
Lyrics: my rich-est gain I count but loss,
Analysis: I | vi | ii V | I

Measures 13–16:
Chords: F | C Dm | Gm/B♭ C | F
Lyrics: and pour con-tempt on all my pride.
Analysis: I | V vi | ii^6 V | I

A common trend in popular music is the use of chord charts. A **chord chart** consists of simply lyrics with chord symbols over them and has no actual music notation to indicate *pitch* or *rhythm*. The hymn used in examples 5.24 and 5.25 is shown in *chord chart* format in example 5.26.

Example 5.26

```
F        Dm    Gm C    F
When I survey the wondrous cross

F          Bb/F  F C/E  Dm Dm/C  E°/Bb F/A  C
on which the Prince of        Glo-     ry           died,

F        Dm    Gm   C   F
my richest gain I count but loss

F          C     Dm  Gm/Bb C   F
and pour contempt on   all    my pride.
```

Chord charts present obvious limitations, especially when the music is unfamiliar. Because of the prevalent use of chord charts among musicians with limited training and ability, many songs are learned and even taught incorrectly (in regard to rhythm, pitch, and accuracy of chords). Chord charts for almost any popular song may be found on the internet, but **surfer beware!** Many chord charts available on the internet are *inaccurate transcriptions* resulting from uneducated guesswork.

This concludes the introduction to triads and harmonic analysis. Chapter six covers notational elements other than pitch and rhythm.

Assignments and Drills

Assignment 5.01

The objective of this assignment is efficient identification of triad qualities in root position.

Instructions: Identify the quality of each root position triad below. The first two are done for you. Try to complete the assignment in less than fifteen minutes. REFER BACK TO EXAMPLES 5.01 — 5.05 IF NECESSARY.

Assignment 5.02

The objective of this assignment is efficient triad creation in root position.

Instructions: Create root position *major* triads as indicated below. Do not alter the note provided. Numbers 1, 11, and 21 are done for you. Try to complete the assignment in less than fifteen minutes. REFER BACK TO EXAMPLES 5.01 AND 5.02 IF NECESSARY.

The note supplied in measures 1 - 10 is the *root*.

The note supplied in measures 11 - 20 is the *third*.

The note supplied in measures 21 - 30 is the *fifth*.

Assignment 5.03

The objective of this assignment is efficient triad creation in root position.

Instructions: Create root position *minor* triads as indicated below. Do not alter the note provided. Numbers 1, 11, and 21 are done for you. Try to complete the assignment in less than fifteen minutes. REFER BACK TO EXAMPLES 5.01 AND 5.02 IF NECESSARY.

The note supplied in measures 1 - 10 is the *root*.

The note supplied in measures 11 - 20 is the *third*.

The note supplied in measures 21 - 30 is the *fifth*.

Assignment 5.04

The objective of this assignment is efficient triad creation in root position.

1. Create root position *diminished* triads as indicated in measures 1 - 15.
2. Create root position *augmented* triads as indicated in measures 16 - 30.
3. Do not alter the note provided.

Try to complete the assignment in less than fifteen minutes.
REFER BACK TO EXAMPLES 5.01 — 5.05 IF NECESSARY.

The note supplied in measures 1 - 5 is the *root*.

The note supplied in measures 6 - 10 is the *third*.

The note supplied in measures 11 - 15 is the *fifth*.

The note supplied in measures 16 - 20 is the *root*.

The note supplied in measures 21 - 25 is the *third*.

The note supplied in measures 26 - 30 is the *fifth*.

Assignment 5.05

The objective of this assignment is efficient triad creation in root position.

Instructions: Create root position triads as indicated below. Do not alter the note provided. Try to complete the assignment in less than fifteen minutes. REFER BACK TO EXAMPLES 5.01 — 5.05 IF NECESSARY.

The note supplied in measures 1 - 5 is the *root*.

1	2	3	4	5
M	m	d	A	M

The note supplied in measures 6 - 10 is the *third*.

6	7	8	9	10
m	d	A	M	m

The note supplied in measures 11 - 15 is the *fifth*.

11	12	13	14	15
d	A	M	m	d

The note supplied in measures 16 - 20 is the *root*.

16	17	18	19	20
A	M	m	d	A

The note supplied in measures 21 - 25 is the *third*.

21	22	23	24	25
M	m	d	A	M

The note supplied in measures 26 - 30 is the *fifth*.

26	27	28	29	30
m	d	A	M	m

Assignment 5.06

The objective of this assignment is efficient triad creation in root position.

Instructions: Create root position triads as indicated below using accidentals instead of key signatures. Numbers one and two are done for you. Try to complete the assignment in less than 40 minutes. REFER BACK TO EXAMPLES 5.01 — 5.07 IF NECESSARY.

#	Key: Chord
1	F: ii
2	E: ii
3	B♭: I
4	A: iii
5	D: V
6	F: vi
7	E♭: IV
8	B: ii
9	B: iii
10	G: vii°
11	A♭: vi
12	C: iii
13	D: vi
14	F#: V
15	C♭: ii
16	F: IV
17	G: iii
18	E♭: vi
19	A♭: vii°
20	B♭: IV
21	B: V
22	C♭: vi
23	C#: I
24	G♭: V
25	E: iii
26	E: vi
27	A♭: iii
28	D: ii
29	A: IV
30	A: ii

Assignment 5.07

The objective of this assignment is efficient triad creation in root position.

Instructions: Create root position triads as indicated below using accidentals instead of key signatures. Most answers will be in *harmonic* minor, but some will be in *natural* minor. Numbers one and two are done for you. Try to complete the assignment in less than 30 minutes. REFER BACK TO EXAMPLES 5.01 — 5.07 IF NECESSARY.

1	2	3	4	5
Cm: III+	Em: V	Dm: VI	Am: vii°	Bm: iv

6	7	8	9	10
Fm: ii°	C#m: i	Gm: VII	B♭m: V	F#m: VI

11	12	13	14	15
Cm: vii°	Fm: iv	Dm: V	Em: v	A#m: III

16	17	18	19	20
Bm: V	Bm: ii°	E♭m: i	Gm: iv	Am: III+

21	22	23	24	25
G#m: VI	E♭m: vii°	Dm: III	Dm: iv	Gm: III+

26	27	28	29	30
Fm: VI	A♭m: VII	Em: VI	Em: ii°	A♭m: vii°

Assignment 5.08

The objective of this assignment is efficient triad creation in root position.

Instructions: Create root position triads as indicated below using accidentals instead of key signatures. Try to complete the assignment in less than 20 minutes. REFER BACK TO EXAMPLES 5.01 — 5.07 IF NECESSARY.

1. G#m: III
2. F: IV
3. Em: iv
4. B: vii°
5. B♭m: ii°
6. Dm: III+
7. B: ii
8. G: vii°
9. Cm: III+
10. Fm: VI
11. A: vi
12. D: iii
13. Dm: iv
14. G: V
15. C#m: iv
16. E: vii°
17. D♭: vi
18. F#m: ii°
19. A: ii
20. Em: iv
21. Dm: VI
22. Gm: v
23. B: vii°
24. Bm: VII
25. F: vii°
26. Fm: iv
27. G#m: ii°
28. D: IV
29. Am: III+
30. C: vi

Triads and Harmonic Analysis

Assignment 5.09

The objective of this assignment is efficient triad creation in root position.

Instructions: Create root position triads as indicated below using accidentals instead of key signatures. Try to complete the assignment in less than fifteen minutes. REFER BACK TO EXAMPLES 5.01— 5.07 IF NECESSARY.

1. supertonic in Em
2. mediant in C
3. mediant in G
4. subdominant in Bm
5. dominant in A♭
6. subtonic in Fm
7. leading tone in Fm
8. supertonic in B
9. supertonic in Am
10. submediant in B
11. submediant in Cm
12. submediant in E♭
13. supertonic in F
14. mediant in Gm (har)
15. dominant in C
16. subdominant in Fm
17. leading tone in Bm
18. submediant in A
19. supertonic in Bm
20. dominant in F#m (nat)
21. dominant in D♭
22. subdominant in D♭
23. leading tone in Cm
24. tonic in F#
25. tonic in Fm
26. supertonic in Dm
27. subtonic in G#m
28. mediant in F#
29. submediant in G♭
30. supertonic in F#m

Assignment 5.10

The objective of this assignment is efficient identification of triad relationships within a key.

Instructions: Indicate the key for each chord below. Numbers one and two are done for you. Try to complete the assignment in less than 10 minutes. REFER BACK TO EXAMPLES 5.01— 5.07 IF NECESSARY.

1. C: iii
2. Am: VI
3. III
4. ii
5. ii°
6. iii
7. V
8. VI
9. IV
10. iv
11. III+
12. vii°
13. ii°
14. vi
15. III+
16. III+
17. ii
18. iv
19. v
20. VI
21. vii°
22. iii
23. IV
24. ii°
25. III+
26. I
27. III
28. ii°
29. vii°
30. vi

Assignment 5.11

The objective of this assignment is recollection of triad qualities according to their scale degrees in major and minor keys.

Instructions: Fill in the blanks in the charts below. Only refer back to examples 5.06 and 5.07 to check your work when finished.

SCALE DEGREE	MAJOR	natural minor	harmonic minor
TONIC	I	i	i

Key of C	C	C#/D♭	D	D#/E♭	E	F	F#/G♭	G	G#/A♭	A	A#/B♭	B
DIATONIC TRIADS in major	I											
DIATONIC TRIADS in natural minor	i											
DIATONIC TRIADS in harmonic minor	i											

Assignment 5.12

The objective of this assignment is identification of quality, inversion, and spacing of triads in chorale style, as well as accurate labeling of triads using pop-chord symbols.

1. Indicate the triad *root, quality,* and *inversion* by labeling each chord with *pop-chord symbols* above.
2. Indicate the *spacing* of each triad by writing open or close between the staves.
3. Indicate the *inversion* of each triad *below* the grand staff. Root position should be left blank, first inversion indicated with ^{6}, and second inversion indicated with $^6_4$.

Measures 1 through 3 have been done for you.

REFER BACK TO EXAMPLES 5.01— 5.05, 508, 5.12—5.14, AND 5.20 IF NECESSARY.

Assignment 5.13

The objective of this assignment is triad creation in first inversion.

Instructions: Write the chord requested in *simple position* on the staves below. The first two have been completed for you. REFER BACK TO EXAMPLES 5.13—5.19 IF NECESSARY.

1. B♭m: iv^6
2. A: vi^6
3. Em: v^6
4. Cm: ii^{o6}
5. A: vii^{o6}

6. C#m: VI^6
7. E♭: iii^6
8. Am: ii$^{o\,6}$
9. D: vi^6
10. G♭: I^6

11. F#: IV^6
12. D: ii^6
13. Gm: iv^6
14. B♭m: III+^{6}
15. F#m: VII^6

16. Am: vii^{o6}
17. E♭: iii^6
18. Gm: vii$^{o\,6}$
19. C♭: ii^6
20. C#m: V^6

21. E♭m: i^6
22. Cm: v^6
23. B: vii^{o6}
24. Dm: III^6
25. E: vii^{o6}

26. A♭m: V^6
27. F#m: ii$^{o\,6}$
28. F: IV^6
29. D#m: VI^6
30. G: vi^6

Assignment 5.14

The objective of this assignment is triad identification using pop-chord symbols.

Instructions: Go back through assignment 5.13 and label each chord above the staff according to pop-chord symbols. For example, number one is E♭m/G♭ and number two is F#m/A. REFER BACK TO EXAMPLES 5.20—5.25 IF NECESSARY.

Assignment 5.15

The objective of this assignment is triad creation in second inversion.

Instructions: Write the chord requested in *simple position* on the staves below. The first two have been completed for you. REFER BACK TO EXAMPLES 5.13—5.19 IF NECESSARY.

1. B♭: ii $_4^6$
2. F#m: iv $_4^6$
3. G: V $_4^6$
4. C: vii° $_4^6$
5. Dm: ii° $_4^6$
6. Gm: III+ $_4^6$
7. B: ii $_4^6$
8. A: vii° $_4^6$
9. D: vi $_4^6$
10. F: vi $_4^6$
11. Em: VI $_4^6$
12. D: iii $_4^6$
13. Dm: iv $_4^6$
14. B♭m: V $_4^6$
15. C#m: iv $_4^6$
16. E: vii° $_4^6$
17. E♭: vi $_4^6$
18. G#m: ii° $_4^6$
19. C: ii $_4^6$
20. G#m: iv $_4^6$
21. Am: VI $_4^6$
22. Gm: v $_4^6$
23. B♭: vii° $_4^6$
24. Dm: VII $_4^6$
25. C#: vii° $_4^6$
26. E♭m: iv $_4^6$
27. G#m: ii° $_4^6$
28. D: IV $_4^6$
29. Cm: III+ $_4^6$
30. G♭: vi $_4^6$

Assignment 5.16

The objective of this assignment is triad identification using pop-chord symbols.

Instructions: Go back through assignment 5.15 and label each chord above the staff according to pop-chord symbols. For example, number one is Cm/G and number two is Bm/F#. REFER BACK TO EXAMPLES 5.20—5.25 IF NECESSARY.

Questions for Review

1. What are the four functional *qualities* of triads and how is each constructed?

2. What is meant by *first inversion* and what is the numeric symbol for a first inversion triad?

3. What is meant by *second inversion* and what is the numeric symbol for a second inversion triad?

4. What is meant by *open* and *close spacing*?

5. What is *simple position*?

6. What is the term used when analyzing music for tones that *do not* belong to the chords? Notes representing these tones were circled in the examples.

7. What is the technical term for the use of roman numerals and inversion symbols?

8. What is the term for symbols above the staff that use letter names for triads and slashes to indicate inversions?

9. What do roman numerals indicate that pop-chord symbols do not? What are some advantages of using roman numerals?

Assignments for Use with Anthology

A5.01 Provide *harmonic analysis* for the Christmas carol *Es ist ein' Ros' entsprungen* in Appendix B of the anthology (page 629). At this point, *do not* attempt to analyze the two triads that use accidentals. Circle any notes that do not belong to the harmony (*nonharmonic tones*).

A5.02 On a sheet of staff paper, write out a *simple position reduction* for all the triads in <u>measures 87-96</u> of Schubert: *Erlkönig*, D. 328. Anthology page 323. Do *not* attempt harmonic analysis of these triads. Write the name and inversion of each chord above your reduction using *pop-chord symbols*. NOTE: SKIP THE FIRST TWO BEATS OF MEASURE 88. FOR NOW, CIRCLE NOTE **D** IN MEASURES 89 AND 90 AS NONHARMONIC. CIRCLE **C** IN MEASURES 91 AND 92 AS NONHARMONIC. CIRCLE **F** IN MEASURES 93—96 AS NONHARMONIC.

A5.03 Follow the instructions below pertaining to Beethoven: *Piano Sonata No. 15 in D Major*, Opus 28, third movement (Scherzo). Anthology page 282.

- Provide harmonic analysis of <u>measures 5-8.</u> Circle **G** in measure 7 as nonharmonic at this time.

- Provide harmonic analysis of <u>measures 13-16</u>. Consider these measures to be in the key of *A major*. Circle **D** in measure 15 as nonharmonic at this time.

- Compare harmonic analyses of <u>measures 5-8</u> and <u>measures 13-16</u>.

- Provide harmonic analysis of <u>measures 21-24</u> (key of *D*). Compare with <u>measures 5-8</u>.

- Provide harmonic analysis of <u>measures 29-32</u> (key of *A*). Compare with <u>measures 13-16</u>.

Chapter 6
Beyond Pitch Notation

The notation of pitch (covered in chapter one) is the foundational visual means of communication from composer to performer. Of the four *properties of sound* (pitch, intensity, timbre, and duration), music theory emphasizes the study of pitch (and duration). However, music performance is a form of human *expression* that transcends mere pitch. This chapter focuses on notational devices other than pitch that are absolute necessities for composers and performers.

Intensity is indicated by *dynamics*. **Dynamics** are indications in a musical score that instruct the performer how softly or loudly the music should be played or sung. Dynamic markings indicate approximations and therefore do not identify exact decibel levels. The two basic dynamic markings, derived from Italian, are *piano* (soft) and *forte* (loud). All other dynamic markings are variations of these two.

Example 6.01 shows dynamic markings from softest to loudest, along with their *approximate* decibel levels.

Example 6.01

dynamic marking (Italian abbreviation)	*pp*	*p*	*mp*	*mf*	*f*	*ff*
technical term	*pianissimo*	*piano*	*mezzo piano*	*mezzo forte*	*forte*	*fortissimo*
description	very soft	soft	"medium soft"	"medium loud"	loud	very loud
approx. decibels	32-43 dB	44-55 dB	56-67 dB	68-79 dB	80-91 dB	92-103 dB

The full name of the instrument known as the *piano* is *pianoforte*, meaning that it can be played at a variety of amplitude levels. Prior to the invention of the piano in the eighteenth century, keyboard instruments were not *touch sensitive*, meaning that they could only play at a fixed dynamic level.

The term crescendo (abbreviated *cresc.*) means to gradually get louder, and decrescendo (abbreviated *decresc.*) is the instruction to gradually get softer.

The symbols for crescendo and decrescendo are shown in example 6.02, along with their respective abbreviations. In a piece of music, either the symbol will be used or the abbreviation, but not both. The term *diminuendo* (abbreviated *dim.*) is often used instead of *decrescendo*.

Example 6.02

cresc.   *decresc.*

Some composers will use **ppp** or **fff** to indicate *extreme* variations of soft and loud.

fp (*fortepiano*) indicates loud, immediately followed by soft.
sub. p (*subito piano*) means *suddenly soft*.

The term **articulation** has to do with the *timbre* of a sound and is the term that describes the *technique* with which a note is performed, primarily in relation to how pitches are *attacked* and *released*. Again, the names for *articulations* are derived from Italian. There are hundreds of articulations that may be assigned to various musical instruments. Only a few of the most common are presented here.

Legato means that the region of music is played or sung *as a phrase*, with each note *smoothly* progressing to the next. Legato notes are indicated with a *slur*.

The opposite of *legato* is **staccato**, which means that the notes are to be *detached* from one another. Staccato is indicated with a dot *above* or *below* the note (opposite the direction of the stem).

Cantabile (pronounced *cahn-TAH-bee-lay*) means songlike, and indicates graceful expression.

Accents indicate that each note should be *articulated very distinctly* and slightly *louder*. They are indicated by the symbol **>**.

Tenuto markings instruct the performer to *carefully articulate the note, giving it its full duration*. The symbol for *tenuto* is - above or below the note head.

Pizzicato (abbreviated *pizz.*) is a term for stringed instruments that indicates *plucking* the strings instead of playing them with a bow. **Arco** is used to tell the performers to return to *bowing* the music.

If music is to be *muted* (brass instruments have mutes that are placed in the bell of their instruments to muffle the sound), the term **con sordino** (with mute) is used until **senza sordino** (without mute) is indicated.

Glissando (abbreviated *gliss.*) is a term that indicates a slide in pitch from one note to the next, and is easily performed vocally or on a slide whistle. A *glissando* is indicated by a wavy line from one note to the next.

Example 6.03 illustrates each of the articulations mentioned in the preceding section.

Example 6.03

Measure one indicates *two legato* phrases; measure two indicates *staccato*; measure three *cantabile;* measure four *accents;* measure five *tenuto;* measure six *plucked;* measure seven *bowed;* measure eight *muted;* measure nine *unmuted;* and measure ten *glissando*.

While technically a dynamic marking, **sforzando** (**sf**) indicates the articulation of a very strong accent.

Ornaments refer to symbols in the music that are shorthand versions of embellishments. Instead of writing out each note, a composer places a simple symbol above or below the note to be *decorated*. *Trills, mordents* and *turns* are the most frequent ornaments, and are featured in example 6.04.

Example 6.04

Note that the performance of the **trill** in measure one begins with the note *above*. The **mordent** in measure two is an *upper mordent* and the **mordent** in measure three is a *lower mordent* (indicated by the vertical line through the mordent symbol). Measure four shows a **turn**.

Tempo markings may be either *approximations* or *exact indications* of the *speed* with which to perform the music. The most common *approximate* tempo designations are shown below in example 6.05.

Example 6.05

tempo marking (Italian)	grave	largo	lento	adagio	andante	moderato	allegretto	allegro	vivace	presto	prestissimo
description	extremely slow	very slow	slow	slow and gentle	evenly paced	neither slow nor fast	relatively fast	fast	fast and lively	very fast	extremely fast
beats per minute (BPM)	slower than 40	40-52	53-65	66-76	77-99	100-112	113-124	125-145	146-160	160-200	faster than 200

Exact tempo designations are described in terms of *beats per minute* (*BPM*) such as ♩ = 60, for instance, meaning 60 quarter notes per minute (or one per second). The type of note indicated prior to the equal sign represents the *unit*.

When composers want to indicate a *change* in tempo, they simply indicate the new tempo in the music (either approximate or exact). If the change is meant to be *gradual*, then the term **accelerando** *(accel.)* is used for speeding up the tempo, and **rallentando** or **ritardando** (frequently just *ritard* or *rit.*) are used for slowing down. The term **a tempo** is used to tell the performer to return to the previous speed after an *accel.* or *rit.*

When the *meter* of a piece changes, it is important for the composer to indicate whether the *tempo* changes as well. For example, when a composition switches from 4/4 to 6/8, the performer is at a loss as to how fast to consider the new *unit* unless the composer provides clarification.

If the composer specifies ♪ = ♪, this indicates that the tempo will actually sound like it has *changed*. If the quarter note in common meter had equaled 60 BPM, then the eighth note equals 120 BPM since there are *two* eighth notes for every quarter note. Since the eighth note stayed at 120 BPM but the *unit* changed to a dotted quarter note (*three* eighth notes per beat), the new *unit* (dotted quarter note) equals 40 BPM.

If, contrarily, the composer specifies ♩ = ♩., at the meter change, the *unit* maintains the same tempo (formerly the quarter note at 60 BPM, now the *dotted* quarter note at 60 BPM). In this case, the rate of the eighth note shifts from 120 BPM to 180 BPM.

It is helpful if one of the two types of indications shown in the two paragraphs above is used when music changes *meter*. If the composer does *not* use one of these indications, the performer is to assume that *the rate of the common denominator* (an eighth note in this case) *does* not *change*.

Percussion notation differs from standard pitch notation because its purpose is purely rhythm. Percussion notation uses a *percussion clef* instead of one of the standard pitch clefs, and the lines and spaces of the staff are assigned to various *instruments*.

In percussion notation *there is no absolute standard of how the lines and spaces on the staff are to be used* for three reasons:
1. Drum notation varies among composers and publishers.
2. There is no set standard in terms of what even comprises a drum set.
3. There is an amazing abundance of non-kit percussion instruments.

At the outset of a composition using percussion notation for non-pitched percussion instruments, it is the responsibility of the composer or arranger to include a *legend*. A **legend** defines each line and space on the staff, as well as other symbols and different types of note heads used. Example 6.06 shows a typical legend for a drum kit.

Example 6.06

DRUMS | CYMBALS

tom-toms: high, low, floor

kick (bass), snare, rim shot, cross stick

hi-hat, open hi-hat, 20" ride, 22" ride, 18" crash, 10" splash

pedaled hi-hat

Example 6.07 shows a *rhythm pattern* using the legend above.

Example 6.07

When a measure is to be *repeated exactly* in the following measure, the **repeat symbol** is used to fill the second measure.

Example 6.08

When a two-measure pattern, such as the one in example 6.07 is to be *repeated exactly* in the following two measures, the repeat symbol is modified to form the **two-bar repeat symbol** as shown in example 6.09.

Example 6.09

These repeat symbols are used primarily in percussion notation, but not exclusively. In standard pitch notation, the one-bar and two-bar repeat symbols are often used for *ostinati*. **Ostinato** is the term for a persistently repeating melodic idea or short phrase. An example of ostinato is the bass line of Canon in D[1] by Johann Pachelbel.

Example 6.10

In Pachelbel's *Canon*, this ostinato figure appears 28 times in succession. In such cases, the music may be notated with *multiple* two-bar repeats as shown in example 6.11.

Example 6.11

Repeat signs are often used for entire *sections* of music, not just one or two measures. Instead of copying music to be repeated a second time, composers use repeat signs.

Example 6.12

Example 6.13

When the *repeat sign* in example 6.12 is encountered, the performer looks back through the music already performed up to that point for its retrograde (backward) equivalent, shown in example 6.13, and repeats from that point. If no **retrograde repeat symbol** is found, the performer is to go back to the *beginning* of the composition or movement.

When a composer wants the performer to repeat music from the *beginning*, the abbreviation *D.C.* may be used instead of the repeat symbols. **D.C.** stands for **da capo**[2] (literally meaning *the head*, as in *cap*, *captain* or *capstone*), instructing the performer to go back to "the top."

When a composer wants the performer to repeat music from a *specific point* in the music, the abbreviation *D.S.* may be used. **D.S.** stands for **dal segno**, which means *the sign*. The performer looks back for the **sign**, represented by the symbol 𝄋, and proceeds from that point onward.

---

[1] Canon in D: *Music by Johann Pachelbel, circa 1680. Public Domain.* Ostinato bass lines in the Baroque era of music history such as the one in *Canon in D* were called *ground bass* or *basso ostinato* (literally "obstinate bass").

[2] Capo is pronounced *KAH-po* in this context (not *KAY-po*, which is a device used to shorten guitar strings).

When the words **al fine** (pronounced *al FEE-nay*) appear following a *D.C.* or *D.S.*, the performer is to repeat as instructed but *stop* at the word *fine* (Italian for *end*).

When a *D.C.* or *D.S.* is followed by the words **al coda**, the performer is to repeat as instructed until the *coda sign* (or the instruction *second time to coda*) is reached. At this point, all other music is skipped over until the word *coda* is found, also accompanied by the **coda sign** (⊕).

Multiple endings allow a composer to repeat large portions of music, modifying the way these sections end or lead into other sections. When an ending such as the one in example 6.14 is reached, the performer finishes the measure and then repeats (either from the *retrograde repeat symbol* or the *beginning* of the piece) until this same point is reached again. Then, the first ending is *skipped* and the *second ending* is taken.

Example 6.14

If the second ending also ultimately repeats back to the beginning or to another portion of the composition, the performer repeats the music again until the *third* ending is reached, and so on. *In measure numbering, both measures in example 6.14 share the same number.*

Another musical shorthand device for notation is the use of **measured tremolo**. Instead of writing out four consecutive sixteenth notes, composers have indicated this rhythmic pattern by writing a quarter note with two slashes on the stem. Example 6.15 provides a translation of various measured tremolo markings. Such notation is common for percussion, but is also found on occasion for strings, woodwinds, and brass instruments.

Example 6.15

When a composer calls for **undulating tremolo** (usually in orchestral music), the performer plays two pitches as indicated back-and-forth as rapidly as possible over the duration of the written notes. Example 6.16 provides an *approximate* translation. Undulating tremolos are not *measured* unless the composer places a number along the beam of the tremolo.

Example 6.16

approximate | exact
(unmeasured) (unmeasured) (unmeasured) (measured)

Example 6.16 illustrates the only acceptable type of instance of *beamed half notes*.

An important part of musical notation is understanding when musical instructions such as dynamics or tempo are placed *above* the staff and when they are placed *below* the staff. In vocal and choral music, dynamics and instructions for expression appear on the *opposite side* of the staff as the *lyrics*. In most cases, the lyrics are *below* the staff, so dynamic and expression indications are placed *above*. However, in choral music, for instance, when tenor and bass parts share the bass clef, their lyrics are often *above* the staff. In such cases, other musical instructions must be placed *below*. Tempo designations appear only *above the top staff* in choral music.

For instrumental music (such as orchestra or band), *tempo* designations are placed *above* the *highest* staff and *dynamics* are placed *below each staff*. Other indications, such as muting, are placed *above each staff*.

Mixed meter is a term that describes *a composition that frequently changes time signatures*. Most music since the beginning of the common practice era is composed with a single time signature for the entire composition or movement. However, mixed meter was a common feature of renaissance motets and has become increasingly popular since the end of the Romantic era of music history.

When a composition *alternates* between two time signatures throughout the piece, it is identified as one of *two types* of alternating meter. Leonard Bernstein's *America*[3] from the musical *West Side Story* is an example of the first type, which is simply a **substitute notation** in *every-other measure* where a *single* time signature could have sufficed for the entire piece. Examples 6.17 and 6.18 illustrate this.

Example 6.17

I like to be in A - mer - i - ca! O. K. by me in A - mer - i - ca!

---

[3] America: *Music by Leonard Bernstein, lyrics by Stephen Sondheim. © 1956, 1957 Amberson Holdings LLC and Stephen Sondheim. Copyright renewed. Leonard Bernstein Music Publishing Company LLC, Publisher.*

Example 6.18

I like to be in A-mer-i-ca! O. K. by me in A-mer-i-ca!

The measures with quarter notes are simply examples of *hemiola*. Strictly speaking, the music in example 6.18 should be notated as shown in example 6.19 below. However, the music in example 6.18 is notated acceptably, following the same principle as *alternate beaming* in example 2.37 from chapter two.

Example 6.19

I like to be in A-mer-i - ca! O. K. by me in A-mer-i - ca!

If a composition alternates repeatedly between $\frac{6}{8}$ and $\frac{2}{4}$, with the *unit* (not the eighth note) remaining constant, it is *also* an example of the first type of alternating time signature (*substitute notation*). Both meters are duple and the only difference between them is how their beats are divided. The rhythms in all three *systems* of example 6.20 produce the exact same musical result as each other.

Example 6.20

The second and third systems in example 6.20 require borrowed division, but avoid the need to change meters every measure.

The second type of alternating meter that alternates back and forth between two time signatures is **true alternating mixed meter**. In this type, the meter literally *must* change each measure and *cannot* be effectively accomplished by substitute notation. An example of true alternating mixed meter is Stuart Townend's contemporary hymn *How Deep the Father's Love for Us*,[4] excerpted in example 6.21.

---

[4] *How Deep the Father's Love for Us: Lyrics and music by Stuart Townend. © 1995, Kingsway's Thankyou Music (administered by EMI CMG Publishing). Tune name: Father's Love.*

Example 6.21

How deep the Fath-er's love for us, how vast be-yond all meas - ure,

For simplicity in notation, composers often elect to indicate *alternating* mixed meters (whether *true* or *substitute notation*) at the *beginning* of the work, as shown in example 6.22.

Example 6.22

How deep the Fath-er's love for us, how vast be-yond all meas - ure,

The Bach chorale[5] in example 6.23 includes several *fermatas*. A **fermata** (𝄐) is a symbol that instructs the performer to hold the note(s) above/below it for a *longer* duration than indicated by the note value. The exact length of the fermata is left completely up to the performer.

Example 6.23

The word *fermata* shares the same root as the English word *ferment*. The concept, then, is to allow the note to linger. Each fermata in example 6.23 above indicates the presence of a **cadence**, which is the term for the *end of a musical phrase*. In most modern music, *cadences* are written with longer *note values*, but the custom of the chorales was the use of fermatas. Notice that chorales (as well as modern hymns) do not abide by the pervasive convention of *indenting* the first musical system.

---

[5] Hinunter ist der Sonnenschein: *Common chorale harmonized by J.S. Bach, circa 1725. Public Domain.*

Before moving on to further study tonal music, a final concept to be grasped is *transposition*. As stated in chapter four, **transposition** is the process of *restating the music at a higher or lower pitch*. It is sometimes very helpful and even necessary to transpose to a higher or lower key to suit an instrumental or vocal *range*.

Another significant reason for mastering the valuable skill of transposition involves musical instruments known as *transposing instruments*. **Transposing instruments** produce a different *pitch* when played than the *note* that is read. For all transposing instruments, WRITTEN C PRODUCES THE SOUND OF THE KEY OF THE INSTRUMENT.

Most trumpets, for instance, are B-flat trumpets.[6] This means that when a trumpeter reads the note *C*, the trumpet produces the note *B-flat*, a major second below. Therefore, all music written for B-flat trumpet must be *written* a major second *higher* so they will sound where desired.

Instruments that are *not* transposing instruments are commonly called *C instruments*, meaning that written *C* produces the pitch *C*. Most instruments are not transposing instruments, playing all written notes at identical *concert pitch*. **Concert pitch** is the term for *sounding pitch* (the actual pitch that is *heard,* regardless of how it is notated).

Example 6.24 is a chart of common transposing instruments, along with their *written* and *sounding* ranges. The transposition of instruments denoted with an asterisk should be committed to memory.

Example 6.25 is a chart of common *C instruments*, along with their *ranges*. Notice that the piccolo, contra-bassoon, guitar, double bass, and electric bass all produce sounds in a different octave register than written. The piccolo is the only instrument (other than certain pitched percussion instruments) that sounds *higher* than written.[7] All others sound *lower* than written, and therefore must be written *above* where they sound.

Example 6.26 is a chart of common pitched percussion instruments (all of which are C instruments).

The *written* ranges for the instruments in example 6.24, 6.25, and 6.26 indicate the appropriate *clefs* for those particular instruments.

> "Never smile encouragingly
> at the brass section."
> - *conductor and cellist Marlin Owen*

---

[6] Unless specified, B-flat trumpet is assumed, even though there are trumpets in C, D, and E-flat.
[7] The D clarinet, E-flat clarinet, and D trumpet also sound higher than written, but these are very rare.

Example 6.24   transposing instruments

written *(key of C)*   **sounding** *(key of ...)*

woodwinds

English Horn (F) — sounds P5↓
- written: B3, C5, G6
- sounding: E3, F4, C6

*****Clarinet** (Bb) — sounds M2↓
- written: E3, C5, C7 (8va)
- sounding: D3, Bb4, Bb6 (8va)

Clarinet (A) — sounds m3↓
- same as for Bb clarinet
- sounding: C#3, A4, A6 (8va)

Bass Clarinet (Bb) — sounds M9↓
- written: Eb3, C5, G6
- sounding: Db2, Bb3, F5

Soprano Saxophone (Bb) — sounds M2↓
- written: Bb3, C5, F#6
- sounding: Ab3, Bb4, E6

***Alto Saxophone** (Eb) — sounds M6↓
- sounding: Db3, Eb4, A5

***Tenor Saxophone** (Bb) — sounds M9↓
- all saxophones share the same written range (see sop. sax.)
- sounding: Ab2, Bb3, E5

Baritone Saxophone (Eb) — Sounds M13↓ (M6 + octave)
- sounding: Db2, Eb3, A4

brass

***Horn in F** (French Horn) — sounds P5↓
- written: F#2, C5, C6
- sounding: B1, F4, F5

***Trumpet** (Bb) — sounds M2↓
- written: F#3, C5, D6
- sounding: E3, Bb4, C6

Baritone (Bb) — sounds M9↓
- written: F#3, C5, C6
- sounding: E2, Bb3, Bb4

Example 6.25 C instruments (written)

woodwinds:
- Piccolo (sounds P8 ↑): D4 to C7
- Flute: C4 to D7
- Oboe: Bb3 to A6
- Bassoon & Contra-bassoon (contra sounds P8 ↓): Bb1 to Eb5

brass:
- Trumpet (most trumpets are in Bb, but some are in C): F#3 to D6
- Trombone: E2 to Bb4
- Euphonium: Bb1 to Bb4
- Tuba: D1 to F4

plucked strings:
- Harp: Cb1 to G#7
- Guitar (sounds P8 ↓): E3 to E6

bowed strings (except for electric bass):
- Violin: G3 to G7
- Viola: C3 to E6
- Cello: C2 to G5
- Double Bass / Electric Bass (sounds P8 ↓): E2 to D5

Example 6.26 pitched percussion (written)

- Timpani (kettle drums): D2 to A3
- Glockenspiel (orchestra bells) (sounds P15 ↑): G3 to C5
- Xylophone (sounds P8 ↑): C4 to C6
- Vibraphone: F3 to F5
- Marimba: A2 to C6
- Chimes: C4 to G5
- Celesta (sounds P8 ↑): C3 to C6

Timpani, while pitched, cannot play *every* note in the ranges shown in example 6.26 without making tuning adjustments during a performance. It takes four timpani to cover the range displayed above, and often only two are used (usually due to limited availability of a full set).

Vocal ranges are shown below in example 6.27. These ranges are *generalizations* (some vocalists have a range larger than that of their vocal part), covering each vocal section of the choir (SATB). **THE LOWEST NOTE AND HIGHEST NOTE OF EACH RANGE INDICATED BELOW SHOULD BE WRITTEN VERY SPARINGLY.**

Example 6.27

soprano   alto   tenor   bass

In most of the examples of chorale style music in this textbook, the music is notated on the *grand staff* with sopranos and altos sharing the treble clef while tenors and basses share the bass clef. Sometimes it is necessary or desirable for composers to give each part its own staff. Often in these instances, the tenor part is notated using a *modified treble clef* to avoid excessive ledger lines that frequently occur when tenor parts are written in bass clef. The tenor range shown in example 6.27 is replicated below in example 6.28 using an *octave clef*.

Example 6.28

Any time one of the standard clefs has the octave designation (*8*) attached to its top or bottom, it becomes an **octave clef**. The small number eight simply indicates that the music is to be ***realized*** (made real in performance) an octave above or below where written. If the symbol *8* is attached to the *bottom* of the clef, then it designates an octave *below*, and if it is attached to the *top* of the clef, it indicates an octave *above*.

Example 6.28 above clearly shows that the center of the tenor range is in the middle of the treble clef (octave clef version), not the bass clef, which makes this clef an ideal choice when the tenor part is on its own staff.

This concludes the introduction to intermediate notation topics, and brings a close to part one of this textbook. The study of music theory continues in part two, which focuses on diatonic melody and harmony.

"Music does not excite until it is performed."
- composer Benjamin Britten

Assignments and Drills

Assignment 6.01

The objective of this assignment is increased understanding of transposing instruments.

Instructions: Follow the directions below, using the proper clef and key signature for each. The first one has been started for you. REFER BACK TO EXAMPLE 6.24 IF NECESSARY.

Write out the notes that would be heard if the melody provided were played on the B-flat trumpet.

Write out the notes that would be heard if the melody provided were played on the French horn.

Write out the notes that would be heard if the melody provided were played on the Alto saxophone.

Write out the notes that would be heard if the melody provided were played on the B-flat clarinet.

Write out the notes that would be heard if the melody provided were played on the tenor saxophone.

Assignment 6.02

The objective of this assignment is increased efficiency in transposing.

Instructions: Memorize the transpositions of the instruments identified in assignment 6.01. For trumpet and clarinet, always assume they are B-flat instruments unless specified otherwise. REFER BACK TO EXAMPLE 6.24 IF NECESSARY.

Assignment 6.03

The objective of this assignment is efficient and accurate transposition.

Instructions: The music example below is in concert pitch.

1. Rewrite the music for the instruments identified on each staff so that when played, the music will *sound* at concert pitch.
2. Use the appropriate clefs and key signatures for each instrument.

The first one has been started for you.

REFER BACK TO EXAMPLE 6.24 IF NECESSARY.

trumpet

French horn

alto saxophone

clarinet

tenor saxophone

Assignment 6.04

The objective of this assignment is efficient and accurate transposition.

Instructions: The music example below is in concert pitch.

1. Rewrite the music for the instruments identified on each staff so that when played, the music will *sound* at concert pitch.
2. Use the appropriate clefs and key signatures for each instrument.

REFER BACK TO EXAMPLES 6.24 — 6.25 IF NECESSARY.

concert pitch

French horn

clarinet

alto saxophone

trumpet

viola

guitar

tenor saxophone

Assignment 6.05

The objective of this assignment is efficient and accurate transposition.

Instructions: The music example below is in concert pitch.

1. Rewrite the music for the instruments identified on each staff so that when played, the music will *sound* at concert pitch.
2. Use the appropriate clefs and key signatures for each instrument.

REFER BACK TO EXAMPLES 6.24 — 6.25 IF NECESSARY.

concert pitch

tenor saxophone

bassoon

celesta

guitar

alto saxophone

viola

French horn

Assignment 6.06

The objective of this assignment is efficient and accurate transposition.

Instructions: The music example below is in concert pitch.

1. Rewrite the music for the instruments identified on each staff so that when played, the music will *sound* at concert pitch.
2. Use the appropriate clefs and key signatures for each instrument.

REFER BACK TO EXAMPLES 6.24 — 6.25 IF NECESSARY.

concert pitch

French horn

trumpet

euphonium

alto saxophone

soprano saxophone

viola

tenor saxophone

Assignment 6.07

The objective of this assignment is efficient and accurate transposition.

Instructions: The music example below is in concert pitch.

1. Rewrite the music for the instruments identified on each staff so that when played, the music will *sound* at concert pitch.
2. Use the appropriate clefs and key signatures for each instrument.
3. Do the work completely from memory. Do not refer back to chapter six.

concert pitch

trumpet

alto saxophone

French horn

tenor saxophone

viola

clarinet

Questions for Review

1. Define *articulation*.

2. Without referring back to example 6.05, write out six or seven tempo designations in order from slowest to fastest.

3. What is a *legend* and why is it necessary to include one when writing for percussion?

4. Explain what is meant by *ostinato*.

5. What is the difference between the designations *D.C.* and *D.S.*?

6. Explain where the dynamics, expression indications, and tempo designations are placed in relation to the staff when notating vocal music.

7. Explain the term *mixed meter*.

8. What is the difference between alternating meter that is merely *substitute notation* and that which is *true alternating meter*?

9. What is the function of a fermata?

10. Why is transposition a necessary skill for musicians?

Assignments for Use with Anthology

A6.01 On a separate sheet of paper, write out a *map* for each composition. The first one is done for you.

- Chopin: *Mazurka 5 in B-flat Minor*, Opus 7, No. 1. Anthology pages 355-356.

    Map:
    Ms. 1-44.
    Pickup to ms. 25-64 (first ending).
    Pickup to ms. 45-64 (second ending).

- Haydn: *Symphony No. 101 in D Major*, fourth movement (Vivace). Anthology pages 159-168.

- Chopin: *Mazurka 6 in A Minor*, Opus 7, No. 2. Anthology pages 357-358.

A6.02 Identify the metrical device used in Bartók: *Music for String Instruments, Percussion, and Celesta*, first movement (Andante). Anthology pages 484-489.

A6.03 On a sheet of staff paper, write out a *simple position reduction* for all the triads in measures 1-8 of Haydn: *Symphony No. 101 in D Major*, third movement (Allegretto). Anthology page 154. Do *not* attempt harmonic analysis of these triads.

A6.04 On a sheet of staff paper, transpose the clarinet in measures 5-15 of Brahms: *Sonata in F Minor for Clarinet and Piano*, Opus 120, No. 1, first movement (Allegro). Anthology page 398. Transpose to sounding (concert) pitch. NOTE: IN GERMAN, THE NOTE ***B*** IS ***B-FLAT***. THUS, THE DESIGNATION *KLARINETTE IN B* MEANS *CLARINET IN B-FLAT*.

A6.05 Provide *harmonic analysis* of measures 1-16 of Mozart: *Menuet and Trio* from *Serenade in C Minor*, K. 388, third movement. Anthology page 207. Do your best to determine which notes are part of a triad and which ones are nonharmonic. Circle the nonharmonic tones. NOTE: *CORNO* IS ITALIAN FOR *HORN* AND *FAGOTTO* IS ITALIAN FOR *BASSOON*. THE HORNS HERE ARE PITCHED IN E-FLAT, AND THE CLARINETS IN B-FLAT.

A6.06 On a sheet of staff paper, transpose the Horn parts in measures 1-16 of Mozart: *Menuet and Trio* from *Serenade in C Minor*, K. 388, third movement. Anthology page 207. Transpose to concert pitch.

A6.07 The trumpet part of *Anthropology* by Charles Parker and Dizzy Gillespie is shown in concert pitch in Appendix A of the anthology (page 617). Transpose measures 1-8 on a sheet of staff paper for the B-flat trumpet.

PART THE SECOND: DIATONIC MELODY AND HARMONY

Music that never deviates from the established key is purely **diatonic**. **Dia**, as in *dia*gonal or *dia*metric, literally means *through* or *across*. **Tonic** means *tones*, or more specifically, *key*. **Diatonic** music, therefore, goes *through the tones* (or *across the key*). Foreign elements to the key are **chromatic**. Both diatonic and chromatic harmony comprise the field of study known as **tonal analysis**.

The study of diatonic music was introduced back in chapter four on scales and keys. This middle section of the textbook is devoted to the study of musical elements and devices that are exclusive to the key. Three types of analysis will be presented. Music will be analyzed up close, or in the foreground; at a slight distance, in the middle ground; and with the entire composition in sight, in the background. Because all three perspectives are vital to musical comprehension, a well-rounded perception of what is happening musically from each vantage point contributes to the overall musicianship of the music theorist.

In *tonal analysis*, the foreground perspective deals primarily with chords. Middle-ground analysis explores how those chords relate to the tonic and each other through *harmonic progression* and ultimately *cadence*. Background analysis examines musical *texture* and *form*.

Foreground, middle-ground, and background analysis are not only useful in understanding harmony, but they enlighten the musician regarding melody as well. Short musical ideas called *motifs*, along with a variety of methods of developing those motifs, are studied in the foreground. Phrases and phrase relationships, called *periods*, are middle-ground elements of melodic analysis. The overall contour of the melody is considered in background analysis.

Chapter 7
Seventh Chords and Figured Bass

As noted in chapter five, three-note chords are called *triads*. Often, however, composers wish to use a fuller, more expanded **sonority**.[1] The result is a combination of tones ranging from four to as many as eleven pitch classes. In diatonic music, a four-note chord is a seventh chord, a five-note chord is a ninth chord, a six-note chord is an eleventh chord, and a seven-note chord is a thirteenth chord. Chords consisting of more than seven notes include chromaticism and are usually referred to as *clusters* or *simultaneities*.

Example 7.01 illustrates the diatonic palette of tertian harmonic options constructed on **C**.

Example 7.01

interval   triad   seventh   ninth   eleventh   thirteenth

A **seventh chord** gets its name from the interval from the root of the chord to the highest note when the chord is arranged in thirds (root position). The chord consists of a root, third, fifth, and seventh.

While a *triad* may be one of *four* functional qualities (Major, minor, diminished, or augmented), there are *five* functional qualities of *seventh chords*. Seventh chord qualities are determined as follows:

- **Major** seventh chords: (*Major triad* with a
    The *triad* is *major* (M).   *major third* on top.)
    The interval from the *root to the seventh* is *major* (M7).
- **Minor** seventh chords: (*Minor triad* with a
    The *triad* is *minor* (m).   *minor third* on top.)
    The interval from the *root to the seventh* is *minor* (m7).
- **Dominant** seventh chords: (*Major triad* with a
    The *triad* is *major* (M).   *minor third* on top.)
    The interval from the *root to the seventh* is *minor* (m7).
- **Diminished** seventh chords: (*Diminished triad*
    The *triad* is *diminished* (d).   with a *minor*
    The interval from the *root to the seventh* is diminished (d7).   *third* on top.)
    NOTE: ALL THIRDS ARE *MINOR THIRDS* IN THE DIMINISHED SEVENTH CHORD.
- **Half-diminished** seventh chords: (*Diminished triad*
    The *triad* is *diminished* (d).   with a *major*
    The interval from the *root to the seventh* is *minor* (m7).   *third* on top.)

---

[1] *Sonority refers to harmonic simultaneity of pitches. An interval is the most basic sonority.*

Example 7.02 illustrates the seventh chords that are created on every degree of a major scale. The quality of each seventh chord is labeled below.

Example 7.02

major 7th chord — minor 7th chord — minor 7th chord — major 7th chord — dominant 7th chord — minor 7th chord — half-diminished 7th chord

In harmonic analysis, the qualities of seventh chords are indicated as follows:

- *Major* seventh chords:
  Uppercase roman numerals followed by the integer 7 in superscript.
  IV^7, for example.
- *Minor* seventh chords:
  Lowercase roman numerals followed by superscript 7.
  ii^7, for example.
- *Dominant* seventh chords:
  Uppercase roman numeral V followed by superscript 7.
  V^7.
- *Diminished* seventh chords:
  Lowercase roman numerals followed by superscript o7.
  vii^{o7}, for example.
- *Half-diminished* seventh chords:
  Lowercase roman numerals followed by superscript ø7.
  $vii^{ø7}$, for example.

Example 7.03 illustrates the seventh chords that are created on every degree of a major scale along with the harmonic analysis of each chord labeled below.

Example 7.03

I^7 — ii^7 — iii^7 — IV^7 — V^7 — vi^7 — $vii^{ø7}$

Example 7.04 on the following page is an updated version of the chart first presented in chapter five in example 5.07. It now includes analysis of diatonic seventh chords for major keys.

Example 7.04

Key of C	C	C#/D♭	D	D#/E♭	E	F	F#/G♭	G	G#/A♭	A	A#/B♭	B
DIATONIC TRIADS	I		ii		iii	IV		V		vi		vii°
DIATONIC TRIADS in natural minor	i		ii°	III		iv		v		VI		VII
DIATONIC TRIADS in harmonic minor	i		ii°	III+		iv		V		VI		vii°
SEVENTH CHORDS	I^7		ii^7		iii^7	IV^7		V^7		vi^7		$vii^{ø7}$

Just as triads seldom appear in their most basic forms in music, seventh chords are also often spread among instruments or voice parts.

Example 7.05 is a reproduction of the musical excerpt used in example 5.11 in chapter five. The circled note within the arpeggio was not considered harmonic at that time because it did not fit into the triad. However, the circled note is the *seventh* of a *dominant seventh* chord.

Example 7.05

Instead of being an A major *triad* (A, C#, E), the chord is a *dominant seventh* (A, C#, E, G) in the key of D (remember that this piece has *modulated* from **G** to **D** at this point). The dominant seventh *quality* (Major triad, minor seventh) is present and the chord appears on the fifth (dominant) scale degree of the key.

This example is replicated below in example 7.06 with the inclusion of *harmonic analysis* and without the circle around the seventh of the V^7 (the circle will be reserved for *nonharmonic tones*). Example 7.07 shows the same example with the inclusion of *pop-chord analysis*.

Example 7.06

D: ii^6 I^6_4 V^7

Example 7.07

Em/G   D/A   A7

Like intervals and triads, seventh chords may be *inverted*. Each *interval* has only *one* inversion, each *triad* has *two* inversions (*plus root position*), and each *seventh chord* has *three* inversions (*plus root position*).

Example 7.08 shows a dominant seventh chord in root position plus all of its inversions.

Example 7.08

root position   first inversion   second inverson   third inversion

The same chord appears on the *grand staff* in example 7.09 below in a variety of inversions and spacings. Measures three through seven are in *chorale style*.

Example 7.09

- The seventh chord in measure three is in root position and open spacing.
- The chord in measure four is in third inversion and close spacing.
- The chord in measure five is in first inversion and close spacing.
- The chord in measure six is in second inversion and open spacing.
- The chord in measure seven is in third inversion and open spacing.

Notice that since four notes constitute the chord, there is no doubling of pitches. At times, for purposes of smooth leading within the vocal parts, a composer will prefer to double a note instead of include all four notes of the seventh chord. When this occurs, the *fifth of the chord* is omitted. Each chord in example 7.10 is still considered a dominant seventh chord in C major.

Example 7.10

Seventh chord *inversions* are included in *harmonic analysis* by numeric symbols. The symbol for a *root position* seventh chord is ^{7}, the symbol for a *first inversion* seventh chord is $^6_5$, the symbol for a *second inversion* seventh chord is $^4_3$, and the symbol for a *third inversion* seventh chord is $^4_2$. These symbols are shown below in examples 7.11 and 7.12.

Example 7.11

C: V^7 V^7 V^7 V^4_2 V^6_5 V^4_3 V^4_2

Example 7.12

C: V^7 V^7 V^7 V^4_2 V^6_5 V^6_5 V^4_2

Seventh chords are indicated in *pop-chord notation* as illustrated in example 7.13.

Example 7.13

seventh chord	major	minor	dominant	diminished	half-diminished
root position	Cmaj7	Cm7	C7	C°7	Cm7(♭5)
first inversion	Cmaj7/E	Cm7/E♭	C7/E	C°7/E♭	Cm7(♭5)/E♭
second inversion	Cmaj7/G	Cm7/G	C7/G	C°7/G♭	Cm7(♭5)/G♭
third inversion	Cmaj7/B♭	Cm7/B	C7/B♭	C°7/B♭♭	Cm7(♭5)/B♭

In *jazz* pop-chord notation, the symbol for a *major seventh chord* is a hollow triangle (△) instead of *maj7*. In all types of pop-chord notation, the *fully-diminished sevenths* may be notated as *dim^7* instead of ^{o7}. Some theorists use to the term **fully-diminished** to distinguish between a *diminished seventh chord* and a **half**-*diminished seventh* chord.

The chords in root position in example 7.13 are shown in their simplest position on the staff in example 7.14 on the following page.

Example 7.14

Cmaj7   Cm7   C7   C°7   Cm7(♭5)

In regard to seventh chord quality, *major sevenths* and *minor sevenths* provide distinctive *color* to the sound. That is, the presence of the seventh modifies the triad in a way that alters the sound but does not affect the *function* of the chord. Conversely, *dominant, diminished,* and *half-diminished* sevenths all contribute to the *activity* of the chord. This will be explained in more detail in chapter nine on *harmonic progression*.

Example 7.15 is an excerpt from the first Prelude[2] in J. S. Bach's landmark keyboard collection, *The Well-tempered Clavier*. Measures two and three of this example are seventh chords.

Example 7.15

To help with analysis, the chords in example 7.15 are shown in *simple position reduction* in example 7.16 on the following page. Example 7.17 shows the excerpt with a *textural reduction*. **Textural reduction** is similar to simple position reduction except that it retains all octave designations of all notes present instead of reducing them by pitch class.

---

[2] The Well-tempered Clavier, Prelude I, BWV 846: *J.S. Bach, 1722. Public Domain.*

Example 7.16

The chord in measure two, when arranged in thirds, is D, F, A, C. Since the seventh of the chord (**C**) is on the bottom, the chord is in *third* inversion.

When arranged in thirds, the chord in measure three is G, B, D, F. The third of the chord, **B**, is the lowest-sounding tone, so the chord is in *first* inversion.

Example 7.17

If pop-chord symbols were to be used for analysis, the chord in measure two would be *Dm7/C*, and the chord in measure three would be *G7/B*.

Textural reduction will be covered in greater detail in chapter ten on *melody and texture*.

Example 7.18 is another excerpt from the Mozart piano sonata used in chapters two, five, and earlier in this chapter. Harmonic analysis is provided.

Example 7.18

G: I V_3^4 V_5^6 I

Note that none of the notes are circled as *nonharmonic* in example 7.18 because every note fits into the harmony indicated. At first glance, the **C** in measure 3 may appear to be nonharmonic, but it is the seventh of a V^7 chord in first inversion.

The *inversion symbols* that are used in *harmonic analysis* that have been studied so far are compiled on the chart in example 7.19. These symbols originated in the Baroque era of music history in a notational shorthand system called *figured bass*.

Example 7.19

	triad	seventh chord
root position		7
first inversion	6	6 5
second inversion	6 4	4 3
third inversion		4 2

"Are we not formed,
as the notes of music are,
For one another,
though dissimilar?"
- poet Percy Bysshe Shelley

Just as modern day *pop-chord notation* substitutes mere symbols for entire chords and their inversions, **figured bass** saved time for composers in the Baroque era. Composers wrote the *bass line* to the music and placed symbols underneath the bass line, informing the performers of what chords and inversions to play. ALL NUMBERS AND SYMBOLS IN THE FIGURED BASS APPLY TO INTERVALS ABOVE THE BASS.

Example 7.20 shows C major triads in root position, first inversion and second inversion on the staff with the intervals above the bass indicated below the staff.

Example 7.20

```
            5       6       6
            3       3       4
```

The *bass note* in the first triad is **C**. The notes above it (**E** and **G**) are a third and a fifth above the bass.

The *bass note* in the second triad is **E** (but the *root* of the chord is still **C**). The intervals above the bass (**G** and **C**) are a third and a sixth above the bass.

The *bass note* in the third triad is **G** (but the *root* of the chord is still **C**). The intervals above the bass (**C** and **E**) are a fourth and a sixth above the bass.

Since *root position* chords occur with the most frequency, composers of the Baroque era just left the space below the bass note *blank* instead of writing in a **5** and a **3**. If *nothing* was written in the *figured bass*, the performers knew to include a third and a fifth above the bass.

Also, since the third above the bass is extremely frequent, occurring in root position *and* first inversion triads, the number **3** was not typically written in figured bass symbols at all. Therefore, the symbol for a first inversion triad became merely **6** instead of both a **6** and a **3**.

Example 7.21 juxtaposes the actual intervals above the bass with the figured bass symbols used.

Example 7.21

triads	actual intervals above the bass	figured bass symbol
root position	5 3	
first inversion	6 3	6
second inversion	6 4	6 4

"A painter paints pictures on canvas. But musicians paint their pictures on silence."
- conductor *Leopold Stowkowski*

Example 7.22 below shows G (dominant) seventh chords in root position, first inversion, second inversion, and third inversion on the staff with the intervals above the bass indicated below the staff.

Example 7.22

```
      7     6     6     6
      5     5     4     4
      3     3     3     2
```

Example 7.23

seventh chords	actual intervals above the bass	figured bass symbol
root position	7 5 3	7
first inversion	6 5 3	6 5
second inversion	6 4 3	4 3
third inversion	6 4 2	4 2

"Music washes away from the soul the dust of everyday life."
- poet Berthold Auerbach

Example 7.24

Other symbols that frequently occur in figured bass: ♯ ♭ ♮ / \ +

Integers are not the only components of figured bass. Other symbols often appear below the bass line as well. The most common of these symbols are sharps, flats, naturals, slashes, backslashes, and plus signs, shown in example 7.24 above.

When any of these symbols are placed *next to a number* (on *either* side of the number), they affect *that interval above the bass*. This is shown in example 7.25, where *root of a first inversion triad* is raised. Since the triad is in *first inversion*, the symbol *6* is used, and since the *root* of the chord is a *sixth above the bass* in first inversion, the *6* is followed immediately by a sharp to indicate that it is raised.

Example 7.25

6♯   equals ⟶

A *slash* (or backslash) *through a number* means to *raise the pitch one half step*. It means exactly the same thing as a sharp in front of or behind that number. Further, a *plus sign* before or after a number means the same thing as a sharp next to number or a slash (or even backslash) through a number.

Example 7.26

6♯ equals ♯6 equals ⑥ equals ♮6 equals 6+ equals +6 equals ⟶

A *flat* placed *next to a number* means to *lower* that interval above the bass *one half step* as shown in example 7.27.

Example 7.27

$$\begin{array}{c}6\\4\flat\end{array} \text{ equals } \uparrow \text{ equals } \begin{array}{c}6\\\flat 4\end{array}$$

A *natural* next to a number simply means to alter *that interval above the bass* as indicated. This is shown in example 7.28 as both a raised and lowered alteration.

Example 7.28

$$\begin{array}{c}6\natural\\4\\3\end{array} \text{ equals } \begin{array}{c}\natural 6\\4\\3\end{array} \text{ equals } \uparrow \qquad \begin{array}{c}6\\\natural 5\end{array} \text{ equals } \begin{array}{c}6\\5\natural\end{array} \text{ equals } \uparrow$$

When accidentals are not used in figured bass, the performer follows the key signature.

The second inversion seventh chord in the first measure of example 7.28 is normally indicated in the figured bass by merely $\begin{smallmatrix}4\\3\end{smallmatrix}$, with the sixth above the bass *implied*. However, since the sixth above the bass (the *third* of the chord) needed to be altered (raised, in this instance), the number **6** had to be included along with the natural symbol.

The first inversion seventh chord in the second measure of example 7.28 required a natural to *lower* the fifth above the bass (the *seventh* of the chord) a half step.

When a musician performs according to figured bass symbols, the term that is used to describe the performance is *figured bass* **realization**. That is, the performer is *making real*, or **realizing**, the music indicated by the shorthand notation.

Sometimes in figured bass, a symbol is written below the staff all by itself (not next to a number). When this occurs, a root position triad is assumed and the *symbol* applies to the *third above the bass*.

Example 7.29

♯ equals ⟶ ↑   / equals ⟶ ↑   ♭ equals ⟶ ↑   ♮ equals ⟶ ↑

Similarly, any symbol written *below* a number applies to the *third above the bass*, as shown in example 7.30 on the following page.

Example 7.30

6 equals ♭6
7 equals +7
6 equals 6/5/♭

Sometimes a composer will use the figured bass to indicate a particular doubling. In chorale style, ³⁄₃ would be used to signify a *root position triad* with a *doubled third*. ⁶⁄₆ would indicate a *first inversion triad* with a *doubled sixth above the bass* (root). If ⁸⁄₆ were to be used, it would signify a *first inversion triad* with the *bass* (third of the triad) *doubled in another octave*.

Example 7.31

3 equals 3/3
6 equals 6/6
8 equals 8/6

At other times, composers may use figured bass to indicate notes that are not part of the harmony. Although these *nonharmonic* tones will be studied in detail in chapter eight, it is worthwhile to have a present awareness of them in figured bass.

If the number **4** appears by itself, it indicates a note *suspended* (held over or repeated) from a previous chord. The *suspended note* will be a *fourth above the bass*, and will temporarily substitute for a *third above the bass* in a *root position triad*. Therefore, the presence of a **4** signifies a *root position triad* with a *fourth* above the bass *instead of a third*. When the suspended fourth *resolves* down to the third of the triad, it is indicated in the figured bass as shown in examples 7.32 and 7.33.

Example 7.32

4   3

Example 7.33

4   #

When a bass note is held or tied in figured bass (even across bar lines), the numbers and symbols that applied to the first note still apply to the tied note unless otherwise indicated. Example 7.34 on the following page illustrates this.

Example 7.34

Sometimes composers have opted to use $^5_4$ in the figured bass instead of just ^{4} in the case of a suspended fourth. This is shown in example 7.34 above.

No symbols are ever put in the figured bass to indicate changes to the *bass note* itself. The sharp in the figured bass in example 7.35 has nothing to do with the bass note, applying simply to the *third above the bass note*.

Example 7.35

Example 7.36

Note that flats and sharps may co-exist in a chord, as shown in example 7.36.

If the fifth of a root position chord must be altered, then 5 must appear in the figured bass with the appropriate alteration, as shown in example 7.36 above.

When the bass note changes, but the notes from the previous chord are to remain the same, this is indicated by a horizontal line as shown in example 7.37.

Example 7.37

"If it's worth saying, it's sung."

– unknown

Numbers appear in parenthesis in the figured bass when it is necessary to indicate the chord inversion, but the interval above the bass that is specified is already present. For instance, sometimes the **outer voices** (soprano and bass) of a chorale are written out in addition to figured bass symbols to be *realized* on a keyboard. In such cases, the figured bass indication often includes an interval above the bass that is already present in the melody. This is demonstrated on the following page in example 7.38. The **inner voices** (alto and tenor) appear without stems to indicate that they are the *realization* of the figured bass.

Example 7.38

"It is incontestable that music induces in us a sense of the infinite and the contemplation of the invisible."
— poet Victor de LaPrade

In the event that a chord is affected by an accidental and the following chord in the same measure has the same bass note (regardless of octave), the accidental need not be repeated in the figured bass. This is shown in example 7.39. However, if a note is affected by an accidental twice in a measure but not successively, it is common practice to repeat the inclusion of the accidental in the figured bass for clarity, as shown in example 7.40.

Example 7.39

Example 7.40

In *harmonic analysis*, the *numbers* from figured bass are used but the *symbols* are not. Further, figured bass, like pop-chord notation, only indicates which chords are present and does not signify their relation to the key. Figured bass lines do not indicate the key and do not utilize roman numerals.

This concludes the introduction to seventh chords and figured bass. *Nonharmonic tones* will be covered in chapter eight.

SEVENTH CHORDS AND FIGURED BASS

Assignments and Drills

Assignment 7.01

The objective of this assignment is efficient seventh chord creation in root position.

Instructions: Create *seventh chords* in *root position* as instructed. The note provided is the *root* of each chord and is not to be altered. The first two have been done for you. REFER BACK TO EXAMPLES 7.01 AND 7.02 IF NECESSARY.

1	half-diminished
2	minor
3	diminished
4	dominant
5	major
6	major
7	diminished
8	half-diminished
9	dominant
10	minor
11	dominant
12	major
13	half-diminished
14	diminished
15	minor
16	major
17	minor
18	diminished
19	dominant
20	diminished
21	dominant
22	major
23	diminished
24	minor
25	half-diminished
26	diminished
27	major
28	dominant
29	half-diminished
30	minor
31	dominant
32	minor
33	half-diminished
34	major
35	diminished
36	major
37	dominant
38	diminished
39	half-diminished
40	minor

Assignment 7.02

The objective of this assignment is identification of seventh chord qualities.

Instructions: Identify the *root* and *quality* of each *seventh chord* using *pop-chord* abbreviations:
Maj7 = major seventh.   m7 = minor seventh.
7 = dominant seventh.   °7 = diminished seventh.
m7(♭5) = half-diminished seventh.

The first two have been done for you.
REFER BACK TO EXAMPLES 7.01, 7.02, AND 7.13 IF NECESSARY.

Assignment 7.03

The objective of this assignment is efficient seventh chord identification in various keys and inversions.

Instructions: Provide the correct *roman numeral* and *inversion* symbol for each chord. The first two have been done for you. REFER BACK TO EXAMPLES 7.01, 7.02, 7.03, 7.08, 7.19, 7.22, AND 7.23 IF NECESSARY.

1. Am: vii°4/2
2. Em: ii ø 4/3
3. D:
4. B♭:
5. F:
6. D♭:
7. D:
8. B:
9. B♭:
10. F:
11. Dm:
12. D:
13. Em:
14. F:
15. G:
16. E:
17. E♭:
18. Bm:
19. A:
20. Am:
21. E:
22. C#:
23. D♭:
24. Dm:
25. G:
26. G♭:
27. G#m:
28. Dm:
29. Am:
30. B♭m:
31. F:
32. D:
33. B:
34. B♭:
35. Em:

Assignment 7.04

The objective of this assignment is efficient seventh chord creation in various keys and inversions.

Instructions: Write each chord as indicated. Do not use key signatures. The first two have been done for you. REFER BACK TO EXAMPLES 7.01, 7.02, 7.03, 7.08, 7.19, 7.22, AND 7.23 IF NECESSARY.

1. G: vii°$^6_5$
2. Cm: vii°$^4_2$
3. Bm: iiø$^6_5$
4. A: vi$^4_3$
5. F: IV^7
6. B♭: V$^4_2$
7. Gm: ii°$^4_3$
8. D: vii°$^6_5$
9. Em: iv$^4_2$
10. Am: V$^4_3$
11. C: vi$^6_5$
12. D♭: ii^7
13. E: iii$^6_5$
14. B: vi$^4_3$
15. F: vii°^{7}
16. A: iii$^4_3$
17. B♭: ii$^4_2$
18. C: vii°$^6_5$
19. Dm: iv^7
20. Em: V$^4_2$
21. Fm: VI$^6_5$
22. G: I$^4_3$
23. A♭m: iv$^4_3$
24. A♭: IV$^6_5$
25. B: vi^7
26. Cm: iiø^7
27. D: iii$^4_3$
28. E: vii°$^6_5$
29. F♯: V$^6_5$
30. F♯m: v$^4_2$
31. G♯m: i$^4_2$
32. A♭: ii$^4_2$
33. A♭m: iv^7
34. Em: VI$^6_5$
35. Dm: iiø^7
36. A: ii^7
37. C: iii$^6_5$
38. E♭: I$^4_2$
39. Fm: VI$^4_3$
40. G♭: IV$^6_5$

Assignment 7.05

The objective of this assignment is accurate harmonic analysis of music in chorale style.

Instructions: Provide *harmonic analysis* for the chorale below.[3] REFER BACK TO EXAMPLES 7.01, 7.02, 7.03, 7.08, 7.19, 7.22, AND 7.23 IF NECESSARY.

O come, let us a-dore Him, O come, let us a-dore Him, O come, let us a-dore Him, Christ the Lord.

Assignment 7.06

The objective of this assignment is accurate harmonic analysis of music in chorale style.

Instructions: Provide *harmonic analysis* for the chorale excerpt below.[4] REFER BACK TO EXAMPLES 7.01, 7.02, 7.03, 7.08, 7.19, 7.22, AND 7.23 IF NECESSARY.

Come, Thou fount of ev-ery bless-ing, tune my heart to sing Thy grace;

---

[3] O Come, Let Us Adore Him *(refrain only)*: Traditional music and lyrics. Public Domain. *Tune name:* Adeste Fideles.

[4] Come, Thou fount of Every Blessing: *Lyrics by Robert Robinson, 1758; traditional American melody, circa 1800. Public Domain. Tune name:* Nettleton.

Assignment 7.07

The objective of this assignment is accurate harmonic analysis of music in chorale style.

Instructions: Provide *harmonic analysis* **for the chorale below.**[5] REFER BACK TO EXAMPLES 7.01, 7.02, 7.03, 7.08, 7.19, 7.22, AND 7.23 IF NECESSARY.

When I sur-vey the won-drous cross

on which the Prince of Glo-ry died,

my rich-est gain I count but loss,

and pour con-tempt on all my pride.

---

[5] When I Survey the Wondrous Cross: *Lyrics by Isaac Watts, 1707; music attributed to Lowell Mason, 1824, based on Gregorian chant (not the same harmonization as examples 5.24-5.26). Public Domain. Tune name:* Hamburg.

Assignment 7.08

The objective of this assignment is accurate and efficient harmonic analysis of music for piano.

Instructions: Provide *harmonic analysis* for the excerpts below. The beginning of the first measure of the first excerpt has been done for you. REFER BACK TO EXAMPLES 7.15 — 7.18 IF NECESSARY.

The Wild Horseman (Opus 68, No. 8): *Robert Schumann, 1848. Public Domain.*

Am: i

Sonata Facile, *Opus 49, No. 2, second movement (Minuet): Ludwig van Beethoven, 1805. Public Domain.*

Assignment 7.09

The objective of this assignment is efficient creation of figured bass symbols below the staff.

Instructions: Provide *figured bass* **for the chorale below.**[6] REFER BACK TO EXAMPLES 7.19 — 7.39 IF NECESSARY.

When I sur-vey the won-drous cross

on which the Prince of Glo-ry died,

my rich-est gain I count but loss,

and pour con-tempt on all my pride.

---

[6] When I Survey the Wondrous Cross: *Lyrics by Isaac Watts, 1707; music attributed to Lowell Mason, 1824, based on Gregorian chant. Public Domain. Tune name:* Hamburg.

Assignment 7.10

The objective of this assignment is efficient creation of figured bass symbols below the staff.

Instructions: The Bach chorale used in example 6.23 appears below in simplified form. Provide the *figured bass* below the staff. Do not attempt harmonic analysis. Ignore circled (nonharmonic) notes. REFER BACK TO EXAMPLES 7.19 — 7.39 IF NECESSARY.

Assignment 7.11

The objective of this assignment is efficient creation of figured bass symbols below the staff.

Instructions: Provide the *figured bass* for the following Bach chorale[7] below the staff. Do not attempt harmonic analysis. Ignore circled (nonharmonic) notes. REFER BACK TO EXAMPLES 7.19 — 7.39 IF NECESSARY.

---

[7] Komm, Gott Schöpfer, Heiliger Geist: *Common chorale harmonized by J.S. Bach, circa 1725. Public Domain. Simplified for analysis.*

Assignment 7.12

The objective of this assignment is efficient creation of figured bass symbols below the staff.

Instructions: Provide the *figured bass* for the following simplified Bach chorale[8] below the staff. REFER BACK TO EXAMPLES 7.19 — 7.39 IF NECESSARY.

Assignment 7.13

The objective of this assignment is efficient creation of figured bass symbols below the staff.

Instructions: Provide the *figured bass* for the following simplified Bach chorale[9] below the staff. REFER BACK TO EXAMPLES 7.19 — 7.39 IF NECESSARY.

---

[8] O wie selig seid ihr doch, ihr Frommen: *Common chorale harmonized by J.S. Bach, circa 1725. Public Domain.*
[9] Vom Himmel hoch da komm ich her: *Common chorale harmonized by J.S. Bach, circa 1725. Public Domain.*

Seventh Chords and Figured Bass

Assignment 7.14

The objective of this assignment is accurate figured bass realization.

Instructions: Realize the *figured bass* for the following bass lines. The first measure of the first exercise is done for you. REFER BACK TO EXAMPLES 7.19 — 7.39 IF NECESSARY.

205

Questions for Review

1. Why is a four-note chord called a *seventh chord*?

2. Identify the *quality* of the *triad* and the quality of the interval of the *seventh from the root* in each of the following types of seventh chords:

    Major seventh:

    Minor seventh:

    Dominant seventh:

    Diminished seventh:

    Half-diminished seventh:

3. What is the *figured bass symbol* for a *seventh chord* in each of the following inversions?

    Root position:

    First inversion:

    Second inversion:

    Third inversion:

4. If one of these symbols (♯ ♭ + ♮ / \ ) is used in figured bass *next to a number*, what is the performer to do?

5. If one of the symbols in question 4 is used in figured bass *by itself*, what is the performer to do?

6. If one of the symbols in question 4 is used in figured bass *below a number*, what is the performer to do?

Assignments for Use with Anthology

A7.01 Complete the *figured bass realization* for Corelli: *Violin Sonata*, opus 5, No. 1 (Adagio). Anthology pages 63-64. A treble clef is provided with the first chord done for you. *Unlike* the chord done for you, write the chords in the inversion indicated by the figured bass.

A7.02 Complete the *figured bass realization* for Handel: *Messiah*, Recitative No. 27, Thy Rebuke Hath Broken His Heart. Anthology page 95. A treble clef is provided for the figured bass realization.

A7.03 *Realize the figured bass* for the Gesangbuch chorale, *Jesu, Jesu, du bist mein*. Anthology page 634. Do not attempt to write inner voices (alto and tenor) in chorale style, but rather, write notes belonging to each chord in the treble clef below the melody. Do not duplicate the bass or soprano notes; just fill in the chord tones that are missing.

A7.04 *Realize the figured bass* for the Gesangbuch chorale, *So gehst du nun, mein Jesu, hin*. Anthology page 639. Do not attempt to write inner voices (alto and tenor) in chorale style, but rather, write notes belonging to each chord in the treble clef below the melody. Do not duplicate the bass or soprano notes; just fill in the chord tones that are missing.

A7.05 *Realize the figured bass* for the Gesangbuch chorale, *So gibst du nun, mein Jesu, gut Nacht*. Anthology page 639. Do not attempt to write inner voices (alto and tenor) in chorale style, but rather, write notes belonging to each chord in the treble clef below the melody. Do not duplicate the bass or soprano notes; just fill in the chord tones that are missing.

A7.06 Write out *figured bass* for the Franck chorale, *Ach, wie flüchtig, ach wie nichtig*. Anthology pages 624-625.

A7.07 Write out *figured bass* for the Hammerschmidt chorale, *Freuet euch, ihr Christen alle*. Anthology page 630.

A7.08 Write out *figured bass* for the Teschner chorale, *Valet will ich dir geben*. Anthology page 640.

Chapter 8
Nonharmonic Tones

Not all notes in a melody belong to the chord that harmonizes the melody at that given point. When a note that is foreign to the chord appears, it is called a *nonharmonic tone*. Simply put, **nonharmonic tones** do not belong to the harmony and are therefore considered *dissonances*. Nonharmonic tones may appear in any voice or instrumental part and are *circled* and *labeled* in harmonic analysis.

If a nonharmonic tone occurs *between beats*, it is considered *unaccented*. If it occurs *on a beat*, it is *accented*.

Nonharmonic tones provide relief from the constancy of chord tones and serve a specific compositional purpose. There are ten different types of nonharmonic tones, each with its own function:

- Passing tone (PT)
- Neighboring tone (NT)
- Escape tone, also called *échappée* (ET)
- Appoggiatura (APP)
- Anticipation (ANT)
- Changing tones, also called *cambiata* (CT)
- Pedal tone (PD)
- Suspension (SUS)
- Retardation (RET)
- Free tone (FT)

"Music is the shorthand of emotion."
- author Leo Tolstoy

Passing tones move *stepwise* from one chord tone to the next as shown in example 8.01.

Example 8.01

Neighboring tones move *stepwise* from one chord tone *back to that same chord tone* as shown in example 8.02.

Example 8.02

Neighboring tones (NT) that step *downward* and then back are called **lower neighbors** (LN), and neighboring tones that step *upward* and then back are called **upper neighbors** (UN).

At first glance, the *nonharmonic tone* in example 8.03 may *appear to be* a passing tone.

Example 8.03

Nonharmonic tones are always identified within the melodic line of a *single voice*. The *alto line* in example 8.03 moves from **E** to **F** and *back to E* (*not up to G*). Therefore, the **F** is an (unaccented) *upper neighbor*.

Escape tones move *away by step* from one chord tone, followed by a *leap* to the next chord tone as shown in example 8.04.

Example 8.04

Escape tones (ET) *usually*:
- appear as *unaccented* nonharmonic tones
- step one way, then leap the *opposite direction*
- leap the interval of a *third*

Appoggiaturas are the opposite of escape tones, *leaping away* from one chord tone, followed by *stepwise motion* to the next chord tone as shown in example 8.05. The word appoggiatura[1] is derived from an Italian word meaning *to lean upon*. Thus, it is a *leaning tone*, functioning toward its resolution.

Example 8.05

Appoggiaturas (APP) *usually*:
- appear as *accented* nonharmonic tones
- leap one way, then step the *opposite direction*

Appoggiaturas are sometimes written as *grace notes*. **Grace notes** are written as miniature notes before a beat that actually sound *on the beat*. They may or may not have a slash through their stems and flags, as shown in example 8.06.

Example 8.06   grace note appoggiaturas[2]

Anticipations are simply *early arrivals* of chord tones, appearing just *ahead of* the chord to which they belong. Example 8.07 on the following page shows two anticipations.

---

[1] In 2005, eighth-grader Anurag Kashyap of Poway, California, won the National Spelling Bee by correctly spelling *appoggiatura*. The thirteen-year-old won $30,000 in the competition, which just goes to show that it (literally) pays to know your music theory.

[2] In the modern era, grace notes are usually performed as incidental notes (sometimes referred to as acciaccaturas) that are played very quickly and are immediately replaced by the more significant note that follows. These grace notes are written with a slash through the stem and flag. However, performance practices of earlier historical eras, such as the Baroque period, place greater rhythmic emphasis on grace notes as important ornamentations. Example 8.06 illustrates Baroque notation and performance of grace note appoggiaturas.

Example 8.07

Anticipations (ANT) are *always un*accented.

Changing tones are two consecutive, or successive, nonharmonic tones that *function* similarly to neighboring tones in three ways:

- They leave by step.
- They approach by step.
- They *usually* return to the same chord tone they left.

Between the departure and approach, however, there is a skip. Changing tones are shown in example 8.08 below.

Example 8.08

Changing tones (CT) are *usually* unaccented.

Pedal tones are repeated or held notes that alternate between chord tones and dissonant non-chord tones, and are shown in example 8.09 on the following page.

Example 8.09

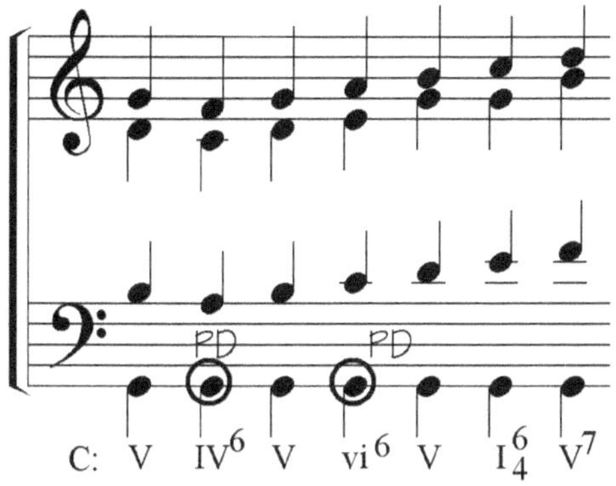

Pedal tones (PD) are found most frequently in the *bass* voice, but may appear in any voice.

Notice that when a pedal tone is in the bass voice, the chord tone in the *tenor* becomes the one from which to determine the chord *inversion*.

C: V IV⁶ V vi⁶ V I⁶₄ V⁷

The pedal tone gets its name from organ music and frequently occurs in the pedals on the organ as shown in example 8.10.[3]

Example 8.10

The terms *pedal point* and *organ point* describe the type of *pedal tones* in example 8.10.

---

[3] *Fantasia and Fugue in C Minor, BWV 537: J.S. Bach, circa 1724. Public Domain.*

Example 8.11 below illustrates pedal points that are *not* in the bass in J.S. Bach's landmark *Toccata and Fugue in D Minor*.[4]

Example 8.11

Organ

In this case, the *melody* is heard on *every-other* note; that is, every note that is not **A**. The notes on **A** are *pedal points*.

Suspensions are special kinds of nonharmonic tones that require extra attention. As stated in chapter seven, a *suspension* is a note that is *held over* or *repeated* from a previous chord. It is harmonic in the original chord, but creates a *dissonance* when held over into the new chord, until it *resolves* down to a *consonant harmony* once again.

Example 8.12 shows several suspensions, illustrating how each one is *prepared, suspended* and *resolved*.

Example 8.12

C: V⁷ I   I   ii⁶   IV⁶₄ I   IV   I⁶

Preparation:
*same note
in same voice*

Suspension:
note held/repeated

Resolution:
down by step

The suspension in measure one of example 8.12 above is in the tenor (**D**). The **D** is *suspended* from the G7 chord when **D** is repeated with the C major triad. It then resolves down by step to **C**, which is, of course, harmonic. The suspension is *prepared* by the same note (**D**) in the same voice (tenor), it is then *suspended* against the new chord until it *resolves* down by step (to **C**).

---

[4] *Toccata and Fugue in D Minor, BWV 565 (fugue only): J.S. Bach, circa 1705. Public Domain.*

The suspension in measure two of example 8.12 occurs when the soprano note (*E*) is held over from the C major triad into the D minor triad. The circle on beat two in the soprano indicates that the half note from beat one is still sounding on beat two and becomes *nonharmonic* at that point.

All suspensions are *accented* nonharmonic tones and are categorized as one of four types:

- 9-8
- 7-6
- 4-3
- 2-3

The 9-8, 7-6 and 4-3 suspensions are labeled as such because of their relationship to the bass note. For instance, in a *9-8 suspension*, the suspended note will be found at the *interval* of a *ninth* above the bass, resolving to an *octave* from the bass. In a *7-6 suspension*, the suspended note is found a *seventh* above the bass and resolves to a *sixth* from the bass.

The *4-3 suspension* has already been examined briefly in examples 7.32 and 7.33 of chapter seven. In those examples, notice how the suspensions are prepared by the same note in the same voice and how they create the interval of a fourth from the bass resolving down by step to a third from the bass.

The *2-3 suspension* actually occurs in the bass voice and creates the interval of a *second between the bass and another voice* at the point of suspension. When the suspended note in the bass resolves down by step against the non-moving voices, that second is expanded to become a *third*.

The suspensions in example 8.12 are shown in example 8.13 with their proper labels. When identifying suspensions in harmonic analysis, these labels should be used.

Example 8.13

Notice that when a suspension occurs in the bass voice, the chord tone of the *resolution* becomes the one from which to determine the chord *inversion*.

C: V⁷ I   I   ii⁶   IV⁶₄ I   IV   I⁶

In the *2-3 suspension* in measure four, the *interval* from the *bass to the soprano/alto* is a *second* at the point of suspension, and a *third* at the point of resolution.

When a suspension is embellished by the addition of brief notes around it, it is called a *decorated suspension*. A *decorated suspension* is shown in example 8.14.

Example 8.14

While this could be considered a 4-3 suspension followed by a lower neighboring tone, the preferred analysis is simply a decorated 4-3 suspension.

C: IV$^6_4$ I

Retardations are similar to suspensions, *except that they resolve upward*. Unlike suspensions, they are not labeled with numeric classification. They are *prepared* by the same note in the same voice, they are *held or repeated* against the new harmony and they *resolve up by step*.

Example 8.15

Retardations (RET) are *always accented* nonharmonic tones.

C: V I   I IV

Care must be taken when analyzing music that *harmonic* tones are not mistaken for *nonharmonic* tones. At times, certain notes that belong to the chord may appear to be nonharmonic, as shown in example 8.16 on the following page.

Example 8.16

C: I   ii^6 I   I

C: I   ii^6 I   I

At first glance, the circled **C** in measure one of example 8.16 may appear to be an appoggiatura. However, just because a note leaps from the first chord tone and then steps to the next, does not mean it is *nonharmonic*. Upon closer examination, the **C** is clearly part of the harmony. For a note to be qualified as *nonharmonic*, it must, by definition, be *foreign* to the chord against which it sounds.

In measure two of example 8.16, it may appear at first that the circled notes are double upper neighboring tones. However, these tones actually create a new sonority, namely, a subdominant chord in second inversion. The *correct* analysis for *measure one* of example 8.16 and the *preferred* analysis for *measure two* of example 8.16 are shown below in example 8.17.

Example 8.17

C: I   ii^6 I   IV$^6_4$ I

In the case of measure two, musical judgment must be exercised. Even if the moving notes do form a chord, it must be determined if that chord is part of the *function* of the harmony or if it is the *incidental* simultaneity of nonharmonic tones. Experience with harmonic progressions and harmonic rhythm (see chapter nine) will help the theorist discern the most appropriate analysis.

At times, it can be difficult to discern whether a note is part of the harmony or if it is *non*harmonic. This is particularly an issue when an apparent nonharmonic tone actually forms what could be considered to be a *seventh chord*. In such cases, the resulting *quality* of the chord helps determine whether a seventh chord is present or the note is nonharmonic. If the quality of the seventh chord is *dominant, diminished* or *half-diminished*, then the chord *is* a seventh and the note in question is *harmonic*. These types of seventh chords are *active chords* and progress in a manner consistent with their activity (see chapter nine). When the seventh of a seventh chord appears *as if it were* a passing tone (called a **passing seventh**), it *always* moves *downward*.

Example 8.18 shows five instances where the status of various notes is determined by the musical context and the *quality* of seventh chords they would produce.

Example 8.18

- In measure one, the *quality* of the seventh chord is not *dominant, diminished, or half-diminished* (it is *major*). Therefore it is a *lower neighboring tone*.

- In measure two, again, the *quality* of the seventh chord is *major*. Because the note in question is simply an *early arrival* of a part of the upcoming harmony, it is an *anticipation*.

- In measure three, the *quality* of the seventh chord is *dominant* (major triad, minor seventh from the bass) and the seventh resolves down by step. The note should not be circled or labeled as nonharmonic and the harmonic analysis should be V^7.

- The *quality* of the seventh chord in measure four is *minor*, so the **C** should be categorized as a *lower neighboring tone*.

- The **C** in measure five creates a minor seventh chord. However, since the **C** resolves down by step, this could *either* be considered a ii chord (with a passing seventh) *or* ii7.

All of the chords in example 8.19 below are seventh chords regardless of quality. The only time the seventh is called into question is when it is moving against stationary notes (as in example 8.18).

Example 8.19

Note that the diminished seventh chord in measure four of example 8.19 is *not technically diatonic* in the key of C major because of the A-flat. However, because of the unique quality of the fully-diminished seventh chord and the strength with which it *leads* to tonic, composers often use this chord freely as a substitute for the diatonic half-diminished seventh chord. This will be explained in greater detail in chapter thirteen on *borrowed chords*.

If a note is clearly not part of the harmony, but is also not one of the nonharmonic tones explained up to this point, it is a ***free tone***. *Free tones* are very rare in music literature, primarily because they do not serve a purpose. Passing tones, neighboring tones, escape tones, appoggiaturas, anticipations, changing tones, pedal tones, suspensions, and retardations all *function* in unique ways that add interest and creativity to the music.

Free tones are one of two types as shown in example 8.20.

Example 8.20

Some theorists consider the free tone in measure three of example 8.20 to be a pedal tone. In the classic sense, however, a pedal tone is both preceded and followed by the same note in the same voice.

This concludes the introduction to nonharmonic tones. *Harmonic progression* will be covered in chapter nine.

NONHARMONIC TONES

Assignments and Drills

Assignment 8.01

The objective of this assignment is identification of nonharmonic tones.

Instructions: Provide *harmonic analysis* for each excerpt below,[5] including *circling and labeling of nonharmonic tones*. Measure one of number one has been done for you. REFER BACK TO ALL EXAMPLES IN CHAPTER EIGHT IF NECESSARY.

1.

G: ii I$^6_4$ V V$^4_2$ I^6 I

2.

3.

---

[5] *Brief excerpts from chorales harmonized by Bach. Public Domain.*

Assignment 8.02

The objective of this assignment is identification of nonharmonic tones.

Instructions: Provide *harmonic analysis* for each excerpt below,[6] including *circling and labeling of nonharmonic tones.* REFER BACK TO ALL EXAMPLES IN CHAPTER EIGHT IF NECESSARY.

[6] *Brief excerpts from chorales harmonized by Bach. Public Domain.*

Assignment 8.03

The objective of this assignment is identification of nonharmonic tones.

Instructions: Provide *harmonic analysis* for each excerpt below,[7] including *circling and labeling of nonharmonic tones*. TRY TO COMPLETE THE ASSIGNMENT WITHOUT REFERRING BACK TO ANY EXAMPLES IN CHAPTER EIGHT.

*melodic minor

[7] *Brief excerpts from chorales harmonized by Bach. Public Domain.*

Assignment 8.04

The objective of this assignment is identification of nonharmonic tones.

Instructions: Provide *harmonic analysis* for each excerpt below,[8] including *circling and labeling of nonharmonic tones*. Be prepared to identify chords in all forms of minor from now on. TRY TO COMPLETE THE ASSIGNMENT WITHOUT REFERRING BACK TO ANY EXAMPLES IN CHAPTER EIGHT.

[8] *Brief excerpts from chorales harmonized by Bach. Public Domain.*

Assignment 8.05

The objective of this assignment is identification of nonharmonic tones.

Instructions: Provide *harmonic analysis* for the excerpt below,[9] including *circling and labeling of nonharmonic tones*. TRY TO COMPLETE THE ASSIGNMENT WITHOUT REFERRING BACK TO ANY EXAMPLES IN CHAPTER EIGHT.

---

[9] Elijah (oratorio), If with All Your Hearts (aria): *Felix Mendelssohn, 1846. Abbreviated. Public Domain.*

Assignment 8.06

The objective of this assignment is identification of nonharmonic tones.

Instructions: Provide *harmonic analysis* for the excerpt below,[10] including *circling and labeling of nonharmonic tones*. TRY TO COMPLETE THE ASSIGNMENT WITHOUT REFERRING BACK TO ANY EXAMPLES IN CHAPTER EIGHT.

---

[10] String Quartet, Opus 18, No. 1. Second movement (Adagio), measures 1-6: *Ludwig Van Beethoven, circa 1798. Public Domain.*

Assignment 8.07

The objective of this assignment is identification of nonharmonic tones.

Instructions: Provide *harmonic analysis* for the excerpt below,[11] including *circling and labeling of nonharmonic tones*. TRY TO COMPLETE THE ASSIGNMENT WITHOUT REFERRING BACK TO ANY EXAMPLES IN CHAPTER EIGHT.

---

[11] Symphony No. 41 ("Jupiter") KV 551, First movement (Allegro Vivace), measures 260-264: *W. A. Mozart, 1788. Public Domain.*

Assignment 8.08

The objective of this assignment is creation of nonharmonic tones.

Instructions: Rewrite the music in the staves provided as instructed. The first one is done for you. REFER BACK TO ALL EXAMPLES IN CHAPTER EIGHT IF NECESSARY.

1. add unaccented PT in bass
2. add accented PT in bass
3. add accented LN in alto
4. add ET in alto

5. add 4-3 SUS in alto
6. add APP in tenor
7. add RET in soprano
8. add CT in tenor

Assignment 8.09

The objective of this assignment is creation of nonharmonic tones.

Instructions: Create *suspensions* as directed. REFER BACK TO EXAMPLES 8.12 — 8.14 IF NECESSARY.

1. 9-8
2. 4-3
3. 7-6
4. 2-3

5. 4-3
6. 7-6
7. 9-8
8. decorated 4-3

Assignment 8.10

The objective of this assignment is creation of nonharmonic tones.

Instructions: On a separate sheet of staff paper, rewrite the chorale below,[12] adding at least seven different kinds of nonharmonic tones. Nonharmonic tones may be added to any voice *except for soprano*. REFER BACK TO ALL EXAMPLES IN CHAPTER EIGHT IF NECESSARY.

Assignment 8.11

The objective of this assignment is identification of nonharmonic tones.

Instructions: Go back through assignments 7.08, 7.10, 7.11, 7.12, and 7.13 in chapter seven and label the nonharmonic tones circled. Circle any 4-3 suspensions that are present (indicated by figured bass).

---

[12] Herr Gott, Dich loben alle wir: *Common chorale harmonized by J.S. Bach (nonharmonic tones removed), circa 1725. Public Domain. Tune name:* Old 100th.

Questions for Review

1. Why do nonharmonic tones exist? What purposes do they serve?

2. When referring to nonharmonic tones, what is meant by the terms *accented* and *unaccented*?

3. What is the difference between a passing tone and a neighboring tone?

4. What is the difference between an escape tone and an appoggiatura?

5. What is the difference between a suspension and a retardation?

6. How are various suspensions classified? Explain each classification.

7. How are pedal tones approached and left?

8. How do you determine the chord inversion when a pedal tone is in the bass?

9. What is the determining factor when distinguishing between nonharmonic tones and chord sevenths?

10. How do you determine the chord inversion when an accented nonharmonic tone is in the bass?

Assignments for Use with Anthology

A8.01 Circle and label the nonharmonic tones in the Franck chorale, *Ach, wie flüchtig, ach wie nichtig*. Anthology pages 624-625.

A8.02 Circle and label the nonharmonic tones in the Bach chorale, *Christ lag in Todesbanden*. Anthology page 627.

A8.03 Circle and label the nonharmonic tones in the Bach chorale, *Freuet euch, ihr Christen alle*. Anthology page 630.

A8.04 Circle and label the nonharmonic tones in the Bach chorale, *Jesu, meine Freude*. Anthology page 635.

A8.05 Circle and label the nonharmonic tones in the Bach chorale, *Komm, Gott Schöpfer, heiliger Geist*. Anthology page 636.

A8.06 Circle and label the nonharmonic tones in the Teschner chorale, *Valet will ich dir geben*. Anthology page 640.

Chapter 9
Harmonic Progression

Harmonic progression is the term used to describe movement from chord to chord. Because of harmonic *patterns* and tendencies, progressions are described on a scale from strong to weak, according to the frequency with which they are used. Chords are no longer viewed merely in the *foreground* as individual entities, but are now considered in the *middle-ground* where they express their functions as they relate to other chords.

Most compositions begin and end with the tonic triad. The tonic is the "home" triad of the key, and the function of the *other* chords is to provide *contrast* and *interest* along the compositional journey from home and back. Strong harmonic progressions provide direction toward the tonic while weak movements between chords lack musical purpose.

The pitches within a given scale are described as either *active tones* or *inactive tones*. **Inactive tones** are those that belong to the tonic triad. They are considered *passive* because they themselves are the target of activity. They are the *resolution*, or *resting point*, of active tones.

Active tones are those that *do not* belong to the tonic triad. Their *tendency* is toward the closest inactive tone, as shown in a major key in example 9.01. If an active tone is equidistantly positioned between two inactive tones, it is attracted toward the stronger of the two. The root of the tonic triad is the strongest, the third is the next strongest, and the fifth is the weakest.

Example 9.01

$\hat{1}$ $\hat{2}$ $\hat{3}$ $\hat{4}$ $\hat{5}$ $\hat{6}$ $\hat{7}$ $\hat{8}$

Each caret (^) in example 9.01 simply refers to a *scale degree*. Whenever a caret is placed above a numeric symbol in music theory, it applies to the scale degree indicated by the number. Scale degrees 1, 3, and 5 are inactive, while 2, 4, 6, and 7 are active.

Again, active tones *tend* toward the inactive tones as indicated above in example 9.01, but they do not *always* resolve as shown. Because their *tendencies* are to resolve to the closest inactive tones, it is helpful to understand these inclinations when sight-reading, composing, or performing.

Just as active *tones* function directionally toward inactive tones, *chords* function in various ways toward the tonic triad. The strongest chords are major triads, and the major triad with the strongest inclination toward tonic is the dominant. When tonal compositions are analyzed in the middle-ground and background, the ultimate pattern of *tonic—dominant—tonic* becomes prevalent. When a musical phrase ends on tonic, the *strongest* progression to the tonic comes from the dominant. This is illustrated with *active tones* in chorale style in example 9.02.

Example 9.02

C: V   I

"Life can't be all bad when for ten dollars you can buy all the Beethoven sonatas and listen to them for ten years."
- author William F. Buckley, Jr.

When the dominant triad is replaced by a dominant seventh chord, the tendencies of the active tones are even stronger and increase the function of the dominant chord toward tonic.

When progressing to tonic, the seventh of a dominant seventh chord should always resolve down by step, as it does in the bass voice of example 9.03 below. The seventh of a V^7 chord is $\hat{4}$, which leans strongly toward $\hat{3}$.

Example 9.03

C: V^4_2 I^6

Example 9.04

C: vii^{o6}_4 I^6

The vii^o triad functions in the same way as the dominant seventh chord for two reasons. First, it is called a *leading tone* chord, meaning that it leads to tonic; and second, it has *all of its notes in common with the V^7*. Compare example 9.04 (above right) with example 9.03 (above left). The vii^o triad may be considered a "rootless" V^7.

When sevenths are added to leading tone triads, the resulting vii^{o7} and $vii^{ø7}$ chords also function like dominant triads and sevenths (toward tonic).

The conclusion of a musical phrase is called a *cadence*. Rhythmically, cadences typically involve longer note durations, providing a reprieve from constant motion. Harmonically, cadences are characterized by specific chord progressions.

The strongest (and most frequent) type of harmonic cadence is the *authentic cadence*. This cadence is characterized by movement from dominant (or dominant substitute) to tonic. Authentic cadences are shown below in example 9.05.

Example 9.05

Authentic cadences are one of two types: perfect or imperfect. A *perfect authentic cadence* (abbreviated *PAC*) is formed when all three of the following criteria are met:

- Both chords must be in root position.
- The first chord must be V (or V^7), not vii°.
- The tonic note of the final chord must be in the soprano.

Conversely, an *imperfect authentic cadence* (abbreviated *IAC*) occurs when *any* of the following is present:

- At least one of the chords is inverted.
- vii° substitutes for V.
- The tonic note of the final chord is *not* in the soprano.

In example 9.05 above, *perfect authentic cadences* are found in measures one, five, and six (even though the fifth is missing in the V^7 in measure six). All the others are *imperfect authentic cadences*.

When a cadence *begins on the dominant but does not resolve to tonic*, it is called a ***deceptive cadence*** (abbreviated *DEC*). The most frequent deceptive cadence is the progression of V - vi in major (V - VI in minor). Deceptive cadences are shown below in example 9.06.

Example 9.06

C: V vi   V$^6_5$ vi   V$^4_3$ iii

Cm: V VI   V^7 VI^6 V^7 iv$^6_4$

A cadence that ends on the dominant is called a ***half cadence*** (*HALF*). A half cadence is used to conclude a phrase that is dependent upon a subsequent phrase. Some theorists refer to these phrase relationships as *antecedent-consequent* (or *question-answer*) phrases. *Authentic cadences* provide a strong sense of finality and are used to conclude *consequent phrases*. Half cadences may be analogous to sentences that end with a question mark. Phrases that end with half cadences are dependent on (answer) phrases to bring the music to a satisfying completion, ultimately back on the tonic triad. Example 9.07 on the following page illustrates several half cadences in both major and minor modes.

Example 9.07

C: I V | ii V | IV V

Cm: i v | ii° V | iv V

The final type of cadence is the **plagal cadence** (*PLAGAL*), which progresses from subdominant to tonic. The plagal cadence is sometimes called the "amen" cadence because of its frequent appendage to hymns as an *amen*. A first inversion supertonic triad may substitute for the subdominant triad, but this is rare. Plagal cadences are shown in example 9.08 below.

Example 9.08

C: IV I | ii^6 I | Cm: iv i

In music composition, the standard *tonic—dominant—tonic* harmonic progression is made interesting by the inclusion of other chords called *pre-dominant chords* between the tonic triad that commences the music and the dominant triad that initiates the final authentic cadence. Example 9.09 illustrates the middle-ground view of this standard structure.

Example 9.09

Tonic (T) — Pre-dominant (PD) ———————→ Dominant (D) — Tonic (T)

I - - - - - - - - V I

It is important to consider the way that chords relate to each other when selecting harmonies to use in the *pre-dominant* stage. The chords chosen should progress naturally until the ultimate destination of an *authentic cadence* is reached. Examples 9.10, 9.11, and 9.12 are different harmonizations of the final phrase of the familiar melody *Amazing Grace*.[1]

Example 9.10

F: I^6 vi I^6_4 V^7 I

Example 9.11

F: V^6 vi ii^7 V^7 I

"A jazz musician is a juggler who uses harmonies instead of oranges."
— pianist Benny Green

Example 9.12

F: V IV vi I iii^7 ii^6_5

Examples 9.10 and 9.11 progress with purpose toward the tonic at the end, utilizing strong harmonic movement between chord roots. While each chord in example 9.12 was carefully chosen to be harmonic with the melody, the progressions are weak and do not lead to resolution at the end of the phrase.

Example 9.13 on the following page is a ranking of chord progressions from strongest to weakest. The progressions are determined based on the movement from one chord *root* to the next, regardless of chord inversions.

---

[1] Amazing Grace: *Lyrics by John Newton, 1779; early American melody, circa 1831. Public Domain.*

Example 9.13

STRENGTH	PROGRESSION	DESCRIPTION	EXAMPLE
VERY STRONG	ROOT DESCENDS A FIFTH	↓5	V - I
STRONG	ROOT DESCENDS A FOURTH	↓4	I - V
STRONG	ROOT ASCENDS A SECOND	↑2	IV - V
MEDIUM	ROOT DESCENDS A THIRD	↓3	I - vi
WEAK	ROOT ASCENDS A THIRD	↑3	I - iii
VERY WEAK	ROOT DESCENDS A SECOND	↓2	vi - V

The progression in example 9.10 is I - vi - I - V - I.
Root movement, then, is ↓3 - ↑3 - ↓4 - ↓5. The chord movements are primarily strong.

The progression in example 9.11 is V - vi - ii - V - I.
Root movement, then, is ↑2 - ↓5 - ↓5 - ↓5. The chord movements are all strong, making the overall progression extremely strong.

The progression in example 9.12 is V - IV - vi - I - iii - ii.
Root movement, then, is ↓2 - ↑3 - ↑3 - ↑3 - ↓2. The chord movements are all weak and the phrase fails to cadence.

The consecutive descending fifth progressions in example 9.11 are known as *circle progressions*. They are called *circle progressions* because the roots of the chords are descending fifths apart, just like the letter names on the *circle of fifths* when read counter-clockwise. A full circle progression in a major key is I - IV - vii° - iii - vi - ii - V - I. The letter names designating these chord roots in C major, for example, are **C, F, B, E, A, D, G, C**; and using pop-chord symbols, the chords are identified as C, F, B°, Em, Am, Dm, G, C.

When identifying circle progressions in a completed harmonic analysis, the roman numerals of the chords creating the circle progression may be encompassed in an ellipse as demonstrated in example 9.14 on the following page.

Example 9.14

was blind but now I see.

F: V⁶ vi ii⁷ V⁷ I
↑2

The term **retrogression** is used to describe a particular usage of weak movement between chords. When the V triad or seventh is immediately followed by IV (iv in minor), this specific descending second movement is a *retro*gression because it is moving *away* from tonic. Chords with *strong* movement between roots gravitate *toward the dominant*, which leads ultimately to tonic. When the strong V chord is followed by IV, natural progression toward tonic is abandoned. Retrogressions are almost never found in music of the common practice era. In the extremely rare instances when they are found, the subdominant chord is voiced in first inversion, so the aural perception is of the bass line moving upward (from the root of the dominant chord to the third of the subdominant). Nonetheless, it is a good rule of thumb for anyone harmonizing music according to common practice to avoid retrogressions altogether.

Harmonic rhythm is the term that describes the rate of chord changes. In most *chorales*, the harmonies generally change on *every beat*. In popular and folk music, the harmonic rhythm is frequently one chord *per measure*.

An important factor of *harmonic rhythm* is that chord changes occur at musically logical moments. If syncopation is not a rhythmic feature of the melody, the changes in harmony generally should be aligned with strong beats (if they do not occur on every beat or just once per measure). Example 9.15 shows plausible patterns of *harmonic rhythm* in various meters.

Example 9.15

Example 9.16 shows *illogical* harmonic rhythm that should be used sparingly or avoided completely.

Example 9.16

"Music is the art which is most nigh to tears and memory."
- playwright *Oscar Wilde*

Additionally, harmonic rhythm *between beats* should be avoided at this stage, and harmonic rhythm that does not occur at least on each downbeat is rare.

One of the weaknesses of example 9.10 was that the harmony changed on beat three of the first measure and was not followed by a new chord on the downbeat of the following measure. Otherwise, the harmonization in that example was acceptable.

Any time a chord is repeated, even if the inversion changes, the harmonic rhythm is not changed.

In harmonic progressions, chords are primarily voiced in root position. The choices to use *inversions* of chords are always intentional, based on several musical factors.

The most important factor in determining whether or not to use a chord inversion is the contour of the bass line. This will become a vital factor in chapter eleven on voice leading. For the time being, note that chord roots often necessitate a bass line with numerous leaps if inversions are not used. Opting for smoother, more stepwise bass lines, composers have used nonharmonic tones and chord inversions.

Second inversion triads are unique sonorities requiring very special care. In the common practice era, composers only used $^6_4$ chords in limited contexts, since the interval of a fourth from the bass to the next chord tone was considered less stable than the interval of a third. Because chords appear primarily in root position (and occasionally in first inversion), the ear of the listener is subconsciously conditioned to the sound of a third above the bass.

Thus, second inversion triads only appear in four limited contexts:

1. The passing bass $^6_4$
2. The arpeggiated bass $^6_4$
3. The pedal bass $^6_4$
4. The cadential $^6_4$

> "Why waste money on psychotherapy when you can listen to the B Minor Mass?"
> – composer Michael Torke

In the *passing bass* $^6_4$, the inclusion of a second inversion triad creates a stepwise bass line where there would have been leaps otherwise, as shown in example 9.17.

Example 9.17

E♭: ii   vi$^6_4$ IV
         ↑
    passing bass $^6_4$

E♭: ii   vi   IV
         ↑
    without passing bass

The *arpeggiated bass* $^6_4$ utilizes the second inversion triad in the process of outlining that chord in the bass line.

Example 9.18

A: I   I^6 I$^6_4$ I
              ↑
      arpeggiated bass $^6_4$

> "Alas for those who never sing, but die with all their music in them!"
> – physician and author Oliver Wendell Holmes

The *pedal bass* $^6_4$ is merely the presence of a second inversion triad over a stationary bass line.

Example 9.19

G: I   IV$^6_4$ I
         ↑
     pedal bass $^6_4$

"My heart, which is so full to overflowing, has often been solaced and refreshed by music when sick and weary."
— theologian Martin Luther

The *cadential* $^6_4$ is a second inversion tonic triad immediately preceding a dominant chord at a cadence point. The tonic $^6_4$ "acts like" V in this context, and serves as an embellishing anticipation of the V chord.

Example 9.20

C: I$^6_4$ V   I
    ↑
cadential $^6_4$

"Musical compositions, it should be remembered, do not inhabit certain countries, certain museums, like paintings and statues. The Mozart Quintet is not shut up in Salzburg: I have it in my pocket."
— conductor Henri Rabaud

This concludes the introduction to harmonic progression. *Melody* and *texture* will be covered in chapter ten.

Assignments and Drills

Assignment 9.01

The objective of this assignment is the identification of cadences.

Instructions: Each measure below represents a cadence. Provide harmonic analysis of each measure and identify the type of cadence present. Measures 1-10 are in major keys; measures 11-20 are in minor. Measure one has been completed for you. REFER BACK TO EXAMPLES 9.05 — 9.08 IF NECESSARY.

Assignment 9.02

The objective of this assignment is the harmonization of simple diatonic melodies.

Instructions:
1. Choose harmonic rhythms and chord progressions for the melodies[2] below.
2. Use logical, patterned harmonic rhythm.
3. Employ weak progressions sparingly and avoid retrogressions altogether.
4. Approach cadences purposefully. Identify each cadence as PAC, IAC, DEC, HALF, or PLAGAL.
5. Write pop-chord symbols above the staff and corresponding roman numerals below.
6. Identify each harmonic progression.
7. Be prepared to defend usage of all chord *inversions*.

The first melody has been done for you as an example.

REFER BACK TO EXAMPLE 9.13 FOR CHORD PROGRESSIONS, 9.15 AND 9.16 FOR HARMONIC RHYTHM, AND 9.05 — 9.08 FOR CADENCES.

1. The first no-el, the an-gel did say was to certain poor shepherds in fields where they lay.
   Chords: D F#m G D G D/F# D/A A7 D
   D: I ↑3 iii ↑2 IV ↓4 I IV ↓4 I^6 I$^6_4$ ↓4 V7 I
   PLAGAL   IAC

2. Be Thou my vi-sion, O Lord of my heart; naught be all else to me, save that Thou art;

3. O for a thou-sand tongues to sing my great Re-deem-er's praise, the glo-ries of my God and King, the tri-umphs of His grace!

---

[2] The First Noel: *19th c. English carol.* Be Thou My Vision: *Lyrics by Eleanor Hull, 1912; traditional Irish melody. Tune Name:* Slane. O for a Thousand Tongues to Sing: *Lyrics by Charles Wesley; music by Carl Gläser, 1828. Tune name:* Azmon. *All Public Domain.*

HARMONIC PROGRESSION

Assignment 9.03

The objective of this assignment is the harmonization of simple diatonic melodies.

Instructions:
1. Choose harmonic rhythms and chord progressions for the melodies[3] below.
2. Use logical, patterned harmonic rhythm.
3. Employ weak progressions sparingly and avoid retrogressions altogether.
4. Approach cadences purposefully. Identify each cadence as PAC, IAC, DEC, HALF, or PLAGAL.
5. Write pop-chord symbols above the staff and corresponding roman numerals below.
6. Identify each harmonic progression.
7. Be prepared to defend usage of all chord *inversions*.

REFER BACK TO EXAMPLE 9.13 FOR CHORD PROGRESSIONS, 9.15 AND 9.16 FOR HARMONIC RHYTHM, AND 9.05 — 9.08 FOR CADENCES.

1. *I am a poor wayfaring stranger, trav'lin through this world of woe. There's no sickness, toil, or danger in that bright land to which I go.*

2. *For he's a jolly good fellow, for he's a jolly good fellow, for he's a jolly good fellow, which nobody can deny!*

3. *Amazing grace, how sweet the sound that saved a wretch like me!*

---

[3] Poor Wayfaring Stranger; For He's a Jolly Good Fellow; Amazing Grace: *Traditional folk songs. Public Domain.*

Assignment 9.04

The objective of this assignment is the identification of harmonic progressions and cadences.

Instructions:
1. Provide *harmonic analysis* for the chorale[4] below.
2. Identify each harmonic progression.
3. Identify each cadence as PAC, IAC, DEC, HALF, or PLAGAL.

The first measure has been completed for you.

REFER BACK TO EXAMPLE 9.13 FOR CHORD PROGRESSIONS AND 9.05 — 9.08 FOR CADENCES.

[4] *Chorale melody from* The Christian Lyre, *1831*: Pleading Savior. *Public Domain.*

Assignment 9.05

The objective of this assignment is the identification of harmonic progressions and cadences.

Instructions:
1. Provide *harmonic analysis* for the chorale[5] below.
2. Identify each harmonic progression.
3. Identify each cadence as PAC, IAC, DEC, HALF, or PLAGAL.

REFER BACK TO EXAMPLE 9.13 FOR CHORD PROGRESSIONS AND 9.05-9.08 FOR CADENCES.

---

[5] *For the Beauty of the Earth:* Lyrics by Folliot Pierpoint, 1864; music by Conrad Kocher, 1838. Public Domain. *Tune name:* Dix.

Questions for Review

1. What is meant by the term *harmonic progression*?

2. Explain T – PD – D – T.

3. What are *active tones* and how do they typically function?

4. In music theory, when a caret (^) appears above a numeric symbol, what does it mean?

5. What chord leads most strongly to tonic? How might this information be useful when modulating from one key to another?

6. How many notes does a vii° triad have in common with a V^7? What implications are there, then, regarding the functions of these two chords whose roots are technically a third apart?

7. What is meant by the term *cadence*? In addition to the *harmonic* properties of a cadence, what other factor is present?

8. Explain the differences between a *perfect* authentic cadence (PAC) and an *imperfect* authentic cadence (IAC).

9. What chord can substitute for the subdominant chord in a plagal cadence?

10. What is meant by the term *circle progression*?

11. Rank each harmonic progression in order from strongest to weakest.

12. What is meant by the term *retrogression*? Why are retrogressions seldom found in common practice literature?

13. Explain the term *harmonic rhythm*.

14. Why are second inversion triads treated with special care, and therefore typically found in only four unique contexts? What are the four acceptable uses of $^6_4$ chords?

Assignments for Use with Anthology

A9.01 Using pop-chord symbols above the staff, identify the chords in <u>measures 18-22</u> of Corelli: *Allemanda* (from *Trio Sonata,* Opus 4, No. 11). Anthology page 68. Encompass each circle progression in your analysis in an ellipse.

A9.02 Using pop-chord symbols above the staff, identify the chords in <u>measures 189-193</u> of Mozart: *Piano Sonata in B-flat Major* (K. 333), third movement (Allegretto). Anthology page 194. Identify each chord progression.

A9.03 Harmonic analysis of various measures of Beethoven: *Piano Sonata No. 15 in D Major*, Opus 28, third movement (Scherzo) was completed in assignment A5.03. Anthology page 282. Go back through your analysis and identify the circle progressions.

A9.04 Using pop-chord symbols above the staff, identify the chords in <u>measures 105-109</u> of Beethoven: *Piano Sonata No. 21 in C Major ("Waldenstein")* Opus 53, first movement (Allegro). Anthology page 289. Identify each chord progression.

A9.05 Examine the chorale, *Herr Gott, dich loben alle wir* in Appendix B of the anthology (pages 631-632). Version "a" was harmonized by Praetorius, version "b" by J.S. Bach. <u>Identify the cadences in each harmonization</u>. Note that both versions transition between relative keys. The melody of this chorale is commonly known today as *Old 100th* (or *The Doxology*).

Chapter 10
Melody and Texture

Most common practice theory focuses on harmony, and much of this book up to this point has been concerned with harmonic intervals, chords, and harmonic progression. It is the *melodic line*, however, that primarily captures the imagination and interest of the listener. The combination of successive intervals with creative rhythms, especially when presented with some element of repetition, gives each melody its unique character.

Like harmony, melody may be analyzed in the foreground (individual intervals), middle ground (motifs and phrases), and background (periods and formal sections).

A ***motif*** is a short recurring musical idea. A motif may be purely rhythmic, but usually motifs are wholly melodic (pitch and rhythm). One of the most famous and instantly recognizable melodic motifs in all of Western music is exploited in the expositional material of the first movement of Beethoven's Fifth Symphony, shown in example 10.01.[1]

Example 10.01

The primary melodic material that comprises the foundation for the entire movement (approximately 7—8 minutes) comes from only two pitches. The first is played three times in rapid eighth notes, followed by the second pitch (of longer duration), down a major third.

Example 10.02

---

[1] Symphony No. 5 in C minor, Opus 67, first movement (Allegro), *simplified piano reduction: Ludwig van Beethoven, 1809. Public Domain.*

The motif recurs with various modifications at various pitch levels throughout the theme.

Example 10.03

In measures 3-5, the melodic interval between the two pitches is a *minor* third, and the last note of the motif is held out longer. In measures 7-8, the melodic interval is reduced to a minor *second* and the motif recurs before it is fully completed in the previous statement. In measures 9-10, the interval is expanded to a *perfect fourth*. Despite these differences, each statement is considered a variation of the original motif.

J.S. Bach's C minor fugue from *The Well-tempered Clavier* also demonstrates the use of motif.[2]

Example 10.04

The fugue *subject*, just two measures in length, contains three identical statements of a simple motif, and five statements of the rhythmic motif, as shown in example 10.05 on the following page.

---

[2] Fugue II for three voices in C minor (BWV 847): *J. S. Bach, 1722. Public Domain.*

Example 10.05

Notice the top staff in measures 3-5. It is the same material as the subject, only stated at the dominant instead of the tonic, with one note adjusted for harmonic purposes. In a fugue, this is called the *answer*, and the ongoing material opposite the answer is called the *countersubject*. Therefore, in just four measures of music, there are two statements of the primary material (subject and answer), including six statements of the primary motif and ten statements of the rhythmic motif.

When a motif is immediately restated in the same voice at a higher or lower pitch level, the result is a ***sequence***, as shown in example 10.06 below.[3]

Example 10.06

As the melody sequences in example 10.06 above, the harmony sequences as well. The bass line ascends chromatically while the chord roots sequence above it. Each measure consists of a circle progression, which ascends as the melody climbs, as illustrated in example 10.07.

---

[3] *I Want to Know Christ: Lyrics by Michael Hudson. Music by Gary Driskell. © 1986 by Ariose Music (administrated by EMI Christian Publishing).*

Example 10.07

> I press t'ward the goal; His good-ness un-folds. March on, O my soul;

The sequences in example 10.07 followed a stepwise ascending pattern. Those in examples 10.08 and 10.09[4] are sequenced in stepwise descending fashion.

Example 10.08

Example 10.09

Notice how there are two voices in example 10.09; an upper voice and a lower voice, even though both are played simultaneously on solo violin. Both voices move in sequence. This "economy of means" is a valuable compositional device. In addition to sequences, composers will arrange their motifs in *contoural inversion* (sometimes called *contrary motion*), *retrograde motion*, and even (rarely) *retrograde inversion*.

Contoural inversion is the process of flipping the contour of the motif upside-down. Beethoven uses this device between voices in his fifth symphony, as shown in example 10.10.[5]

Example 10.10

---

[4] *Chaconne from Partita No. 2 in D minor for Violin Solo (BWV 1004), measures 57-59: J. S. Bach, circa 1720. Public Domain.*

[5] *Symphony No. 5 in C minor, Opus 67, first movement (Allegro), measures 14-21. Simplified piano reduction: Ludwig van Beethoven, 1809. Public Domain.*

Retrograde motion is the process of reversing the order of the notes in a motif so that the motif is performed backwards. Among other devices, Bartók uses retrograde in his landmark composition, *Music for Strings, Percussion, and Celesta*, shown in Example 10.11.[6]

Example 10.11

After stating the motif in measure 46, Bartók immediately presents its retrograde form in measure 47. Note that he also doubles it at the octave, and drastically changes the dynamic level for contrast. The motif is restated in its original form (down an octave) in measure 48, before being restated again in a higher octave in measure 49. In measure 49, the rhythmic values of each note are half as long as they were in the original. This technique of halving note durations is called **rhythmic diminution** because the rhythms have been made shorter. Thus, the term for doubling (or otherwise elongating) note values is **rhythmic augmentation**.

Retrograde inversion is the process of notating a motif in contoural inversion *and* retrograde. This is very rare in music literature prior to the 20th century.

Sequences may be created at any interval from the original motif (not necessarily stepwise), and are one of two types: real or tonal. A **real sequence** is an exact transposition of the motif. A **tonal sequence** conforms to the key signature and is not concerned with replicating the *quality* of the original intervals.

The first sequence of Beethoven's Fifth Symphony (see example 10.01) is a *tonal* sequence since the interval between the pitches of the motif in measures 1-2 is a *major* third and the interval between the pitches of the sequence in measures 3-4 is a *minor* third. If it were to have been a *real* sequence, the note in measure four would have been **D-flat** instead of **D-natural**, which would have produced a drastically different effect.

In a **false sequence**, part of the motif is repeated and the rest is sequenced (or vice versa), as shown below.[7]

Example 10.12

---

[6] *Music for Strings, Percussion, and Celesta*, third movement (Adagio) *right hand of piano part only, measures 47-50*: Béla Bartók, © 1937, Universal Edition. Copyright renewed.
[7] *Cassation, Menuet (K. 99)*: Wolfgang Amadeus Mozart, 1769. Public Domain.

A ***modified sequence*** keeps the overall shape of the motif intact, but embellishes it.

Example 10.13

At first glance, example 10.13 above may not appear to be a sequence at all. Upon listening, however, it becomes apparent that measures two and three are sequenced embellishments of measure one.

A ***phrase*** is a passage of music that represents a more substantial idea than a motif, ending in a cadence. Typically a phrase is four measures in length, but may be longer or shorter, depending on a variety of factors such as meter and tempo. A fast piece of music in cut time or $\frac{2}{4}$ meter, for instance, may consist of eight-measure phrases. Frequently, phrases are comprised of motifs or sequences. The example below[8] contains two phrases.

Example 10.14

Examination of this melody, even without the presence of harmony at this point, reveals that the first phrase ends with a half cadence and the second ends authentically. Further, the second phrase begins as if it is a sequence of the first. When two adjacent phrases are in antecedent-consequent relationship such as this, the result is a ***period***. The opening phrase of a period always ends with a weaker cadence than the concluding phrase, which usually ends with an authentic cadence. Two repeated phrases, then, do not form a period.

Periods are typically two phrases, but may also be three phrases in length (A A B or A B B), or even four (often called a *double period*).

The excerpt in example 10.14 above is a ***parallel period***. When the second phrase of a two-phrase period begins with the same motivic material as the first phrase (either identically or sequenced), a parallel period is present. If the second phrase begins differently than the first, the phrases form a ***contrasting period***, as shown in example 10.15 on the following page.[9]

---

[8] Polly Wolly Doodle: *Traditional American Folk Song, circa 1880. Public Domain.*
[9] String Quartet No. 17, Allegro ("The Hunt," K. 458): *Wolfgang Amadeus Mozart, 1784. Public Domain.*

Example 10.15

Analysis of an entire melody is a type of background analysis. Motifs, sequences, and phrases are middle ground. In background view, examination of the complete period above reveals that this melody follows one of the most common *contours* in Western tonal music: the gradual ascent to a climax point, approximately two-thirds to three-quarters of the way through, followed by descent to tonic. Further, it should be noted that inactive tones (tones belonging to the tonic triad) comprise the majority of pitches present, and that stepwise motion prevails.

The *range* of a melody is usually kept between a sixth and a tenth. More than a tenth becomes taxing on the ear (and difficult to sing), and the interval of a fifth or less is too narrow for there to be much sense of motion and direction.

Texture refers to the way that a melody is treated harmonically, and is another important aspect of background analysis. There are three primary texture types: *monophony, homophony,* and *polyphony.*[10]

The term **monophony** (or **monophonic** *texture*) refers to a single melody *without* harmonic accompaniment. The melody in example 10.16 below[11] is monophonic. Melodies that are doubled at the octave, or even at other intervals such as thirds or fifths, are still considered monophonic since the harmony is created exclusively from *parallel* renderings of the melody.

Example 10.16

Ut qué-ant lá - xis   re - so - ná - re   fí - bris   Mí - ra ges - tó - rum

fá-mu-li tu - ó - rum,   Sól - ve   pol - lú - ti   lá - bi - i   re - á-tum,   Sánc - te   Jo-án-nes.

---

[10] *The term* heterophony *is a rare fourth type of texture that results from simultaneous embellishments of a melody.*
[11] *Plainchant hymn Ut qué-ant láxis: Guido d'Arezzo, circa A. D. 1015. Public Domain. See also example 1.20.*

The term *homophony* (or *homophonic* texture) refers to melody with accompaniment. This is the most common texture in Western music. The *type* of accompaniment is irrelevant to the overall designation of texture; the mere presence of chords underneath (or above) a melody makes the texture homophonic.

Consider background and middle ground analysis of the homophonic excerpt from Petzold's Minuet in G (example 10.17 below).[12] A double period is formed by the four phrases (A B A B'), whose cadences are PLAGAL, HALF, PLAGAL, PAC respectively. Notice the motifs, sequences, and motif fragments in contoural inversion. An entire melody is spun out of an economy of material.

Example 10.17

The minuet as shown above is not monophonic because the presence of chord symbols indicates harmonic accompaniment. The accompaniment may be realized in a number of ways and with a number of instruments. The following examples illustrate a variety of piano styles that could be employed to harmonize the melody.

Example 10.18 — block chords

---

[12] Harpsichord Suite, Minuet: *Christian Petzold, circa 1710. Often mis-attributed to J.S. Bach because of its inclusion in Bach's* Anna Magdalena Notebook *(BWV Anh 114, 1725). Public Domain.*

Example 10.19 — figurated block chords ("jump bass")

Example 10.20 — broken chords

Example 10.21 — figurated broken chords ("Alberti bass")[13]

Example 10.22 — figurated broken chords

---

[13] *Some theorists refer to this style of accompaniment as* Alberti bass, *after the Baroque composer Domenico Alberti, whose writings show immense fondness for the technique.*

Example 10.23 *broken chords (expanded)*

Example 10.24 *arpeggiated chords*

Example 10.25 *chorale style*

Chorale style voice leading has a special designation within the homophonic texture. Because each voice has essentially the same rhythm (especially when stripped of nonharmonic tones), music written in chorale style is **homorhythmic**. It is still melody with accompaniment (*homophonic texture*); it is just a special kind where the accompaniment is comprised of individual voice lines that move in essentially the same rhythm as the melody.

When music like example 10.25 above is realized on the piano, the performer occasionally needs to re-voice chords as the music is being read. The first harmonic interval in the bass clef, for example, is too far of a stretch for most pianists to play with the left hand. Performers compensate by mentally removing the tenor note from the bass clef and adding it to a playable register in the treble clef for the right hand.

The third texture, **polyphony** (or **polyphonic** *texture*), refers to complex music that contains two or more simultaneous *independent* melodic lines. Since the melodies do not have the same basic rhythms as each other at the same time, they are not considered homorhythmic in texture. In homorhythm, the voices that support the melody are not independent; they are accompanying lines. In polyphony, each melody is strong enough to survive on its own. When combined, these melodies create harmony, yet don't lose their sense of independence.

Example 10.26

"Music's the medicine of the mind."
- senator John Alexander Logan

The example of polyphony above[14] is an intense passage. There are initially five different melodies being played simultaneously, each independent of the others, yet each contributing to a meaningful harmonic whole (I - ii$^6_5$ - V - I - IV - I$^6_4$).

It is also considered polyphony when a melody overlaps with itself at differing rhythmic intervals. This compositional device is a form of *imitation* known as **stretto**, and is illustrated in four voices below.[15]

Example 10.27

---

[14] Symphony No. 41 in C Major ("Jupiter") K. 551, Movement IV (Finale, Allegro), *measures 399-404, strings only*: Wolfgang Amadeus Mozart, 1788. Public Domain.

[15] Symphony No. 41 in C Major ("Jupiter") K. 551, Movement IV (Finale, Allegro), *measures 296-301, strings only*: Wolfgang Amadeus Mozart, 1788. Public Domain.

This concludes the introduction to melody and texture. Voice leading will be covered in chapter eleven.

Assignments and Drills

Assignment 10.01

The objective of this assignment is identification of motivic material.

Instructions: Label motifs in the example below[16] (M1, M2, etc.). Indicate the presence of any real sequences (REAL SEQ), tonal sequences (TONAL SEQ), false sequences (FALSE SEQ), modified sequences (MOD SEQ), contoural inversion (INV), retrograde motion (RETRO), rhythmic diminution (DIM), and rhythmic augmentation (AUG). In the cases of incomplete statements of a motif, use the designation *motif fragment* (M1 FRAG). The first measure has been completed for you. REFER BACK TO EXAMPLES 10.03 — 10.13 IF NECESSARY.

---

[16] Invention No. 1 in C Major: *J. S. Bach, measures 1-7, 1723.*
The primary material of an invention is called a motive, *which is usually longer than a motif and is not to be confused with motif in this context. The* motive *of this invention is the combination of motifs 1 and 2.*

Assignment 10.02

The objective of this assignment is identification of motivic material.

Instructions: Label motifs (M1, M2, etc.) in the example below.[17] Indicate the presence of any real sequences (REAL SEQ), tonal sequences (TONAL SEQ), false sequences (FALSE SEQ), modified sequences (MOD SEQ), contoural inversion (INV), retrograde motion (RETRO), rhythmic diminution (DIM), and rhythmic augmentation (AUG). In the cases of incomplete statements of a motif, use the designation *motif fragment* (M1 FRAG). REFER BACK TO EXAMPLES 10.03 — 10.13 IF NECESSARY.

---

[17] Angels We Have Heard on High: *French carol, lyrics translated by James Chadwick, 1862. Tune name:* Gloria. *Public Domain.*

Assignment 10.03

The objective of this assignment is identification of motivic material.

Instructions: Label motifs (M1, M2, etc.) in the example below.[18] Indicate the presence of any real sequences (REAL SEQ), tonal sequences (TONAL SEQ), false sequences (FALSE SEQ), modified sequences (MOD SEQ), contoural inversion (INV), retrograde motion (RETRO), rhythmic diminution (DIM), and rhythmic augmentation (AUG). In the cases of incomplete statements of a motif, use the designation *motif fragment* (M1 FRAG). REFER BACK TO EXAMPLES 10.03 — 10.13 IF NECESSARY.

[18] Piano Sonata No. 16 in G Major (Op. 31, No. 1), third movement (Rondo), measures 32-42: *Ludwig van Beethoven, 1803*. Public Domain.

Assignment 10.04

The objective of this assignment is identification of motivic material.

Instructions: Label motifs (M1, M2, etc.) in the example below.[19] Indicate the presence of any real sequences (REAL SEQ), tonal sequences (TONAL SEQ), false sequences (FALSE SEQ), modified sequences (MOD SEQ), contoural inversion (INV), retrograde motion (RETRO), rhythmic diminution (DIM), and rhythmic augmentation (AUG). In the cases of incomplete statements of a motif, use the designation *motif fragment* (M1 FRAG). REFER BACK TO EXAMPLES 10.03 — 10.13 IF NECESSARY.

---

[19] *Motet* Lauda Sion (lyrics omitted): *Giovanni Pierluigi da Palestrina, circa 1560. Public Domain.*

Assignment 10.05

The objective of this assignment is identification of motivic material.

Instructions: Label motifs (M1, M2, etc.) in the example below.[20] Indicate the presence of any real sequences (REAL SEQ), tonal sequences (TONAL SEQ), false sequences (FALSE SEQ), modified sequences (MOD SEQ), contoural inversion (INV), retrograde motion (RETRO), rhythmic diminution (DIM), and rhythmic augmentation (AUG). In the cases of incomplete statements of a motif, use the designation *motif fragment* (M1 FRAG).

REFER BACK TO EXAMPLES 10.03 — 10.13 IF NECESSARY.

---

[20] *Chorale prelude* Warum solit ich mich den grämen (version 1): *Johann Walther, circa 1715. Public Domain. A chorale prelude is a polyphonic arrangement for organ of a* cantus firmus *(pre-existing melody). The simple* cantus firmus *for this chorale prelude is shown here.*

Assignment 10.06

The objective of this assignment is identification of periods.

Instructions: Examine each melody below to see if a period is present. If so, identify the type (parallel or contrasting). If not, do nothing. REFER BACK TO EXAMPLES 10.14 — 10.15 IF NECESSARY.

Composition Project

Assignment 10.07

Instructions: Compose an original piece of music *for piano* as follows:

- Homophonic texture, with melody in the right hand and accompaniment in the left (utilize one of the piano styles exemplified in examples 10.18—10.25)
- Motifs present
- Range of melody between a 6th and 10th
- Melody primarily stepwise
- Melodic nonharmonic tones used intentionally according to function (no free tones)
- Period construction
- Traditional cadences
- Strong harmonic rhythm
- Strong harmonic progressions, no retrogressions
- Tempo, dynamics, articulation included
- Minimum 16 measures in length

Questions for Review

1. Define the following terms:

    a. motif

    b. sequence

    c. real sequence

    d. tonal sequence

    e. false sequence

    f. modified sequence

    g. contoural inversion

    h. retrograde motion

    i. retrograde inversion

    j. phrase

    k. period

    l. contrasting period

    m. parallel period

    n. texture

    o. block chords

    p. broken chords

    q. Alberti bass

2. Can monophony exist when more than one voice is present?

3. Explain the differences between analyses in the foreground, middle ground, and background.

4. Explain what is meant by *homorhythmic texture*.

Assignments for Use with Anthology

A10.01 Identify the phrases in *Greensleeves*. Anthology page 41. Identify any periods by type. Identify motifs. Harmonize the melody, using pop-chord symbols above and roman numerals below.

A10.02 Identify the phrases in Petzold's *Minuet in G*. Anthology page 77. Identify periods by type. Identify motivic material.

A10.03 Identify the phrases in measures 58-72 of Schubert: *Erlkönig*, D. 328. Anthology pages 321-322. Identify periods by type.

A10.04 Identify the type of period in measures 1-8 of Beethoven: *Piano Sonata No. 8 in C Minor*, Opus 13, ("Pathétique"), third movement (Allegro). Anthology page 274.

A10.05 Identify the texture of each of the assignments above, as well as:

- *Hymn to St. John the Baptist* (Liber Usualis 1504). Anthology page 4.
- Palestrina: *Sanctus* (from *Missa Aeterna Christi Munera*). Anthology page 27.
- Corelli: *Trio Sonata*, Opus 4, No. 11, Allemanda. Anthology page 67.
- Schubert: *Waltz in A Flat Major,* Opus 9, No. 2 (D. 365). Anthology page 326. (Note also motivic devices.)
- Chopin: *Prelude 6 in B Minor*. Anthology page 349.
- Chopin: *Prelude 20 in C Minor*. Anthology page 354.
- Bartók: *Music for String Instruments, Percussion, and Celesta*, first movement (Andante). Anthology pages 484-489. (Note also motivic devices.)

Chapter 11
Voice Leading

When more than one musical line occurs simultaneously, the technique of composing each line is known as **voice leading**. Voice leading is present in both polyphonic and homophonic textures. This chapter will focus on homophonic voice leading in a "hymn style," or *homorhythmic,* context.

When a melody is harmonized for SATB (soprano, alto, tenor, bass) voices, the individual *melodic lines* of each part must be considered. Typically, the soprano part carries the melody and the other voices combine to provide the harmony. These harmonic voices, however, must not be thought of as merely "filling in the chords." While it is important that these voices do ultimately provide the necessary harmonic structure, the theorist must think linearly as well.

Each vocal part has its own musical *line,* and these lines must possess musical qualities individually. The theorist must think in terms of overall harmony (the vertical dimension) and individual melodies (the horizontal dimension) simultaneously when writing for more than one part. Thus, the term *voice leading* relates to the character of how notes progress one to another within the melodic lines of each part.

The term **cantus firmus** (literally "fixed song") will be used here to indicate a pre-existing melody to be voice led.[1] The first step in voice leading a cantus firmus is determining the harmonic rhythm. The second step is choosing chords for the melody that constitute strong harmonic progressions and purposeful cadences. Once these steps have been taken, *the bass line should be the first vocal part to be added to the soprano*. The bass and soprano parts together are referred to as the **outer voices** and form the complete basis of the composition, both melodically and harmonically.

The theorist must abide by one fundamental standard when voice leading: *each line must be readily "singable."* Even when writing for instruments instead of literal voices, the singability of each line is first priority. Because of this basic requirement, most lines are primarily *stepwise*. Exceptions may be made for bass parts, which sometimes contain more leaps than steps when providing the foundation for root position chords. Otherwise, the theorist must carefully consider the individual lines and ensure that they are all singable and musical. The addition of nonharmonic tones such as passing tones, for instance, is often helpful in achieving stepwise motion.

---

[1] *The term* cantus firmus *is historically reserved for polyphonic works, as seen in footnote 20 of chapter 10 (page 271). It is used throughout this text, however, regardless of texture type, to denote any pre-existing melody.*

Various types of motion *between voices* must also be considered. From one voice to another, it is possible to have four types of motion: parallel, similar, contrary, and oblique.

Example 11.01 — parallel motion

parallel 3rds   parallel 5ths   parallel 6ths*   parallel 8ves   parallel unisons

*compound intervals are reduced when identified

As each part ascends a melodic second in the first measure above, the harmonic interval of a third is maintained between the soprano and alto. The result is parallel thirds (the first third is a m3, the second is a M3, but the thirds are parallel nonetheless). The same type of **parallel motion** is present in each measure that follows.

With **similar motion**, the voices move *in the same direction*, but do not maintain parallel intervals.

Example 11.02 — similar motion

Voices moving in **contrary motion** are going opposite directions from each other.

Example 11.03 — contrary motion

When one voice is stationary and the other one is moving, **oblique motion** is the result.

Example 11.04

For motion to be considered one of these four types, there must be actual melodic movement. In example 11.05 below, there are no parallel fifths or thirds because neither voice is *moving* melodically.

Example 11.05

When voice leading according to common practice, there are a number of very specific guidelines to follow. At first, observing these precepts may seem tedious, but much freedom awaits the creative composer/arranger who is willing to voice lead according to these disciplines. These practices are broken down into **laws, regulations,** and **principles**.

There are **four musical laws** of voice leading that must never be broken. Violations of these fixed practices are simply not part of the fabric of music of the common practice era.

> 1. Do not write parallel perfect octaves, fifths, or unisons.[2]
> 2. Do not write melodic augmented seconds or augmented fourths.
> 3. Do not write outside a voice's range.[3]
> 4. Do not double the leading tone.

---

[2] *Parallel octaves/unisons are permitted in purely monophonic sections.*
[3] *Ranges for vocal parts are shown in example 6.27 on page 168. Remember that the regions near the extreme highest and lowest notes of each range are difficult to produce and should be written very sparingly.*

There are **five regulations** which should be followed when possible. Exceptions to these preferred practices do occur on rare occasion in music of the common practice era.

> 1. Do not cross voices.
> 2. Do not overlap voices.
> 3. Do not exceed an octave between soprano/alto or alto/tenor.
> 4. Do not write *uneven fifths*.
> 5. Do not leave the leading tone unresolved in an outer voice in a cadence.

Voice crossing, also referred to as voicing *out of order*, is shown in example 11.06.

Example 11.06

tenor above alto

soprano below alto

bass above tenor

Voice overlapping occurs when a note appears above or below the *previous* note *in an adjacent voice*. If this regulation is violated on occasion, the overlap should never exceed the interval of a whole step.

Example 11.07

B3 in the alto is m2 lower than previous C4 in tenor

alto note in second chord is m2 higher than soprano note in first chord

overlap occurs between tenor and bass voices

As a general regulation, the distance between soprano and alto pitches should not exceed an octave. Likewise, the distance between the alto and tenor should not exceed an octave. There may be more than an octave between the tenor and bass voices if desired, however. In fact, close intervals, such as thirds, are avoided in low registers (harmonic thirds are sparsely found below C3 in common practice literature).

Uneven fifths (sometimes called *unequal fifths*) are parallel fifths that are not both *perfect* fifths. This term represents the movement between voices of a diminished fifth to a perfect fifth, or a perfect fifth to a diminished fifth, as show below in example 11.08. In certain circumstances, it may be necessary to write uneven fifths. This is a viable option when there are no other reasonable alternatives.

Example 11.08

The leading tone is strongly active, tending toward the tonic. When it is present at the moment of cadence in the soprano or bass, its natural inclination toward tonic should be observed. When the leading tone appears *in an inner voice* at a cadence, it is *not* always necessary to resolve it to the tonic note.

Example 11.09

C: V$^6_5$ I   V   I   V^7 I

When it comes to *doubling*, there are **three principles** that help lead to smooth voice leading and satisfying musical results. Any note of a triad may be doubled (unless it is the leading tone or otherwise causes a violation of laws/regulations), but the following principles should be adhered to whenever possible.

> 1. For **root position** triads, the first choice for doubling is the **bass**.
> 2. For **first inversion** triads, the first choice for doubling is the **soprano**.[4] Doubling the bass is the second choice. When first inversion triads appear in succession, doubling should be alternated between soprano and bass.
> 3. For **second inversion** triads, the first choice for doubling is the **bass**.

---

[4] *One word of caution: diminished triads most often appear in first inversion with the leading tone in the soprano. DO NOT DOUBLE THE SOPRANO when it contains the leading tone.*

When voice leading, remember that the fifth of a chord may be omitted if smooth lines are the result. In the case of triads, both the root and the third may be doubled (so long as one is not the leading tone). Occasionally at cadence points, it may even be desirable to triple the root, leaving three roots and one third, but this is rare.

If two adjacent chords have one or more notes in common, keep the common tone in the same voice whenever possible. While continuously repeating notes may seem boring, they are easily sung or played, and are preferable to unnecessary jumping around from note to note.

Example 11.10

C: I   iii   IV   ii

The first measure of example 11.10 above shows a simple melody and bass part. To complete the harmonization by writing singable, musical alto and tenor parts, the theorist must know all the laws, regulations, and doubling principles. The root is already doubled in the first chord, so the alto and tenor simply complete the full triad, as shown in measure two.

In measure three, the mediant triad is completed simply by *keeping the common tones* from the previous chord. This worked nicely because by keeping the common tones, the bass of the root position mediant triad was doubled (first choice).

In measure four, the subdominant chord is present and the voices are still moving smoothly. Note that the first choice for doubling in this chord, the root, is doubled by the tenor, which simply moves down a half step without causing any parallelism violations.

In measure five, the tenor keeps the common tone which comprises the third of the triad, while the alto doubles the bass (first choice). Not every exercise in voice leading works as easily as this one, however. Sometimes alternate or even irregular doublings must be used in order to avoid law/regulation violations. In some instances, as mentioned above, the fifth must be omitted from a chord in order to otherwise follow convention.

The same simple melody and bass line are harmonized in example 11.11 on the following page, with equal ease, as well as equally satisfying results. This time, the voice leading was done in *close spacing* (less than an octave between the soprano and tenor).

Example 11.11

C: I   iii   IV   ii

Comparing examples 11.10 and 11.11, note that the alto and tenor parts are simply switched. It is important to realize that this technique does not always work in voice leading. Sometimes, when switching the inner voices, unforeseen parallelisms result. For instance, acceptable parallel fourths between voices become unacceptable parallel fifths when the voices switch places. Fortunately, all laws, regulations, and doubling principles were still followed here. Compare the sound of these two examples to see which spacing you prefer.

When voice leading dominant seventh or leading tone seventh chords, *the seventh of the chord must resolve down by step*. Note how the seventh of each chord in example 11.09 resolved down by step to the third of the tonic chord. The seventh of a dominant seventh chord is the fourth degree of the scale, which is an *active tone* that leans toward the third scale degree, only a half step away. Just as the leading tone of the scale naturally leads upward toward tonic, the fourth scale degree, especially when appearing as the seventh of a dominant seventh chord, is a *leaning tone*, tending toward the closest scale degree—the third.

Dominant seventh chords have three types of resolutions:

1. Type one: regular. The root descends a fifth.
2. Type two: deceptive. The root ascends a second.
3. Type three: irregular. The root neither descends a fifth nor ascends a second.

Example 11.12

Type 1: regular   Type 2: deceptive   Type 3: irregular

C: V^6_5 I V^4_3 vi^6 V^4_2 iii

"He who sings scares away his woes."
- author Miguel de Cervantes

It is not unusual for the fifth to be omitted and the root doubled in root position dominant seventh chords, leaving two roots, a third, and a seventh.

As explained in chapter nine, the vii° chord is considered a "rootless" V^7. Because of this, the note on which a diminished chord is constructed is referred to as the ***prime*** instead of the root.

Diminished and half-diminished seventh chords (leading tone sevenths) also have three types of resolutions:

1. Type one: regular. The prime ascends a minor second.
2. Type two: deceptive. At least one chord tone stays the same.
3. Type three: irregular. The prime neither ascends a minor second nor do any chord tones stay the same.

Example 11.13

Type 1: regular   Type 2: deceptive   Type 3: irregular

Cm: vii°^{7} i   vii°$^6_5$ iv   vii°$^4_3$ III

Notice the unusual doubling in the tonic triad in measure one of example 11.13 above. If the tenor had moved stepwise down to C in order to double the bass of the root position resolution chord, the result would have produced *uneven fifths* between the alto and tenor. This is a frequent problem when resolving diminished sevenths.

In order to avoid violating this regulation when voice leading diminished sevenths, it is helpful to follow the resolution principle of **direction of inflection**. Every diminished seventh chord, regardless of inversion, contains two tritones. When the tritone is in the form of an augmented fourth, the inflection of *augmentation* (getting larger) is *outward*. When the tritone is in the form of a diminished fifth, the inflection of *diminution* (getting smaller) is *inward*.

Tritones naturally resolve in the direction of their inflection. If they are augmented, they'll continue to expand; if they are diminished, they'll continue to contract. Augmented fourths resolve outward to sixths, and diminished fifths resolve inward to thirds. This is demonstrated in example 11.14 on the following page.

Example 11.14

[Musical notation showing voice leading example in C major with vii°⁶₅ resolving to I⁶, with A4 marked in first measure and d5 marked in second measure]

C: vii°⁶₅   I⁶

Both tritones resolve in the direction of their inflection. The A4 in the first measure resolves outward; the d5 in the second measure resolves inward. The tritones are put together in measure three to form a diminished seventh chord that naturally resolves correctly. Notice that the seventh of the chord automatically resolves downward as it is supposed to, and the prime ascends the interval of a second, forming a regular (type one) resolution. The third of the tonic triad is doubled, as is normal when resolving diminished sevenths.

Diminished sevenths may appear in a variety of voicings where the tritones are more difficult to spot. Nonetheless, two tritones are always present, and if both are resolved direction of inflection, the result will be smooth voice leading and avoidance of law/regulation violations.

Example 11.15

[Musical notation showing voice leading examples in C minor with various inversions of vii°⁷ resolving to i, with tritone intervals (A4 and d5) labeled throughout]

Cm: vii°⁷   i   vii°⁶₅   i⁶   vii°⁴₃   i⁶   vii°⁴₂   i⁶₄

In every instance of example 11.15, the leading tone progresses to tonic, the seventh of the diminished seventh chord resolves down by step, and each tritone resolves in the direction of inflection. Each progression forms a regular (type one) resolution.

It is not considered "wrong" to only resolve one tritone in direction of inflection so long as the leading tone resolves to tonic and the seventh resolves down by step. However, if the second tritone is not resolved, *uneven fifths* usually result. Since these only occur sparingly, the theorist will choose exceptions wisely when it seems more important to double the root of the tonic chord instead of the third (such as at a final cadence).

Special care must be taken when resolving *half-diminished* seventh chords. Parallel perfect fifths are a common pitfall. It is still important to *resolve the prime up to tonic* in type one resolutions, and *resolve the seventh of the chord down by step*. The half-diminished seventh, however, only has one tritone. Make sure it resolves direction of inflection. When resolving the remaining note (other than the prime, the seventh, and the tritone), make sure no laws or regulations are broken. *When parallel fifths would result, it is standard procedure to double the third of the root position tonic triad.*

Example 11.16

C: vii°7 I   vii°7 I   vii°$\frac{6}{5}$ I^6 vii°$\frac{4}{3}$ I^6

In the example above, only the chord of resolution in the first measure has preferred doubling, even though in all measures, the tritone is resolved in direction of inflection, the leading tone progresses to tonic, and the seventh of each chord resolves down by step.

If the alto in measure two had progressed down to C for the preferred doubling, parallel fifths would have resulted between alto and soprano. In measure three, if the bass had resolved down to the root of the tonic chord, parallel fifths would have resulted between bass and soprano. In measure four, the alto moved up to the third of the chord to avoid parallel fifths with the soprano (as in measure two).

It is important to spend a great deal of time mastering these principles of voice leading. Memorizing all musical laws, regulations, and doubling principles is an excellent start. Practicing, however, and having another theorist review your work with a careful eye and ear for violations is invaluable.

Inadvertently violating the common practices of voice leading is quite typical at first. Remember that failure is the highway to success. The important thing is to keep working until parallelisms and other problems are readily noticed and corrected. Also remember that *both ends of the pencil are useful*. Voice leading is a fine art, and doing it well is rewarding.

This concludes the introduction to voice leading, and brings a close to part two of this textbook. The study of music theory continues in part three, which focuses on chromatic harmony.

Assignments and Drills

Assignment 11.01

The objective of this assignment is proper voice leading according to common practice.

1. Provide harmonic analysis for each brief excerpt below according to the key signature and figured bass provided.
2. Write smooth, singable alto and tenor lines, following the voice leading guidelines presented in chapter eleven.

Measures 1 and 2 have been completed for you. <u>All keys are major.</u>

REFER BACK TO THE FOUR LAWS, FIVE REGULATIONS, AND THREE DOUBLING PRINCIPLES AS NECESSARY.

C: I   V   G: V   I

Assignment 11.02

The objective of this assignment is proper voice leading according to common practice.

1. Provide harmonic analysis for each brief excerpt below according to the key signature and figured bass provided.
2. Write smooth, singable alto and tenor lines, following the voice leading guidelines presented in chapter eleven.

All keys are minor.

REFER BACK TO THE FOUR LAWS, FIVE REGULATIONS, AND THREE DOUBLING PRINCIPLES AS NECESSARY.

Voice Leading

Assignment 11.03

The objective of this assignment is proper voice leading according to common practice.

1. Provide harmonic analysis for each brief excerpt below according to the key signature and figured bass provided.
2. Write smooth, singable soprano, alto, and tenor lines, following the voice leading guidelines presented in chapter eleven.

<u>All keys are major</u>.

<small>REFER BACK TO THE FOUR LAWS, FIVE REGULATIONS, AND THREE DOUBLING PRINCIPLES AS NECESSARY.</small>

Assignment 11.04

The objective of this assignment is proper voice leading according to common practice.

1. Provide harmonic analysis for each brief excerpt below according to the key signature and figured bass provided.
2. Write smooth, singable soprano, alto, and tenor lines, following the voice leading guidelines presented in chapter eleven.

<u>All keys are minor.</u>

REFER BACK TO THE FOUR LAWS, FIVE REGULATIONS, AND THREE DOUBLING PRINCIPLES AS NECESSARY.

Voice Leading

Assignment 11.05

The objective of this assignment is proper voice leading according to common practice.

1. Provide harmonic analysis for each brief excerpt below according to the key signature and figured bass provided.
2. Write smooth, singable alto and tenor lines, following the voice leading guidelines presented in chapter eleven.
3. Sing each line when finished.

REFER BACK TO THE FOUR LAWS, FIVE REGULATIONS, AND THREE DOUBLING PRINCIPLES AS NECESSARY.
DO NOT VIOLATE ANY LAWS, AVOID REGULATION VIOLATIONS IF AT ALL POSSIBLE, AND ADHERE
TO DOUBLING PRINCIPLES UNLESS DOING SO CAUSES A GREATER INFRACTION.

Assignment 11.06

The objective of this assignment is proper voice leading according to common practice.

1. Provide harmonic analysis for each brief excerpt below according to the key signature and figured bass provided.
2. Write smooth, singable alto and tenor lines, following the voice leading guidelines presented in chapter eleven.
3. Sing each line when finished.

REFER BACK TO THE FOUR LAWS, FIVE REGULATIONS, AND THREE DOUBLING PRINCIPLES AS NECESSARY.
DO NOT VIOLATE ANY LAWS, AVOID REGULATION VIOLATIONS IF AT ALL POSSIBLE, AND ADHERE
TO DOUBLING PRINCIPLES UNLESS DOING SO CAUSES A GREATER INFRACTION.

* The nonharmonic tone here is substituting for the third of the triad. Omit the third in lieu of this note.

VOICE LEADING

Assignment 11.07

The objective of this assignment is error identification.

Instructions: Identify voice leading errors in each excerpt below. Label each one and indicate whether it is a violation of a law or a regulation. Also make note of other problems (chords without thirds, retrogressions, etc.).

REFER BACK TO THE FOUR LAWS AND FIVE REGULATIONS AS NECESSARY. ALSO REVIEW EXAMPLES 9.17 — 9.20.

1. E: I I^6 IV V IV^6 V^6 IV^6_4 I IV vi^6_4 V^6_4 IV I^6 IV^6 V

2. F: IV I iii IV vi iii^6 IV I^6 IV iii^6 ii^6_4 IV I V I

3. Em: i i^6_4 III iv III i^6_4 vii^{o6}_4 vii^{o6}_4 VI^6_4 vii^{o6}_4 VI^6_4 V^6 i vii^{o6} i

4. Bm: i V iv V iv^6_4 V i vii^o V^7 i

Assignment 11.08

The objective of this assignment is proper voice leading according to common practice.

1. Harmonize each brief melody below. The harmonic rhythm is one chord change per melody note (inversion changes of repeated chords *are* considered chord changes).
2. Voice lead the alto, tenor, and bass parts. Write the bass line first.
3. Start and end with root position triads.
4. Use second inversion triads only in acceptable contexts (REVIEW EXAMPLES 9.17 — 9.20).
5. Add at least one nonharmonic tone. Check to make sure the additional notes do not create any voice leading errors.
6. Write a complete harmonic analysis below the staff. Enclose circle progressions in ellipses.

<u>All keys are major.</u>

ATTEMPT TO RECALL ALL LAWS, REGULATIONS, AND DOUBLING PRINCIPLES FROM MEMORY.

Assignment 11.09

The objective of this assignment is proper voice leading according to common practice.

1. Harmonize each brief melody below. The harmonic rhythm is one chord change per melody note (inversion changes of repeated chords *are* considered chord changes).
2. Voice lead the alto, tenor, and bass parts. Write the bass line first.
3. Start and end with root position triads.
4. Use second inversion triads only in acceptable contexts (REVIEW EXAMPLES 9.17-9.20).
5. Add at least one nonharmonic tone to each exercise. Check to make sure the additional notes do not create any voice leading errors.
6. Write a complete harmonic analysis below the staff. Enclose circle progressions in ellipses.

<u>All keys are minor</u>.

ATTEMPT TO RECALL ALL LAWS, REGULATIONS, AND DOUBLING PRINCIPLES FROM MEMORY.

Assignment 11.10

The objective of this assignment is harmonization of a melody according to common practice chorale style voice leading.

1. Harmonize the melody below.[5] The harmonic rhythm is one chord per melody note, except when there are beamed eighth notes (one chord per *beat* in such instances).
2. Voice lead the alto, tenor, and bass parts. Write the bass line first.
3. Use second inversion triads only in acceptable contexts (REVIEW EXAMPLES 9.17-9.20).
4. Add nonharmonic tones to enhance the voice leading. Check to make sure the additional notes do not create any voice leading errors.
5. Write a complete harmonic analysis below the staff. Enclose circle progressions in ellipses.

ATTEMPT TO RECALL ALL LAWS, REGULATIONS, AND DOUBLING PRINCIPLES FROM MEMORY.

---

[5] *Chrétien d' Urhan: Rutherford, 1734. Public Domain.*

Assignment 11.11

The objective of this assignment is harmonization of a melody and bass line according to common practice chorale style voice leading.

Harmonize the progression below, first in open spacing, then in close spacing. One of these spacings works quite well, while the other poses significant challenges. Compare with Examples 11.10 and 11.11 on pages 282-283.

C: I   iii   IV   V   C: I   iii   IV   V

Assignment 11.12

The objective of this assignment is harmonization of a melody according to common practice chorale style voice leading.

1. On a separate sheet of paper, harmonize a popular or folk melody of your choice in chorale style (including nonharmonic tones). Write the bass line first.
2. Write a complete harmonic analysis below the staff. Enclose circle progressions in ellipses.

Assignment 11.13

The objective of this assignment is identification of cadences (review).

Instructions: Many of the brief progressions in assignments 11.1 – 11.5 were cadences. Go back through assignments 11.1 – 11.5 and label each cadence you find.

Composition Project

Assignment 11.14

Instructions: Compose an original *chorale* as follows:

- Homophonic texture on grand staff with soprano/alto in treble clef and tenor/bass in bass clef (indicate each part by stem direction)
- Period construction
- Traditional cadences
- Harmonic rhythm changes every beat
- Strong harmonic progressions, no retrogressions
- Keep voices stepwise as much as possible
- No law violations
- Avoid regulation violations as much as possible
- Follow doubling principles unless doing so causes a law/regulation violation
- Include nonharmonic tones
- Minimum 16 measures in length

Questions for Review

1. Why is voice leading more than just filling in the notes of each chord?

2. What is meant by the term *cantus firmus*?

3. List the four musical laws of voice leading.

4. List the five musical regulations of voice leading.

5. List the three doubling principles of voice leading.

6. What is the term for the note on which a diminished triad is constructed? Why is it not called the *root*?

7. In what inversion does a diminished triad appear the most frequently?

8. What are *uneven fifths*?

9. Explain the three types of resolutions of dominant seventh chords.

10. Explain the three types of resolutions of diminished seventh chords.

11. Explain what is meant by *direction of inflection*.

12. How many tritones are present in a diminished seventh chord?

13. Why is irregular doubling of the resolution chord usually necessary when resolving half-diminished seventh chords?

Assignments for Use with Anthology

A11.01 Locate all the harmonic intervals of a tritone in the treble clef of Beethoven: *Piano Sonata No. 8 in C Minor*, Opus 13, ("Pathétique"), first movement (Allegro), <u>measures 11-49 only</u>. Anthology page 265. Do not look for tritones within actual chords in the treble clef—only consider those that appear as two-note intervals. Label each one as A4 or d5, and identify the resolution as outward or inward. Are there any that do not resolve direction of inflection?

A11.02 Voice lead the alto and tenor of the Gesangbuch chorale, *Jesu, Jesu, du bist mein,* in Appendix B of the anthology (page 634). Erase work done in treble clef from assignment A7.03.

A11.03 Voice lead the alto and tenor of the Gesangbuch chorale, *So gehst du nun, mein Jesu, hin,* in Appendix B of the anthology (page 639). Erase work done in treble clef from assignment A7.04.

A11.04 Voice lead the alto and tenor of the Gesangbuch chorale, *So gibst du nun, mein Jesu, gut Nacht,* in Appendix B of the anthology (page 639). Erase work done in treble clef from assignment A7.05.

PART THE THIRD: CHROMATIC HARMONY

Music that never deviates from the established key is purely **diatonic**. **Dia**, as in *dia*gonal or *dia*metric, literally means *through* or *across*. **Tonic** means *tones*, or more specifically, *key*. **Diatonic** music, therefore, goes *through the tones* (or *across the key*). Foreign elements to the key are **chromatic**. Both diatonic and chromatic harmony comprise the field of study known as **tonal analysis**.

If music is *purely* diatonic, it does not include accidentals that vary from the scale on which the music is based (other than the harmonic and melodic forms of the minor scale). Most tonal music is considered diatonic, even though it may contain melodic and harmonic elements from outside the key (chromaticism).

Music that is *purely* chromatic is non-tonal; that is, without a tonic. Such music lies outside the scope of this text. The chromatic harmony explored in the pages to follow deals with how elements from outside a given key relate to those within the key. It is the discovery and enjoyment of "foreign" harmonies and how such devices "work." It is the investigation of a vast wealth of creative opportunities that are simply unavailable in strictly diatonic contexts, as well as the exploration of multiple methods of modulating from key to key.

Chapter 12
Tonicization

Tonicization is the phenomenon that occurs when a chord *other than one built on the first scale degree* "acts like" tonic. That is, a chord that normally serves some *other* function, such as mediant or dominant, for example, is *tonicized*—set up as a temporary "tonic." Tonicization is sort of an "almost modulation," where a new key center is very briefly *suggested*, yet not genuinely established.

Just as the dominant and leading tone chords naturally progress to tonic in an authentic cadence, tonicized chords are *preceded* by chords in *dominant* or *leading tone* relationship to them. These "set-up" chords are the ones that are *chromatically altered* in order to tonicize a diatonic triad within the key. Such tonicizing chords are known as *secondary dominants* or *secondary leading tone chords*.

A ***secondary dominant*** is a *dominant-function* seventh chord or major triad that is constructed on any scale degree other than the *diatonic* dominant. Therefore, it is a diatonic chord that is *chromatically altered* to posses the *quality* of a *major triad* or a *dominant seventh chord*.

In any major key, triads built on the supertonic, mediant, submediant, and leading tone are *not* diatonically major in quality. This is shown below in example 12.01 (a replication of example 5.03).

Example 12.01

C: I ii iii IV V vi vii° I

If any one of these triads (ii, iii, vi, vii°) is *altered* to become *major* in quality, *it ceases to maintain its original function* (as supertonic, mediant, etc.) and takes on the *function* of a dominant triad. In the key of C major, for example, a major triad built on *D* is *not* labeled with an uppercase roman numeral II, because *it is no longer functioning as a supertonic chord*. In this case, the D major triad in the key of C is *acting as a dominant* chord. And if ***D*** is a *dominant* (V), then *its tonic* must be ***G*** (in the key of G, the dominant triad is D). Therefore, ***G*** is briefly tonicized in the key of C by the D major triad. Since ***G*** is the dominant in the key of C, the D major chord is the dominant *of the dominant* (***D*** is the V of ***G***, which is dominant in ***C***).

Example 12.02

C: V/V

In harmonic analysis, a slash is used to indicate the word "of." "Five of five," for example, is written V/V, as shown here in example 12.02.

This same process can be applied to chords built on the mediant, submediant, or leading tone. If, for example, the triad built on the leading tone (B diminished, in the key of C) is *altered* to become major in quality (B, D, F becomes B, D#, F#) the vii° does not become VII. It is no longer functioning as a leading tone toward tonic. The B *major* chord is perceived as a *dominant* triad. The chord it is tonicizing is constructed on E (iii), since **B** is the dominant of **E**. Therefore, the B major triad is a V of **E**. **E** is mediant in **C**, so the harmonic analysis of the B major chord in the key of C major, then, is V/iii.

Example 12.03

C: V/iii

"Were it not for music, we might in these days say, the beautiful is dead."
- British politician Benjamin Disraeli

Example 12.04 below illustrates the roman numeral analysis of major triads built on every scale degree in C major.

Example 12.04

C: I   V/V   V/vi   IV   V   V/ii   V/iii   I

The chart in example 12.05 below (originally presented in example 5.07) has a new row added to indicate secondary dominants.

Example 12.05

Key of C	C	C#/Db	D	D#/Eb	E	F	F#/Gb	G	G#/Ab	A	A#/Bb	B
DIATONIC TRIADS	I		ii		iii	IV		V		vi		vii°
NATURAL MINOR DIATONIC TRIADS	i		ii°	III		iv		v	VI		VII	
HARMONIC MINOR DIATONIC TRIADS	i		ii°	III+		iv		V	VI			vii°
SECONDARY DOMINANTS			V/V		V/vi		(V/vii°)			V/ii		V/iii

Note that every diatonic scale degree may be tonicized except IV (and I, for obvious reasons). This is because the dominant of IV is simply tonic. There is no V/IV — the analysis of a chord in dominant relationship to subdominant is simply I.

Most theorists agree that a diminished triad such as vii° cannot be tonicized since Locrian is the only mode where a diminished chord conceivably could be tonic. Parenthesis are used to surround V/vii° on the chart above to indicate the purely theoretical nature of such a chord.

When the interval of a minor third is superimposed above the fifth of a major triad, the chord becomes a *dominant seventh* in quality. Since "dominant" can only mean "V," all chords of this quality are dominants—either the *diatonic* dominant or a *secondary* dominant. Example 12.06 below illustrates the roman numeral analysis of dominant sevenths built on every scale degree (except IV) in C major.

Example 12.06

C: V^7/IV V^7/V V^7/vi IV V^7 V^7/ii V^7/iii

If a dominant seventh chord were to appear on **F** in the key of C ($\hat{4}$), it would be the dominant of B-flat, which is not in the key (it is the *lowered* seventh scale degree).

The roman numeral chart of chord identification in example 12.07 below now shows secondary dominant *sevenths*.

Example 12.07

Key of C	C	C#/D♭	D	D#/E♭	E	F	F#/G♭	G	G#/A♭	A	A#/B♭	B
DIATONIC TRIADS	I		ii		iii	IV		V		vi		vii°
NATURAL MINOR DIATONIC TRIADS	i		ii°	III		iv		v	VI		VII	
HARMONIC MINOR DIATONIC TRIADS	i		ii°	III+		iv		V	VI			vii°
SECONDARY DOMINANTS	V^7/IV		$V^{(7)}/V$		$V^{(7)}/vi$		$(V^{[7]}/vii°)$			$V^{(7)}/ii$		$V^{(7)}/iii$

Note that V^7/IV now appears on the chart. V^7/IV differs from I^7 in quality. I^7 is a major seventh (C, E, G, B), V^7/IV is a dominant seventh (C, E, G, B♭), *functioning* as a dominant.

The chorale *Ein' Feste Burg* contains an astounding number of secondary dominants (eleven in the eighteen-measure harmonization presented on the following page). Example 12.08[1] demonstrates how these secondary dominants function to tonicize the diatonic chords that follow. Notice that all the chords containing chromatic alterations are enclosed in a rectangle. Each one is a *secondary* dominant that serves to *tonicize* the chord that follows, except for the first one in measure 15, which is immediately followed by another secondary dominant.

---

[1] A Mighty Fortress Is Our God: *Music and lyrics attributed to Martin Luther (lyrics based on Psalm 46), 1529. Public Domain. Tune name:* Ein' Feste Burg.

Example 12.08

Harmonic analysis has been completed for the chorale in example 12.08 except for the secondary dominants. The first one, appearing in measure two, is a dominant seventh chord constructed on **D** (D, F#, A, C). **D⁷** is a dominant seventh in the key of G, and, indeed, **G** is the chord of resolution at the fermata. Therefore, the harmonic analysis of this chord is V^7/V.

The secondary dominant in measure three is an A major triad in first inversion. **A** is the dominant of **D**. **D** is supertonic in the key, so the analysis is V^6/ii.

Measure six is identical to measure two, and measure seven is identical to measure three.

Measure nine includes a D major triad. Again, diatonically, a D chord is minor in the key of C. When it becomes major, the analysis does not change from ii to II. *The analysis symbol* II *does not exist.* When transformed into a major triad, the *function* of the chord ceases to be supertonic and becomes dominant. **D** is the dominant of **G**, which is V in the key of C. Therefore, the analysis of the secondary dominant in measure nine is V/V.

The secondary dominant in measure 12 precedes a vi chord. The submediant triad in **C** is **A minor**. The dominant of **A** is **E**, and as anticipated, an E major triad is the tonicizing chord (V^6/vi).

The only secondary dominant in this example that does not resolve to its tonicized chord is the C⁷ chord in measure 15. This *dominant* seventh chord, constructed on $\hat{1}$, is a V^7/IV, since it tonicizes **F**. It does not resolve to **F** (IV), however. It leads chromatically to *another* secondary dominant—a first inversion dominant seventh of the supertonic. The resolution of the V^7/IV is irregular, but is immediately followed by a regular resolution of the succeeding secondary dominant.

Like primary dominants, secondary dominants have three types of resolution:

1. Type one: regular. The root descends a fifth.
2. Type two: deceptive. The root ascends a second.
3. Type three: irregular. The root neither descends a fifth nor ascends a second.

Example 12.09

The presence of secondary dominants necessitates the designation of a new type of cadence—the **secondary cadence**. Referring back to example 12.08, it is apparent that the cadence at the first fermata resembles both a *half cadence* and an *authentic cadence*. It is certainly a half cadence because it ends on V, and in the middle ground, this is the best designation. But it is simultaneously an authentic cadence because the chords forming the cadence are in dominant-tonic relationship (the V chord has been *toni*cized by its dominant, the V/V). Because of this, the cadence is best seen in the foreground as authentic. The term **secondary authentic cadence** rightfully recognizes authentic function of the cadence that bears a dominant-tonic relationship, but does not end on the actual tonic.

Consider the cadence below in example 12.10.

Example 12.10

The progression is V^6_5/vi - vi. The secondary *dominant seventh* is built on $\hat{3}$ and resolves to *its* tonic (vi). This, too, is a *secondary authentic cadence* because it acknowledges the temporary V-i progression. The designation *secondary authentic* is used to indicate the presence of a dominant-to-tonic cadence that is the result of a *secondary* dominant and its tonicized chord.

In example 12.08, the cadence that occurs on the downbeat of measure 16 actually ends on a secondary dominant (V/vi). This is considered a **secondary half cadence**, because it ends on V, albeit a *secondary* V. Another example of a secondary half cadence is illustrated below in example 12.11. The *resolution* of the secondary dominant, unlike the one in measure 16 of example 12.08, is *classified* as irregular (type three), though not uncommon.

Example 12.11

C: I V^7/vi IV V^7/V IV V^7 I
            SECONDARY HALF   PAC

Notice, also, the deceptive resolution of the V^7/vi chord in the first measure above.

If a secondary dominant resolves deceptively (type two) at a cadence point, as in example 12.12, the result is a *secondary deceptive cadence*.

Example 12.12

[Musical notation showing: C — A/C# — D7 — Em (fermata) — C — G7/B — Csus — C, with Roman numeral analysis in C: I — V⁶/ii — V⁷/V — iii — I — V⁶₅ — I, labeled SECONDARY DEC and IAC]

Notice, also, the resolution of the V⁶/ii chord in the first measure above. Even though it advances to another secondary dominant, it still resolves regularly (type one).

Secondary leading tone chords function similarly to secondary dominants, except that tonicization takes place via *leading tone chords* instead of *dominants*. **Secondary leading tone chords** are diminished triads or sevenths that are constructed on any scale degree other than the *diatonic* leading tone, yet *function* as leading tone chords. Therefore, they are diatonic chords that are *chromatically altered* to posses the *quality* of a *diminished* triad or seventh chord.

Example 12.13 shows the diatonic triads in C major. A chromatically altered version of each diatonic triad follows each one. Each of these six diminished triads is a secondary leading tone chord. Example 12.14 indicates the roman numeral classification of each chord.

Example 12.13

[Musical notation showing diatonic triads and their altered versions in C: I, ii, iii, IV, V, vi, vii°]

Example 12.14

[Musical notation with roman numerals in C: I, vii°/ii, ii, vii°/iii, iii, vii°/IV, IV, vii°/V, V, vii°/vi, vi, (vii°/vii°), vii°]

The chart in example 12.15 below has a new row added to indicate secondary leading tone chords.

Example 12.15

Key of C	C	C#/Db	D	D#/Eb	E	F	F#/Gb	G	G#/Ab	A	A#/Bb	B
DIATONIC TRIADS	I		ii		iii	IV		V		vi		vii°
NATURAL MINOR	i		ii°	III		iv		v	VI		VII	
HARMONIC MINOR DIATONIC TRIADS	i		ii°	III+		iv		V	VI			vii°
SECONDARY DOMINANTS	V^7/IV		$V^{(7)}$/V		$V^{(7)}$/vi		(V/vii°)			$V^{(7)}$/ii		$V^{(7)}$/iii
SECONDARY LEADING TONES		vii°/ii		vii°/iii	vii°/IV		vii°/V		vii°/vi		(vii°/vii°)	

Secondary leading tone chords may appear with or without chord sevenths. These chords may be *fully* diminished or *half* diminished, and are omitted from the chart above for the sake of space.

Example 12.16[2] illustrates the use of a secondary leading tone seventh.

Example 12.16

D: ii⁶   I⁶   V⁶₅   I   V⁴₂/IV   IV⁶   I⁶₄   viiØ⁷/V   V⁷   I

Like primary leading tone chords, secondary leading tone chords have three types of resolution:

1. Type one: regular. The prime ascends a minor second.
2. Type two: deceptive. At least one chord tone stays the same.
3. Type three: irregular. The prime neither ascends a minor second nor do any chord tones stay the same.

---

[2] *Jesus, meine Zuversicht:* Common chorale harmonized by J.S. Bach (simplified), circa 1725. Measures 7-8. Public Domain.

Example 12.16 resolved the secondary leading tone chord in regular (type one) fashion. The excerpt in example 12.17[3] illustrates an effective deceptive (type two) resolution in measure 29, beat two before ultimately resolving regularly (type one) in measure 30.

Example 12.17

Whenever a V/iii is constructed, it is built on the leading tone of the key. It *is* acceptable to double the root of this chord (in any inversion). This is *not* considered doubling the leading tone because the chord is not *functioning* as the leading tone in this context.

However, when voice leading secondary dominants and secondary leading tone chords, one must be careful not to double the leading tone *of the tonicized chord*. Doubling either the third of a secondary dominant or the prime of a secondary leading tone chord is a violation of common practice law.

This concludes the introduction to tonicization. Borrowed chords will be covered in chapter thirteen.

---

[3] Great Is Thy Faithfulness: *Lyrics by Tomas Chisholm, music by William Runyan, 1923. © 1923, renewed in 1951 by Hope Publishing Company. Measures 29-32. Tune name:* Faithfulness.

Assignments and Drills

Assignment 12.01

The objective of this assignment is identification of secondary dominants.

Instructions: Fill in the blanks as requested pertaining to each chord provided. The first one has been completed for you. REFER BACK TO EXAMPLES 12.02 — 12.07 IF NECESSARY.

1. Identify the key according to roman numeral analysis.

   V_5^6 __Eb__ V_5^6/V __Ab__ V_5^6/ii __Db__ V_5^6/III __Cm__ V_5^6/vi __Gb__

2. Identify the key according to roman numeral analysis.

   V^6 _____ V^6/ii _____ V^6/iv _____ V^6/iii _____ V^6/VI _____

3. Identify the key according to roman numeral analysis.

   V^7 _____ V^7/vi _____ V^7/iii _____ V^7/V _____ V^7/ii _____

4. Write the harmonic analysis of this chord in the following keys.

   G: _____   Bm: _____   Em: _____   D: _____   C: _____

5. Write the harmonic analysis of this chord in the following keys.

   $G^\flat$: _____ $D^\flat$: _____ $C^\flat$: _____ $A^\flat$: _____ $B^\flat m$: _____

6. Write the harmonic analysis of this chord in the following keys.

   $B^\flat$: _____ $D^\flat$: _____   Am: _____   C: _____ $E^\flat$: _____

Assignment 12.02

The objective of this assignment is identification of secondary leading tone chords.

Instructions: Fill in the blanks as requested pertaining to each chord provided. REFER BACK TO EXAMPLES 12.13 — 12.17 IF NECESSARY.

1. Identify the key according to roman numeral analysis.

   vii° _____ vii°/V _____ vii°/ii _____ vii°/VI _____ vii°/vi _____

2. Identify the key according to roman numeral analysis.

   vii°6 _____ vii°6/iii _____ vii°6/vi _____ vii°6/III _____ vii°6/IV _____

3. Identify the key according to roman numeral analysis.

   vii°7 _____ vii°7/V _____ vii°7/iii _____ vii°7/vi _____ vii°7/IV _____

4. Write the harmonic analysis of this chord in the following keys.

   E♭: _____ *Cm: _____ Fm: _____ B♭: _____ Gm: _____

5. Write the harmonic analysis of this chord in the following keys.

   G: _____ E: _____ C: _____ F: _____ F#m: _____

6. Write the harmonic analysis of this chord in the following keys.

   G: _____ B♭: _____ Em: _____ F: _____ D♭: _____

*There are *two* possible analyses of the chord at the asterisk. How the chord resolves in context determines the appropriate analysis. Since the resolution is unknown, indicate both possibilities here.

Assignment 12.03

The objective of this assignment is identification of cadences involving tonicization.

Instructions: Go back through example 12.08 on page 306 and identify each cadence. The cadence points are the fermatas and half notes. REFER BACK TO EXAMPLES 12.10 – 12.12 IF NECESSARY.

Assignment 12.04

The objective of this assignment is proper roman numeral identification of diatonic and chromatic chords.

Instructions: Fill in the blanks in the chart below. Only refer back to example 12.15 to check your work when finished.

Key of C	C	C#/Db	D	D#/Eb	E	F	F#/Gb	G	G#/Ab	A	A#/Bb	B
DIATONIC TRIADS												
NATURAL MINOR DIATONIC TRIADS												
HARMONIC MINOR DIATONIC TRIADS												
SECONDARY DOMINANTS												
SECONDARY LEADING TONES												

Assignment 12.05

The objective of this assignment is identification of secondary dominants in literature.

Instructions: Examine the pop-chord analysis provided for example 10.06 back on page 257. Beneath the staff, write the roman numeral analysis (including figured bass inversion symbols) for each chord. Enclose each circle progression in an ellipse.

Assignment 12.06

The objective of this assignment is identification of secondary dominants in literature.

Instructions: Complete the harmonic analysis for the chorale[4] below and identify each cadence. REFER BACK TO EXAMPLES 12.02 — 12.17 IF NECESSARY.

---

[4] *O Jesu Christ, mein's Lebens Licht:* Common chorale harmonized by J.S. Bach, circa 1725. Public Domain.

Assignment 12.07

The objective of this assignment is identification of secondary dominants and secondary leading tone chords in literature.

Instructions: Complete the harmonic analysis for the chorale[5] below and identify each cadence. REFER BACK TO EXAMPLES 12.02 — 12.17 IF NECESSARY.

---

[5] *Zeuch uns nach Dir: Common chorale harmonized by J.S. Bach, circa 1725. Public Domain.*

Assignment 12.08

The objective of this assignment is identification of secondary dominants and secondary leading tone chords in literature.

Instructions: Complete the harmonic analysis for the chorale[6] below. Identify each cadence as well. REFER BACK TO EXAMPLES 12.02 — 12.17 IF NECESSARY.

---

[6] *Hinunter ist der Sonnenschein:* Common chorale harmonized by J.S. Bach, circa 1725. Public Domain.

TONICIZATION

Assignment 12.09

The objective of this assignment is creation of secondary dominant sevenths.

Instructions: Write each chord indicated by harmonic analysis on the staff. REFER BACK TO EXAMPLES 12.02 — 12.07 IF NECESSARY.

1. C: V^6_5/V
2. G: V^7/iii
3. F: V^4_3/IV
4. B♭: V^4_2/ii
5. A: V^7/vi

6. C: V^6_5/iii
7. A♭: V^6_5/V
8. D: V^7/IV
9. F: V^4_2/vi
10. B♭: V^7/V

11. Em: V^7/VI
12. Cm: V^4_3/V
13. F#m: V^6_5/iv
14. Gm: $V^4_2/ii°$
15. C#m: V^4_3/VII

Assignment 12.10

The objective of this assignment is creation of secondary leading tone seventh chords.

Instructions: Write each chord indicated by harmonic analysis on the staff. REFER BACK TO EXAMPLES 12.13 — 12.17 IF NECESSARY.

1. C: $vii°^6_5/V$
2. A: $vii°^7/iii$
3. Fm: $vii°^4_3/IV$
4. Gm: $vii°^7/ii°$
5. D: $vii°^4_2/vi$

6. Am: $vii°^7/VI$
7. B♭: $vii°^4_2/vi$
8. D: $vii°^4_3/V$
9. F: $vii°^7/ii$
10. A♭: $vii°^6_5/iii$

11. Em: $vii°^7/VI$
12. Cm: $vii°^4_3/V$
13. F#m: $vii°^6_5/iv$
14. G: $vii°^4_2/ii$
15. C: $vii°^4_3/vi$

Assignment 12.11

The objective of this assignment is proper voice leading of secondary dominant resolutions.

1. Resolve each secondary dominant as follows:
   - Measures 1-5, type 1
   - Measures 6-10, type 2
   - Measures 11-15, type 1
   - Measures 16-20, type 2

2. Indicate the key and provide harmonic analysis of both chords.

<u>Measures 1-10 are major keys; measures 11-20 are minor keys.</u>
Measures 1, 6, and 11 have been completed for you.

REFER BACK TO EXAMPLE 12.09 IF NECESSARY.

D: V/V V

C: V/vi IV

Em: V$^6_5$/iv iv

* Though technically not altered chromatically, this chord **functions** *as a secondary dominant because the quality of the chord is* **a dominant** *seventh.*

Assignment 12.12

The objective of this assignment is proper voice leading of secondary leading tone resolutions.

1. Resolve each secondary leading tone chord as follows:
   - Measures 1-5, type 1
   - Measures 6-10, type 2
   - Measures 11-15, type 1
   - Measures 16-20, type 2

2. Indicate the key and provide harmonic analysis of both chords. Be careful to adequately notate the quality of the sevenths (diminished or *half*-diminished)

<u>Measures 1-10 are major keys; measures 11-20 are minor keys.</u>

REFER BACK TO EXAMPLES 12.16 — 12.17 IF NECESSARY.

Composition Project

Assignment 12.13

Instructions: Compose an original piece of music *for vocalist* as follows:

- Homophonic texture on treble clef in *lead sheet* format (melody with lyrics below and pop-chord symbols above)
- Lyrics may be original if desired; otherwise any lyrics in Public Domain are acceptable
- Period construction
- Traditional cadences
- Strong pattern of harmonic rhythm
- Strong harmonic progressions, no retrogressions
- Include at least one secondary dominant that resolves regularly (type 1)
- Minimum 16 measures in length

Questions for Review

1. What is *tonicization*?

2. How is a tonicized chord approached? How might this information be useful when modulating from one key to another?

3. Explain the three types of secondary dominant resolution.

4. Explain the three types of secondary leading tone chord resolution.

5. What is a *secondary authentic cadence*?

6. What is a *secondary half cadence*?

7. What is a *secondary deceptive cadence*?

8. Speculate as to why plagal cadences are never classified as *secondary*.

9. Why are diminished chords, such as vii°, generally ruled out as the *object* of tonicization? Can you think of any reason why they *should* be able to be tonicized?

10. A standard circle progression is *iii — vi — ii — V — I*. What would the roman numeral analysis be if iii, vi, and ii were chromatically altered to become major chords? Why is this an even stronger circle progression than in the original form? Could it be altered further to become even stronger?

Assignments for Use with Anthology

For each assignment below, use roman numeral analysis to identify secondary dominants and secondary leading tone chords. Identify each resolution type as well.

A12.01   Purcell: *Dido's Lament*, from the opera *Dido and Aeneas*. Anthology page 69, measures 2-3 (key of C minor).

A12.02   Mozart: *Piano Sonata in B-flat Major*, K. 333, second movement (Andante). Anthology page 189, measures 68-69.

A12.03   Beethoven: *Piano Sonata No. 1 in F Minor*, Opus 2, No. 1, first movement (Allegro). Anthology page 251, measures 41-42.

A12.04   Beethoven: *Piano Sonata No. 8 in C Minor*, Opus 13, ("Pathétique"), first movement (Allegro). Anthology page 264, measure 1.

A12.05   Schubert: *Erlkönig*, D. 328. Anthology page 322, measure 70.

A12.06   Schubert: *Erlkönig*, D. 328. Anthology page 323, measures 91-92.

A12.07   Schumann: *Kleine Studie*, from *Album for the Young*, Opus 68. Anthology page 345, measures 38-45.

A12.08   Brahms: *Intermezzo in A Minor*, Opus 76, No. 7. Anthology page 393, measures 14-15.

Chapter 13
Borrowed Chords

As composers explored opportunities for harmonic expansion beyond the scope of purely diatonic resources, they began the practice of "borrowing" chords from the *parallel* key. *Harmonic* elements may be "borrowed," just as *metric* devices are (triplets, for instance, in simple meter comprise a "borrowed division" of the beat from compound meter). Composers discovered a great wealth of harmonic options available by simply using elements from a parallel mode. Thus, **borrowed chords** are those that are purely *diatonic in the parallel key,* though chromatically altered in the current key.

In one sense, borrowed harmonies are already familiar. Recall that the *ascending melodic minor* scale borrows the *upper tetrachord* from its *parallel major* counterpart. Even the *major dominant* chord in *harmonic minor* is borrowed from the *parallel major*. The harmonic minor mode replaces the *natural subtonic* with a *borrowed leading tone* from the *parallel key*.[1]

In major keys, it is very common for composers to borrow a chord from the parallel natural minor key. The diminished supertonic (ii°), for instance, provides a creative alternative to the purely diatonic ii chord. When a chord is borrowed from the parallel key, it retains the same function it had diatonically. For example, the *borrowed* subdominant (iv, in major) still functions as its diatonic counterpart (IV). Chords built on each scale degree keep their original function regardless of whether they are diatonic or borrowed.[2] Example 13.01 illustrates triads from parallel modes.

Example 13.01

Comparing the triads above from parallel keys, it is apparent that not one of the chords sharing a single scale degree is identical in quality. Further, notice that the chords built on $\hat{3}$, $\hat{6}$, and $\hat{7}$ are *constructed on different actual notes* between the two modes (E/E♭, A/A♭, B/B♭). Because of this, the roman numeral designation must indicate the chromatic shift in pitch. In major, for example, a borrowed mediant is ♭III, not merely III.

---
[1] *Though these chords are technically borrowed from the parallel major, the term* borrowed chord *is not applied to chords such as V in harmonic minor. The major dominant triad is simply considered the product of raising the seventh scale degree in the harmonic form of the mode; V is considered* diatonic in harmonic minor.

[2] *♭VII is an exception. It does not function like a leading tone, although it is often followed by tonic. Sometimes ♭VII functions as a pre-dominant chord, providing heightened activity near a musically significant return to tonic.*

While any chord may be borrowed from the parallel key, the most common borrowed chords in a major key are ii°, ii°⁷, ♭III, iv, ♭VI, and ♭VII, although ♭VII was somewhat scarce in the common practice era. The v and i triads may be borrowed in major, but are extremely rare (especially i). Some theorists refer to the usage of borrowed chords as **modal mixture**.

There is only one chord in a minor key that is commonly borrowed from major. When concluding a minor composition, composers sometimes choose to end on a final *major* tonic (I). This is known as the **Picardy third**.[3]

The roman numeral chart of chord identification is now expanded to include borrowed chords.

Example 13.02

Key of C	C	C#/D♭	D	D#/E♭	E	F	F#/G♭	G	G#/A♭	A	A#/B♭	B
DIATONIC TRIADS	I		ii		iii	IV		V		vi		vii°
NATURAL MINOR DIATONIC TRIADS	i		ii°	III		iv		v	VI		VII	
HARMONIC MINOR DIATONIC TRIADS	i		ii°	III+		iv		V	VI			vii°
SECONDARY DOMINANTS	V⁷/IV		V⁽⁷⁾/V		V⁽⁷⁾/vi	(V/vii°)				V⁽⁷⁾/ii		V⁽⁷⁾/iii
SECONDARY LEADING TONES		vii°/ii		vii°/iii	vii°/IV		vii°/V		vii°/vi		(vii°/vii°)	
BORROWED CHORDS	I (i)		ii°, ii°⁷	♭III		iv		(v)	♭VI		♭VII	

It should be noted that vii°⁷ technically is not diatonic in a major key. The leading tone seventh is half-diminished (see example 7.03 on page 182). The fully-diminished seventh chord, however, is a highly functional, active chord that is often preferred compositionally to the diatonic half-diminished seventh. To be technical, it *is* borrowed from harmonic minor, as shown in example 13.03. However, its use is so prevalent and its utility so similar to the half-diminished seventh that the fully-diminished leading tone chord is widely considered to function diatonically. Therefore, the designation *borrowed chord* is not applied to vii°⁷.

Example 13.03

C Major — vii°⁷ — B, D, F, A

C harmonic minor — vii°⁷ — B, D, F, A♭

> "If the king loves music, it is well in the land."
> *— Chinese philosopher Mencius*

---

[3] *The origin of this term is uncertain. The practice, however, dates back to the Renaissance.*

Borrowed chords whose roots are on different scale degrees than their diatonic counterparts are made even more interesting when *tonicized*. ♭III, ♭VI, and ♭VII may be approached by chords in dominant or leading tone relationship to them.

Example 13.04

Key of C	C	C#/D♭	D	D#/E♭	E	F	F#/G♭	G	G#/A♭	A	A#/B♭	B
Diatonic triads	I		ii		iii	IV		V		vi		vii°
Natural minor diatonic triads	i		ii°	III		iv		v		VI		VII
Harmonic minor diatonic triads	i		ii°	III+		iv		V		VI			vii°
Secondary dominants	V⁷/IV		V⁽⁷⁾/V		V⁽⁷⁾/vi	(V/vii°)				V⁽⁷⁾/ii		V⁽⁷⁾/iii
Secondary leading tones		vii°/ii		vii°/iii	vii°/IV		vii°/V		vii°/vi		(vii°/vii°)	
Borrowed chords	I (i)		ii°, ii^{ø7}	♭III		iv		(v)	♭VI		♭VII	
And their tonicizers			vii°/♭III	V⁽⁷⁾/♭VI		V⁷/♭VII		vii°/♭VI		vii°/♭VII	V⁽⁷⁾/♭III	

Examine the simple traditional song in example 13.05.[4] The first instance of chromatic alteration is a secondary dominant. The chord chromatically altered in measure 6, however, is a borrowed subdominant.

Example 13.05

[4] God Is So Good: *Traditional. Public Domain.*

The borrowed supertonic is very similar to the borrowed subdominant. The borrowed ii$^{ø6}_5$ in measure two of the hymn below in example 13.06[5] has three notes in common with a borrowed iv. In other words, *all* of the notes in iv are present in ii$^{ø6}_5$.

Example 13.06

[Musical notation: hymn excerpt in 3/4 with lyrics "Search me, O God, and know my heart to-day;"]

Example 13.07[6] shows two successive borrowed chords, ♭VI and ♭VII, used to punctuate a cadence.

Example 13.07

[Musical notation with chord symbols: F#dim7, C/G, Am7, Dm7, G, A♭, B♭, C with lyrics "Bow down and wor-ship, for this is your God."]

Borrowed chords are abundant in popular music. Even the rarely-used borrowed chords, such as v are being celebrated and explored by songwriters. Michael W. Smith's *Purified*, excerpted in example 13.08[7] on the following page, uses the minor dominant as its signature moment at the beginning of the bridge.

---

[5] *Search me, O God: Lyrics by James Orr, 1936 (based on Psalm 139:23); traditional Maori melody. Public Domain. Tune name:* Maori.

[6] *Meekness and Majesty: Lyrics and music by Graham Kendrick.* © 1986, Thankyou Music (admin. By EMI Christian Music Publishing).

[7] *Purified: Lyrics and music by Michael W. Smith and Deborah D. Smith.* © 2001, Word Music, Inc./Smittyfly Music/This Is Your Time Music LLC.

Example 13.08

| E | B m | E | B m | E |

You are ho - ly, You are ho - ly,

The Picardy third was prevalent in common practice music, and continues to find a home in contemporary music of many styles. Twenty-three out of the 24 minor-mode compositions in Book I of Bach's *The Well-Tempered Clavier* end with the Picardy third. One such example is the Fugue in C minor, excerpted in example 13.09.[8]

Example 13.09

This concludes the introduction to borrowed chords. Augmented sixth chords will be covered in chapter fourteen.

---

[8] Fugue II for three voices in C minor (BWV 847), measures 28-31: *J. S. Bach, 1722. Public Domain.*

Assignments and Drills

Assignment 13.01

The objective of this assignment is identification of borrowed chords, secondary dominants, secondary leading tone chords, and diatonic chords.

Instructions: Fill in the blanks as requested pertaining to each chord provided. Put a circle around the roman numeral analysis of borrowed chords, and enclose secondary chords in a box. The first one has been started for you. REFER BACK TO EXAMPLES 13.01 — 13.09 IF NECESSARY.

1. Write the roman numeral analysis of this chord in the following keys.

   D: (♭VII)   B♭: [V/V]   A♭: _____   Cm: _____   E: _____

2. Write the roman numeral analysis of this chord in the following keys.

   C: _____   E: _____   A: _____   Dm: _____   G: _____

3. Write the roman numeral analysis of this chord in the following keys.

   Cm: _____   D♭: _____   E♭: _____   A♭: _____   C: _____

4. Write the roman numeral analysis of this chord in the following keys.

   D: _____   C#: _____   G: _____   Em: _____   F#m: _____

5. Write the roman numeral analysis of this chord in the following keys.

   F: _____   Cm: _____   E: _____   D: _____   B: _____

6. Write the roman numeral analysis of this chord in the following keys.

   C♭: _____   B♭: _____   D♭: _____   E♭: _____   A♭m: _____

Assignment 13.02

The objective of this assignment is identification of borrowed chords, secondary dominants, secondary leading tone chords, and diatonic chords.

Instructions: Fill in the blanks as requested pertaining to each chord provided. REFER BACK TO EXAMPLES 13.01 — 13.09 IF NECESSARY.

1. Identify the key according to roman numeral analysis.

   V _____ V/V _____ ♭VI _____ ♭III _____ ♭VII _____

2. Identify the key according to roman numeral analysis.

   vii° _____ ii° _____ vii°/iii _____ vii°/V _____ vii°/♭VII _____

3. Identify the key according to roman numeral analysis.

   ii _____ iv _____ vi _____ v _____ iii _____

Assignment 13.03

The objective of this assignment is proper roman numeral identification of diatonic and chromatic chords.

Instructions: Fill in the blanks in the chart below. Only refer back to example 13.04 to check your work when finished.

Key of C	C	C#/D♭	D	D#/E♭	E	F	F#/G♭	G	G#/A♭	A	A#/B♭	B
DIATONIC TRIADS												
NATURAL MINOR DIATONIC TRIADS												
HARMONIC MINOR DIATONIC TRIADS												
SECONDARY DOMINANTS												
SECONDARY LEADING TONES												
BORROWED CHORDS												
AND THEIR TONICIZERS												

BORROWED CHORDS

Assignment 13.04

The objective of this assignment is identification of borrowed chords.

Instructions: Complete the harmonic analysis for each brief piano accompaniment figure below.[9] Circle the roman numeral analysis of borrowed chords.

REFER BACK TO EXAMPLES 13.01 — 13.09 IF NECESSARY.

1.

2.

3.

4.

---

[9] *The progression in number four is directly derived from* Variations on a Hungarian Song, Opus 21, No. 2, variation 12, measures 101-102: *Johannes Brahms, 1856. Public Domain.*

Assignment 13.05

The objective of this assignment is identification of borrowed chords in literature.

Instructions: Complete the harmonic analysis for the chorale[10] below and identify each cadence. Circle the roman numeral analysis of borrowed chords. REFER BACK TO EXAMPLES 13.01 — 13.09 IF NECESSARY.

---

[10] O wie selig seid ihr doch, ihr Frommen: *Common chorale harmonized by J.S. Bach, circa 1725. Public Domain. A simplified version of this chorale appears in assignment 7.12.*

Assignment 13.06

The objective of this assignment is identification of borrowed chords in literature.

1. Complete the harmonic analysis for the excerpt[11] below.
2. Write pop-chord symbols for each chord above the staff.

The assignment has been started for you.

REFER BACK TO EXAMPLES 13.01 — 13.09 IF NECESSARY.

D: V^6/vii^o

considered nonharmonic at present

---

[11] String Quartet, Opus 64, No. 5. First movement (Allegro), measures 43-50: *Franz Joseph Haydn, 1790. Public Domain.*

Assignment 13.07

The objective of this assignment is identification of borrowed chords in literature.

1. Complete the harmonic analysis for the excerpt[12] below (including nonharmonic tones).
2. Write pop-chord symbols for each chord above the staff.

REFER BACK TO EXAMPLES 13.01 — 13.09 IF NECESSARY.

---

[12] String Quartet, Opus 64, No. 5. Third movement (Allegretto), measures 9-16: *Franz Joseph Haydn, 1790. Public Domain.*

Assignment 13.08

The objective of this assignment is identification of borrowed chords in literature.

1. Complete the harmonic analysis for the excerpt[13] below (including nonharmonic tones).
2. Write pop-chord symbols for each chord above the staff.

REFER BACK TO EXAMPLES 13.01 — 13.09 IF NECESSARY.

---

[13] Der Wanderer (D. 493), measures 1-10: *Franz Schubert, 1816. Public Domain.*

Assignment 13.09

The objective of this assignment is identification and voice leading of borrowed chords and secondary dominants.

1. Complete the harmonic analysis for each brief melody below.
2. Identify each cadence.
3. Put a circle around the roman numeral analysis of borrowed chords.
4. Write the alto and tenor voices according to common practice.

REFER BACK TO EXAMPLES 13.01 — 13.09 IF NECESSARY.

Composition Project

Assignment 13.10

Instructions: Compose an original piece of music *for solo instrument* as follows:

- Homophonic texture on treble clef in *lead sheet* format (melody below and pop-chord symbols above)
- Period construction
- Traditional cadences
- Strong pattern of harmonic rhythm
- Strong harmonic progressions, no retrogressions
- Include at least one borrowed chord
- Minimum 16 measures in length

Questions for Review

1. From where are *borrowed chords* borrowed?

2. How do borrowed chords typically function? Are there any exceptions?

3. What are the most common borrowed chords in major?

4. What is meant by the term *Picardy third*?

5. Which borrowed chord is so common that it generally is not labeled a borrowed chord?

Assignments for Use with Anthology

For each assignment below, provide complete harmonic analysis.

A13.01 Dominico Scarlatti: *Sonata in D Major (Allegrissimo)*. Anthology page 141, measures 179-199.

A13.02 Mozart: *Clarinet Concert in A Major,* K. 622, first movement (Allegro). Anthology pages 240-241, measures 307-315.

A13.03 Schubert: *Waltz in A Flat Major*, Opus 9, No. 2, D. 365. Anthology page 326, measures 9-10. Consider the F-flat in measure nine nonharmonic at present. For a challenge, examine measures 11-16. The chord in measure thirteen will be explained in chapter fourteen, so leave it blank. *The chord in measure twelve must be considered enharmonically.*

A13.04 Schubert: *Moment Musical No. 6*, from *Sechs Moments Musicaux*, Opus 94, D. 780. Anthology page 328, measures 59-65.

A13.05 Mendellsohn: *Song Without Words*, Opus 19b, No. 1. Anthology page 332, measures 16-19.

A13.06 Chopin: Mazurka 6 in A Minor, Opus 7, No. 2. Anthology pages 357-358, measures 31-40.

A13.07 Brahms: *Wie melodien zieht es mir*. Anthology page 388, measures 23-28.

Chapter 14
Augmented Sixth Chords

Augmented sixth chords are unique sonorities that function as pre-dominant chords. These chords are *not arranged in thirds* but appear in "normal position," where the "sounding root" is in the bass voice.

Augmented sixth chords come in three varieties: Italian, German, and French. Each one contains the interval of an *augmented sixth* between the bass ("sounding root") and an upper voice. Usually, augmented sixth chords appear on the sixth scale degree in minor keys and on the *lowered* sixth scale degree in major keys.

An augmented sixth chord appears in example 14.01 below. Notice these qualities of the chord:

- It is not arranged in thirds. If it were, F-sharp would be on the bottom, A-flat would be in the middle, and C would be on top. The distance from F-sharp up to A-flat is a *diminished third*, which is *enharmonic* with a *major second*. This is one reason why the chord is not arranged in thirds. While the lowest interval of the triad would *look like* a third on paper, the aural perception is clearly a second.
- It contains the interval of an augmented sixth from the bass to an upper voice.
- It is constructed on the lowered sixth scale degree (key of C major).

Example 14.01

- Normal position
- A6 from bottom to top
- Built on lowered sixth in a major key
- Comprised of M3 + A6

Specifically, the chord in example 14.01 is an ***Italian sixth*** chord. The Italian sixth contains the intervals of a *major third* and an *augmented sixth* above the bass. It is the only type of augmented sixth chord comprised of just three notes. When written in a four-voice texture, the third above the bass is doubled.

The ***German sixth***, shown below in example 14.02, contains all of the properties of an Italian sixth, but also includes the interval of a *perfect fifth* above the bass.

Example 14.02

- Normal position
- A6 from bottom to top
- Built on lowered sixth in a major key
- Comprised of M3 + P5 + A6

Because of the appearance of the German sixth, some theorists refer to it as a *German $^6_5$*. For purposes of clarity and ease recalling the distinctions among the types of augmented sixth chords, the designation "German $^6_5$" will be used in this textbook.

Occasionally, the German $^6_5$ is spelled enharmonically, substituting a *doubly-augmented fourth* (AA4) instead of a *perfect fifth* (P5), as shown in example 14.03.

Example 14.03

- Normal position
- A6 from bottom to top
- Built on lowered sixth in a major key
- Comprised of M3 + AA4 + A6

The terms *enharmonic German sixth*, *doubly-augmented $^6_5$*, and *English sixth* are all used to describe this unique spelling.

The German $^6_5$, in either its natural spelling or its alternate enharmonic spelling, is identical in aural *quality* to a *dominant seventh chord* (major triad plus a minor seventh from the root). The German sixth is a major triad plus an augmented sixth. Since the interval of A6 is enharmonic with m7, the sound of an isolated German $^6_5$ is completely enharmonic with the quality of a dominant seventh chord. It does not *function* like a dominant seventh, however. It is not built on the dominant, nor is it acting as a secondary dominant. It is a pre-dominant chord that helps "set up" the dominant; it is not the dominant itself, even though it has the identical *quality* to a dominant seventh chord.

The **French sixth**, shown below in example 14.04, also contains all of the properties of an Italian sixth, but has the additional interval of an *augmented fourth* above the bass.

Example 14.04

- Normal position
- A6 from bottom to top
- Built on lowered sixth in a major key
- Comprised of M3 + A4 + A6

Because of the appearance of the French sixth, some theorists refer to it as a *French $^4_3$*. For purposes of clarity and ease recalling the distinctions among the types of augmented sixth chords, the designation "French $^4_3$" will be used in this textbook.

Since all augmented sixth chords are *pre-dominant* chords that create harmonic interest and heightened activity toward the dominant, it is important to study their resolutions. The interval of the augmented sixth expands outward, in the direction of inflection. Because this interval is augmented, it is expanding.

If the augmented sixth chord is built on the sixth scale degree in minor (or the lowered sixth in major), as it most commonly appears, when its interval of an A6 resolves outward as it should, an octave is created on the dominant.

Example 14.05

C: It^6 V

This direction-of-inflection activity is the expected resolution of the interval of the A6, regardless of whether the augmented sixth chord itself is Italian, German, or French. Once the A6 interval expands to the octave, there are three types of resolution:

1. Type one: regular. To the dominant.[1]
2. Type two: deceptive. To tonic in second inversion.[2]
3. Type three: irregular. To neither the dominant nor tonic $^6_4$.

Example 14.06

type 1: regular   type 2: deceptive   type 3: irregular

C: It^6 V   C: It^6 I$^6_4$ C: It^6 iii^6 C: It^6 ♭III^6

Note that the roman numeral harmonic analysis of the Italian sixth is *It*^{6}. The Italian sixth is not abbreviated I^6, of course, since I is the designation for tonic. The German sixth appears as Gr$^6_5$, and the French sixth is designated Fr$^4_3$. If the enharmonic spelling of the German sixth (using the doubly-augmented fourth) occurs, the most common designation in harmonic analysis is still Gr$^6_5$, although En$^4_3$ may be used alternatively if preferred.

The Italian and French sixths most frequently resolve directly to dominant (type one), although it is not unusual for them to resolve deceptively (type two) *before* arriving at the dominant. The *goal* to which these chords progress, however, is always the dominant (or a secondary dominant).

---

[1] *When augmented sixth chords are constructed on a note other than the sixth scale degree in minor or lowered sixth in major, they typically resolve to a secondary dominant that is constructed a m2 below the augmented sixth chord. This is considered a* type one *resolution, since the A6 chord is resolving to its dominant. (The A6 chord appears in such instances on the lowered sixth of the tonicized chord.)*

[2] *Resolution to a tonicized chord in second inversion is a* type two *resolution as well, since it is resolving to its tonic.*

The German $^6_5$ almost always resolves deceptively (type two). When the German sixth chord resolves *directly* to the dominant (type one), parallel perfect fifths result, as shown in example 14.07.

Example 14.07

C: Gr$^6_5$ V

"I think music in itself is healing. It's an explosive expression of humanity. It's something we are all touched by. No matter what culture we're from, everyone loves music."

- singer/songwriter Billy Joel

The "normal" resolution of the German sixth, then, is to tonic in second inversion, immediately followed by the dominant, as shown in example 14.08.

Example 14.08

C: Gr$^6_5$ I$^6_4$ V

Notice the resolution of each note in the German sixth chord in example 14.08. The outer voices containing the A6 move in the direction of inflection. The third above the bass is a common tone, so it does not move, and the fifth above the bass resolves chromatically. Some consider the chromatic resolution of the fifth above the bass to be *counter* to the direction-of-inflection principle, since the flatted note, which naturally inflects downward, is actually moving upward chromatically.

The enharmonic spelling of the German sixth chord is employed for this very reason (in major keys). When the interval of a doubly-augmented fourth is substituted for the perfect fifth, *all* notes resolve in the direction of inflection in a type two resolution. This is still the preferred resolution, even when the German sixth chord is spelled enharmonically.

Example 14.09

C: Gr$^6_5$ I$^6_4$ V

To become familiar with augmented sixth chords and their resolutions, creating Italian, German, and French augmented sixths in various keys is a helpful exercise. In order to quickly and easily assemble and resolve these unique chords, the following simple formula is recommended.

Example 14.10

Step 1: Choose a key, any key. The key of A major is used here as an example.

Step 2: Create an imaginary octave on the dominant

Step 3: Reduce the imaginary octave by a minor second in each direction.

This produces the interval of an augmented sixth on the lowered sixth scale degree.

Step 4: Add a major third above the bass

If creating an Italian sixth, construction is complete. If creating a German or French sixth, proceed to step five.

Step 5: Add the final note — a P5 from the bass for the German $^6_5$ or an A4 for the French $^4_3$.

Resolution of the augmented sixths chords, whether regular, deceptive, or irregular, is simple. The imaginary octave that was used in creating the augmented sixth becomes the resolution of the interval of the augmented sixth; it is no longer imaginary, and it appears immediately *following* the augmented sixth chord, providing the framework for the chord of resolution.

Example 14.11

type
1 2 3

A note of caution should be mentioned at this point for composers seeking to implement augmented sixth chords. The unique sonorities created by these chords and other chromatic harmonies should be used sparingly. While composers of the common practice era frequently employed multiple secondary dominants throughout a composition, instances of borrowed chords and augmented sixth chords usually occur not more than once over a span of several minutes. Overuse of any unique sonority actually diminishes the effectiveness of these highly specialized chords.

In literature of the common practice era, augmented sixth chords appear more frequently in minor keys than in major keys.[3] A catchy phrase to help remember details about augmented sixth chords goes as follows: *"Augmented sixth chords appear predominantly in minor."* The word "predominantly" is a play on words, meaning "primarily," but also meaning immediately prior to a chord built on $\hat{5}$ ("pre-dominant").

The roman numeral chart of chord identification is now expanded to include augmented sixth chords.

Example 14.12

Key of C	C	C#/Db	D	D#/Eb	E	F	F#/Gb	G	G#/Ab	A	A#/Bb	B
Diatonic Triads	I		ii		iii	IV		V		vi		vii°
Natural Minor Diatonic Triads	i		ii°	III		iv		v	VI		VII	
Harmonic Minor Diatonic Triads	i		ii°	III+		iv		V	VI			vii°
Secondary Dominants	V⁷/IV		V⁽⁷⁾/V		V⁽⁷⁾/vi	(V/vii°)				V⁽⁷⁾/ii		V⁽⁷⁾/iii
Secondary Leading Tones		vii°/ii		vii°/iii	vii°/IV		vii°/V		vii°/vi		(vii°/vii°)	
Borrowed Chords	I (i)		ii°, iiø⁷	bIII		iv		(v)	bVI		bVII	
And Their Tonicizers			vii°/bIII	V⁽⁷⁾/bVI		V⁷/bVII		vii°/bVI		vii°/bVII	V⁽⁷⁾/bIII	
Augmented Sixth Chords									It⁶ Gr⁶₅ Fr⁴₃			

This concludes the introduction to augmented sixth chords. Neapolitan chords and altered/expanded dominants will be covered in chapter fifteen.

---

[3] *Following the common practice era, the use of augmented sixths began appearing in popular songs and hymns. In these contexts, as will be seen in the assignments following this chapter, their appearance is more prominent in major keys.*

Assignments and Drills

Assignment 14.01

The objective of this assignment is creation and resolution of Italian sixth chords.

Instructions: Create Italian sixth chords in normal position where they would typically appear. Resolve each one in type one (regular) fashion. Provide harmonic analysis below the staff. <u>All keys are minor</u>. The first one has been completed for you. REFER BACK TO EXAMPLES 14.01, 14.05, 14.06, 14.10, AND 14.11 IF NECESSARY.

Gm: It⁶   V

Assignment 14.02

The objective of this assignment is creation and resolution of German sixth chords.

Instructions: Create German sixth chords in normal position where they would typically appear. Resolve each one as it would normally resolve (type two — deceptive, *then* to the dominant). Provide harmonic analysis below the staff. <u>All keys are major</u>. The first one has been completed for you. REFER BACK TO EXAMPLES 14.02, 14.06, 14.08, 14.10, AND 14.11 IF NECESSARY.

B♭:   Gr⁶₅   I⁶₄   V

Assignment 14.03

The objective of this assignment is creation and resolution of French sixth chords.

Instructions: Create French sixth chords in normal position where they would typically appear. Resolve each one in type one (regular) fashion. Provide harmonic analysis below the staff. <u>All keys are minor</u>. REFER BACK TO EXAMPLES 14.04, 14.10, AND 14.11 IF NECESSARY.

Assignment 14.04

The objective of this assignment is proper roman numeral identification of diatonic and chromatic chords.

Instructions: Fill in the blanks in the chart below. Only refer back to example 14.12 to check your work when finished.

Key of C	C	C#/D♭	D	D#/E♭	E	F	F#/G♭	G	G#/A♭	A	A#/B♭	B
DIATONIC TRIADS												
NATURAL MINOR DIATONIC TRIADS												
HARMONIC MINOR DIATONIC TRIADS												
SECONDARY DOMINANTS												
SECONDARY LEADING TONES												
BORROWED CHORDS												
AND THEIR TONICIZERS												
AUGMENTED SIXTH CHORDS												

Assignment 14.05

The objective of this assignment is identification of augmented sixth chords and their resolutions.

Instructions: Provide harmonic analysis of each brief excerpt below, and label each resolution as "type 1," "type 2," or "type 3." REFER BACK TO EXAMPLES 14.01—14.06 IF NECESSARY.

Nearer, Still Nearer *Music by Lelia Naylor Morris, 1898. Final phrase. Tune name: Morris. Public Domain.*

Jesus, We Just Want to Thank You *Music by William J. Gaither. © 1974 by William J. Gaither. Second phrase.*

Where He Leads Me *Music by John Samuel Norris, 1890. Final phrase. Tune name: Norris. Public Domain.*

Assignment 14.06

The objective of this assignment is identification of augmented sixth chords and their resolutions.

Instructions: Provide harmonic analysis of each brief excerpt below, and label each resolution as "type 1," "type 2," or "type 3." REFER BACK TO EXAMPLES 14.01—14.06 IF NECESSARY.

Wonderful Grace of Jesus — Music by Haldor Lillenas, 1918. Fourth phrase. Tune name: Wonderful Grace. Public Domain.

Jesus Is All the World to Me — Music by Will Lamartine Thompson, 1904. Final phrase. Tune name: Elizabeth. Public Domain.

Thou Didst Leave Thy Throne — Music by Timothy Richard Matthews, 1876. Refrain. Tune name: Margaret. Public Domain.

Assignment 14.07

The objective of this assignment is identification of augmented sixth chords and their resolutions.

Instructions: Provide harmonic analysis of each brief excerpt below, and label each resolution as "type 1," "type 2," or "type 3." REFER BACK TO EXAMPLES 14.01—14.06 IF NECESSARY.

Wherever He Leads, I'll Go *Music by B.B. McKinney. © 1936, renewal 1964 by Broadman Press. Third phrase of refrain.*

There's Room at the Cross for You *Music by Ira Stanphill. © 1946 by Singspiration Music. Beginning of refrain. Tune name:* Room at the Cross.

Moment by Moment *Music by May Whittle Moody, 1893. Third phrase. Tune name:* Whittle. *Public Domain.*

Assignment 14.08

The objective of this assignment is identification of augmented sixth chords and their resolutions in unusual circumstances.

Instructions: The brief excerpts below contain anomalies in chord spelling or voicing. Provide harmonic analysis, pointing out the departure from convention. REFER BACK TO EXAMPLES 14.01—14.06 IF NECESSARY.

Only One Life *Music by Merrill Dunlop. © 1937, renewed 1964 by Merill Dunlop. Final cadence.*

He Lives *Music by Alfred Ackley. © 1933 by Homer A. Rodeheaver. Renewed 1961 by The Rodeheaver Company (a division of Word, Inc.) Third phrase of refrain.*

He Rose Triumphantly *Music by Oswald Smith. © 1944, renewed 1972 by The Rodeheaver Company (a division of Word, Inc.) First two measures.*

Assignment 14.09

The objective of this assignment is identification of augmented sixth chords and their resolutions in unusual circumstances.

Instructions: The brief excerpts below contain anomalies in chord spelling or voicing. Provide harmonic analysis, pointing out the departure from convention. REFER BACK TO EXAMPLES 14.01—14.06 IF NECESSARY.

I Must Tell Jesus *Music by Elisha Hoffman, 1893. Beginning of final phrase of refrain. Tune name: Orwigsburg. Public Domain.*

There's Something About That Name *Music by William J. Gaither. © 1970 by William J. Gaither. Sixth phrase.*

Assignment 14.10

The objective of this assignment is identification of augmented sixth chords and their resolutions in literature.

Instructions: Go back to assignment 13.06 on page 337 and identify the second chord in measure 48, considering the circled note in the first violin part as harmonic. Instead of ♭III, provide the new harmonic analysis of that chord and identify its resolution.

Assignment 14.11

The objective of this assignment is proper voice leading of augmented sixth chords.

Instructions: Provide augmented sixth chords on the grand staff in chorale style as indicated. Resolve each one in typical fashion. Provide harmonic analysis below the staff. <u>All keys are minor</u>. Remember that Italian sixths have the third above the bass doubled. REFER BACK TO EXAMPLES 14.01, 14.10, AND 14.11 IF NECESSARY.

1. Italian
2. German
3. French
4. Italian
5. German
6. French
7. Italian
8. German

Composition Project

Assignment 14.12

Instructions: Compose an original *chorale* as follows:

- Homophonic texture on grand staff with soprano/alto in treble clef and tenor/bass in bass clef (indicate each part by stem direction)
- Period construction
- Traditional cadences
- Harmonic rhythm changes every beat
- Strong harmonic progressions, no retrogressions
- Keep voices stepwise as much as possible
- No law violations
- Avoid regulation violations as much as possible
- Follow doubling principles unless doing so causes a law/regulation violation
- Include nonharmonic tones
- Include one augmented sixth chord with type 1 or type 2 resolution
- Minimum 16 measures in length

Questions for Review

1. Why are augmented sixth chords named as such?

2. On what scale degree are augmented sixth chords usually constructed in minor? In major?

3. What is the function of augmented sixth chords?

4. Why doesn't the German sixth usually resolve type 1?

5. Why is the German sixth sometimes spelled enharmonically with a doubly-augmented fourth instead of a perfect fifth in major keys?

6. What is the formula for creating an augmented sixth chord in any key?

7. What is a helpful phrase used in remembering details of augmented sixth chords?

Assignments for Use with Anthology

For each assignment below, provide complete harmonic analysis.

A14.01   Bach: *Fugue XVI in G Minor (from* The Well-Tempered Clavier, *Book I),* BWV 861. Anthology page 115, measures 27-28.

A14.02   Beethoven: *Piano Sonata No. 8 in C Minor*, Opus 13, ("Pathétique"), third movement (Allegro). Anthology page 275, measures 44-47.

A14.03   Beethoven: *Piano Sonata No. 8 in C Minor*, Opus 13, ("Pathétique"), third movement (Allegro). Anthology page 279, measure 185.

A14.04   Schubert: *Der Doppelgänger*, from *Schwanengesang*, D. 957. Anthology page 318, measures 38-42.

A14.05   Schubert: *Moment Musical No. 6*, from *Sechs Moments Musicaux*, Opus 94, D. 780. Anthology page 327, measures 15-21.

A14.06   Chopin: *Mazurka 5 in B Flat Major*, Opus 7, No. 1. Anthology page 356, measures 45-52.

A14.07   Chopin: *Mazurka 6 in A Minor*, Opus 7, No. 2. Anthology page 357, measures 17-20.

A14.08   Wolf: *Das verlassene Mägdlein*. Anthology page 410, measures 9-12.

Chapter 15
Neapolitan Chords
and Altered/Expanded Dominants

A ***Neapolitan chord***[1] is a *major triad* built on the *lowered second scale degree*. These chords appear in minor keys primarily, but may be employed in the major mode as well. Usually, the Neapolitan chord is voiced in first inversion so that the diatonic $\hat{4}$ is emphasized in the bass.[2] When in first inversion, the chord is called a ***Neapolitan sixth***.

Example 15.01

Am: N^6

"My idea is that there is music in the air, music all around us; the world is full of it, and you simply take as much as you require."
 - *composer Edward Elgar*

The abbreviation N is used in harmonic analysis. Some theorists refer to the Neapolitan chord as a "Phrygian II" because the triad built on the diatonic second scale degree in Phrygian mode is major, and appears a m2 above tonic (see example 15.02). These theorists use the analysis symbol $\flat$II. In this sense, the chord is "borrowed" from the parallel Phrygian mode, but because the Neapolitan is not considered a borrowed chord, few theorists use this designation.

Example 15.02

E Phrygian: i   II   III   iv   v°   VI   vii   i

A Phrygian: i   II   III   iv   v°   VI   vii   i

Like augmented sixth chords, the Neapolitan is a pre-dominant chord. It is an altered supertonic triad, which naturally progresses to dominant in circle-progression fashion. The unusual aural effect created by the Neapolitan is most pronounced when it is followed immediately by the dominant. This is primarily because the roots of the Neapolitan and the dominant are a tritone apart, as shown in example 15.03.

---

[1] *The origin of this term is unknown.*
[2] *When appearing in a major key, the third of the chord ($\hat{4}$) is the only member of the chord that is diatonic.*

Example 15.03

Bb/D   E

Am: N⁶   V

The root of the Neapolitan is B-flat; the root of the dominant is E.

Because of the abrupt effect of the dominant immediately following the Neapolitan chord, composers often smoothly transition between the Neapolitan and dominant by inserting a cadential tonic $^6_4$ chord between them.

Example 15.04

Bb/D   Am/E   E

Am: N⁶   i$^6_4$ V

"Music cleanses the understanding; inspires it, and lifts it into a realm which it would not reach if it were left to itself."
— theologian Henry Ward Beecher

Another option for minimizing the abrupt effect of the tritone relationship between Neapolitan and dominant is the use of a secondary dominant or secondary leading-tone chord between them. This often creates very smooth bass movement as well.

Example 15.05

Bb/D   B7/D#   E

Am: N⁶   V$^6_5$/V   V

Example 15.06

Bb/D   D#°7   E

Am: N⁶   vii°7/V   V

When voice leading in this context, care must be taken. Note the appearance of uneven fifths in examples 15.05 and 15.06 above.

The third of the Neapolitan chord (typically in the bass) is the note that is doubled, because it is diatonic in the key and usually provides smooth voice leading.

Example 15.07 demonstrates effective voice leading and appropriate doubling.

Example 15.07

B♭/D   B7/D♯   E

Am: N⁶   V$^6_5$/V   V

"Take a music bath once or twice a week for a few seasons. You will find it is to the soul what a water bath is to the body."
- *physician and author Oliver Wendell Holmes*

Sometimes a secondary chord *and* cadential tonic $^6_4$ appear between the Neapolitan and the dominant to make the transition even smoother. This also helps avoid voice leading conflicts.

Example 15.08

B♭/D   D♯°7   Am/E   E

Am: N⁶   vii°⁷/V   i$^6_4$ V

"I don't know whether I like it, but it is what I meant."
- *composer Ralph Vaughan Williams, on his fourth Symphony*

Example 15.09

Key of C	C	C#/D♭	D	D#/E♭	E	F	F#/G♭	G	G#/A♭	A	A#/B♭	B
Diatonic triads	I		ii		iii	IV		V		vi		vii°
Natural minor diatonic triads	i		ii°	III		iv		v		VI		VII
Harmonic minor diatonic triads	i		ii°	III+		iv		V		VI		vii°
Secondary dominants	V⁷/IV		V⁽⁷⁾/V		V⁽⁷⁾/vi		(V/vii°)			V⁽⁷⁾/ii		V⁽⁷⁾/iii
Secondary leading tones		vii°/ii		vii°/iii	vii°/IV		vii°/V		vii°/vi		(vii°/vii°)	
Borrowed chords	I (i)		ii°, ii^{ø}⁷	♭III		iv		(v)	♭VI		♭VII	
and their tonicizers			vii°/♭III	V⁽⁷⁾/♭VI		V⁷/♭VII			vii°/♭VI	vii°/♭VII	V⁽⁷⁾/♭III	
Augmented Sixth Chords									It⁶ Gr$^6_5$ Fr$^4_3$			
Neapolitan chords	vii°/N	N N⁶ N$^?$							V⁽⁷⁾/N			

The appearance of Neapolitan chords in literature is neither abundant nor uncommon. Like augmented sixths, overuse of the unique sonority created by Neapolitans diminishes their effectiveness. Historically, composers wisely used them sparingly for maximum effect at significant moments.

Another interesting and effective use of chromaticism is alteration of the dominant. The function of the dominant chord toward the tonic is intensified in three ways:

1. The *quality* of the triad is altered from major to *augmented* (called **altered dominants**).
2. The triad is expanded to become a dominant seventh chord.
3. The dominant seventh chord is expanded to become a 9th, 11th, or 13th chord (called **expanded dominants**).

If the quality of the dominant triad is *altered* to make the triad *augmented*, the active tones increase their degree of activity. Remember that *active tones* are tones *not* belonging to the tonic triad. These tones gravitate toward those of the tonic triad (review example 9.01 if necessary).

In the dominant triad, the root of the chord is not an active tone, but the third of the chord is the leading tone of the key ("leading" toward tonic). The fifth of the chord is the supertonic scale degree, which normally "leans" toward tonic. However, if the fifth of the chord is raised a half step to create an augmented triad, the note leans in its direction of inflection (upward). Example 15.10 illustrates the natural resolution of active tones for both the diatonic dominant and the altered dominant.

Example 15.10

C: V^7 I   V$^+$ I

The dominant *seventh* chord may also be altered, consisting of an *augmented triad* and *minor seventh*.

Example 15.11

C: V+^{7} I

Another unique augmented triad that deserves mention because of its altered active tone is ♭VI⁺. This chord functions in the same way as a German sixth chord, leading naturally to tonic in second inversion. This chord is a "passing sonority" between the diatonic submediant and tonic $^6_4$, with the altered tone progressing in direction of inflection.

Example 15.12

A m   A♭+   C/G

C: vi   ♭VI⁺   I$^6_4$

> "If I were to begin life again, I would devote it to music. It is the only cheap and unpunished rapture upon earth."
> — writer *Sydney Smith*

In addition to being converted into an augmented triad, the dominant seventh chord may be made more interesting and colorful when notes are *added above the seventh*.

Example 15.13

C: V   V⁷   V⁹   V¹¹   V¹³

Expanded dominants[3] appear in root position only, since they tend to lose their identities when inverted. It may be challenging at times to determine whether a note contributes to the formation of an expanded dominant or is merely nonharmonic. Experience with expanded dominants, as well as considering the perceived function of the nonharmonic tone, will help the theorist make a musically educated choice.

Because of the sheer number of notes in expanded dominants, it is necessary for some of them to be omitted, especially in a four-voice texture. Consider the dominant 13th chord in example 15.13. Since the chord has seven notes, it includes *every* diatonic scale degree! Throughout the common practice era, expanded dominants such as V¹³ did not appear as complete chords with all notes present.

Example 15.14 shows the most common configurations of 9th, 11th, and 13th chords in four-voice writing.

---

[3] *Scale degrees other than the dominant may be expanded to 9th, 11th, and 13th chords, but the vast majority of extended chords are dominants.*

Example 15.14

The 9th chord has the fifth omitted, the 11th chord has the third and fifth omitted (this is the only chord where omitting the third is standard), and the 13th chord has the fifth, ninth, and eleventh omitted.

The dominant 11th chord requires special attention. At a glance, it appears to be a subdominant triad with a nonharmonic tone (probably a pedal tone) in the bass. In fact, the proper pop-chord analysis of the V^{11} chord in the key of C is F/G. In harmonic analysis, however, this designation (IV with pedal tone) should be avoided. The *function* of this sonority is (expanded) *dominant*.

Note the presence of the *root* and *seventh* as the only two consistent notes among the dominant 9th, 11th, and 13th chords. Also notice the consistent omission of the fifth in all three. In modern popular musical styles, and consequently in pop-chord notation, chords with suffixes like "add 2" are common. The element that distinguishes between an "add 2" and a 9th chord is *the presence of the seventh*. The first chord in example 15.14 is not a "G add 2" or even a "G7 add 2;" it is G9. Example 15.15 shows pop-chord analysis of the chords in example 15.14.

Example 15.15

"Music is a means of giving form to our inner feelings without attaching them to events or objects in the world."
- philosopher George Santayana

When there is no seventh to a chord, but additional notes are present that *would have* constituted a 9th, 11th, or 13th chord had the seventh been present, the additional notes are considered nonharmonic. These additional notes are often added to pop-chord analysis, however, as shown in example 15.16.

Example 15.16

In pop-chord analysis, the difference between the designation "G2" and "G (add 2)" is simple. In the case of "G2," the note that is a diatonic second above the chord root *substitutes for the third*. In the case of "G (add 2)," the entire G chord is present, and a diatonic second above the chord root is *added* to the chord.

Example 15.17

G2   G (add 2)

As a point of interest, note that the G2 chord is really an inverted Dsus, with the fourth in the bass. Chords such as this, with no third present, are common in popular music, but foreign to music of the common practice era.

In jazz, expanded chords appear frequently with chromatic alterations (♭9, #11, etc.).

Example 15.18

G13 (♭9 #11)

"The key to the mystery of a great artist is that for reasons unknown, he will give away his energies and his life just to make sure that one note follows another... and leaves us with the feeling that something is right in the world."
- *composer and conductor Leonard Bernstein*

This concludes the introduction to Neapolitan chords and altered/expanded dominants. The roman numeral chart of chord identification is now expanded to include these chords, and appears on the following page. Chromatic mediants will be covered in chapter sixteen.

Example 15.19

Key of C	C	C#/Db	D	D#/Eb	E	F	F#/Gb	G	G#/Ab	A	A#/Bb	B
Diatonic Triads	I		ii		iii	IV		V		vi		vii°
Natural Minor Diatonic Triads	i		ii°	III		iv		v	VI		VII	
Harmonic Minor Diatonic Triads	i		ii°	III+		iv		V	VI			vii°
Secondary Dominants	V7/IV		V(7)/V		V(7)/vi		(V[7]/vii°)			V(7)/ii		V(7)/iii
Secondary Leading Tones		vii°(7)/ii		vii°(7)/iii	vii°(7)/IV		vii°(7)/V		vii°(7)/vi		(vii°[7]/vii°)	
Borrowed Chords and their Tonicizers			ii°, ii°7	bIII		iv		(v)	bVI		bVII	
			vii°/bIII	V(7)/bVI		V7/bVII		vii°/bVI		vii°/bVII	V(7)/bIII	
Augmented Sixth Chords									It6 Gr6/5 Fr4/3			
Neapolitan Chords	vii°/N	N N6 N64							V(7)/N			
Altered Dominants								V+				
Expanded Dominants								V9 V11 V13				

370

Assignments and Drills

Assignment 15.01

The objective of this assignment is creation and proper voice leading of Neapolitan sixth chords.

Instructions: Provide Neapolitan sixth chords on the grand staff in chorale style. Resolve each one directly to the dominant. Provide harmonic analysis below the staff. <u>All keys are minor</u>. Remember that Neapolitan sixths have the bass note (the third of the chord) doubled. Be especially careful to avoid writing melodic A2s and A4s. The first one is done for you. REFER BACK TO EXAMPLES 15.01 AND 15.03 IF NECESSARY.

Gm: N⁶ — V

Assignment 15.02

The objective of this assignment is creation and proper voice leading of Neapolitan sixth chords.

Instructions: Provide Neapolitan sixth chords on the grand staff in chorale style. Resolve each one directly to tonic in second inversion followed by dominant. Provide harmonic analysis below the staff. <u>All keys are major</u>. REFER BACK TO EXAMPLE 15.04 IF NECESSARY.

Assignment 15.03

The objective of this assignment is creation and proper voice leading of Neapolitan sixth chords.

Instructions: Provide Neapolitan sixth chords on the grand staff in chorale style. Resolve measures 1-3 to V^6_5/V followed by the dominant. Resolve measures 4-6 to vii^{o7}/V followed by the dominant. Provide harmonic analysis below the staff. <u>All keys are minor</u>. REFER BACK TO EXAMPLES 15.05—15.07 IF NECESSARY.

Assignment 15.04

The objective of this assignment is creation and proper voice leading of Neapolitan sixth chords.

Instructions: Provide Neapolitan sixth chords on the grand staff in chorale style. Resolve measures 1-3 to V^6_5/V followed by tonic in second inversion, followed by the dominant. Resolve measures 4-6 to vii^{o7}/V followed by tonic in second inversion, followed by the dominant. Provide harmonic analysis below the staff. <u>All keys are major</u>. REFER BACK TO EXAMPLE 15.08 IF NECESSARY.

Assignment 15.05

The objective of this assignment is identification of Neapolitan sixth chords.

Instructions: Provide harmonic analysis for each excerpt below. REFER BACK TO EXAMPLES 15.01—15.09 IF NECESSARY.

Die Liebe hat gelogen *D. 751, Opus 23, No. 1, measures 1-4. Franz Schubert, 1822. Public Domain.*

Der Müller und der Bach *D. 795, Opus 25, No. 19, measures 1-10. Franz Schubert, 1823. Public Domain.*

Assignment 15.06

The objective of this assignment is identification of Neapolitan sixth chords.

Instructions: Provide harmonic analysis for the excerpt below. REFER BACK TO EXAMPLES 15.01—15.09 IF NECESSARY.

Piano Concerto No. 23 — K. 488, second movement, andante (F# Minor), measures 1-11, piano score only. Wolfgang Amadeus Mozart, 1786. Public Domain.

Assignment 15.07

The objective of this assignment is identification of Neapolitan sixth chords.

Instructions: Provide harmonic analysis for the excerpt below. REFER BACK TO EXAMPLES 15.01—15.09 IF NECESSARY.

Ballade No. 1 in G Minor *Opus 23, measures 1-15. Frédérick Chopin, 1836. Public Domain.*

Assignment 15.08

The objective of this assignment is identification of altered dominants.

Instructions: Provide harmonic analysis for each excerpt below. REFER BACK TO EXAMPLES 15.10—15.15 IF NECESSARY.

Erlkönig *D.328. Franz Schubert, 1815, measures 66-72. Public Domain.*

manch bun - - - te Blu - men sind an dem Strand; mei-ne Mut - ter hat manch' gül_____ den Ge - wand".

Great Is Thy Faithfulness *Measures 1-4. Lyrics by Tomas Chisholm, music by William Runyan, 1923. © 1923, renewed in 1951 by Hope Publishing Company. Tune name: Faithfulness.*

Great is Thy faith - ful - ness, O God my Fa - ther,

Assignment 15.09

The objective of this assignment is identification of altered chords.

Instructions: Provide harmonic analysis for the excerpt below. REFER BACK TO EXAMPLE 15.12 IF NECESSARY.

O Holy Night — Measures 16-23. Lyrics by Placide Cappeau, 1847, translated by John Sullivan Dwight, 1855; music by Adolphe-Charles Adam, 1847. Public Domain. This arr. © 2010, Brian Dunbar. Tune name: Cantique De Noel.

Assignment 15.10

The objective of this assignment is identification of expanded dominants.

Instructions: Provide harmonic analysis for each excerpt below. REFER BACK TO EXAMPLES 15.01—15.09 IF NECESSARY.

Artist's Life Waltz *Opus 316, No. 3. Johann Strauss II, 1867. Measures 1-8. Public Domain.*

Grandmother's Minuet *Opus 68, No. 2, measures 1-4. Edvard Grieg, circa 1905. Public Domain.*

Assignment 15.11

The objective of this assignment is proper roman numeral identification of diatonic and chromatic chords.

Instructions: Fill in the blanks in the chart below. Only refer back to example 15.19 to check your work when finished.

Key of C	C	C#/Db	D	D#/Eb	E	F	F#/Gb	G	G#/Ab	A	A#/Bb	B
DIATONIC TRIADS												
NATURAL MINOR DIATONIC TRIADS												
HARMONIC MINOR DIATONIC TRIADS												
SECONDARY DOMINANTS												
SECONDARY LEADING TONES												
BORROWED CHORDS AND THEIR TONICIZERS												
AUGMENTED SIXTH CHORDS												
NEAPOLITAN CHORDS												
ALTERED DOMINANTS												
EXPANDED DOMINANTS												

Questions for Review

1. What is a Neapolitan chord?

2. Why is it usually referred to as a Neapolitan "sixth" chord?

3. Why do some theorists refer to the Neapolitan as a Phrygian II ($\flat$II)?

4. Why does the resolution of Neapolitan-to-dominant create such an unusual aural effect, when it is simply a modified circle progression?

5. What are three techniques established by composers to "smooth out" the resolution from Neapolitan to dominant?

6. When the Neapolitan progresses immediately to V/V, how does each voice progress? (If you are having trouble with this question, spell a Neapolitan in root position; then spell a root-position V/V.) Brainstorm how the dilemma posed by this situation can be avoided.

7. What happens if Neapolitan chords appear frequently in a musical composition?

8. In what way are dominant chords *chromatically* altered to increase their activity toward tonic?

9. In what two ways are dominant chords diatonically altered to intensify their activity toward tonic?

10. To what type of chord does $\flat\text{VI}^+$ bear a similar function?

Assignments for Use with Anthology

For each assignment below, provide complete harmonic analysis.

A15.01 Mozart: *Piano Sonata in D Major*, K. 284, variation VII. Anthology page 175, measure 10.

A15.02 Schubert: *Erlkönig*, D. 328. Anthology page 325, measures 138-140; 143-148.

A15.03 Chopin: *Prelude 20 in C Minor*. Anthology page 354, measure 8.

A15.04 Brahms: *Sonata in F Minor for Clarinet and Piano*, Opus 120, No. 1, first movement (Allegro). Anthology page 398, measures 5-10 (remember to transpose the clarinet).

A15.05 Haydn: String Quartet in G Minor, Opus 74, No. 3, second movement (Largo). Anthology page 152, measure 7.

15.06 Beethoven: *Piano Sonata No. 5 in C Minor*, Opus 10 number 1, second movement (Adagio). Anthology page 262, measures 78-82.

15.07 Oliver: *West End Blues*. Anthology Appendix A (page 609), measures 3-4.

Chapter 16
Chromatic Mediants

Every chord has a mediant[1] relationship with eight triads. Of these eight triads, two are diatonic mediants, and the other six are chromatic. **Chromatic mediants** are triads that contain some sort of deviation from the key and are "a third away" from any diatonic chord within that key (usually tonic). Example 16.01 illustrates all the chords in mediant relationship to a tonic triad in the key of C major.

Example 16.01

C Major:

	MEDIANTS BELOW	TONIC TRIAD	MEDIANTS ABOVE	
DIATONIC	vi		iii	MINOR
CHROMATIC	VI / ♭VI	(tonic triad)	III / ♭III	MAJOR
DOUBLY-CHROMATIC	♭vi		♭iii	MINOR

The chords designated ♭vi and ♭iii are **doubly-chromatic mediants** because of two factors: First, they are of a different quality than the tonic triad; second, and more importantly, they have no notes in common with the tonic triad. When a chord and its doubly-chromatic mediant are heard in succession, the effect is dramatic.

---

[1] *As explained in chapter four, the third scale degree is named "mediant" because it is mid-way between tonic and dominant (ascending). The sixth scale degree is named "submediant" because it is mid-way between tonic and subdominant (descending). In context, "mediant" means "third," either above or below.*

Up to this point, *major* triads built on the diatonic third and sixth scale degrees have been considered secondary dominants (V/vi and V/ii respectively). The context determines which designation the chord should receive (*secondary dominant* or *chromatic mediant*). Consider the two chromatically altered chords in the progression below.

Example 16.02

C   A/C♯   F/C   D   G/D   G7/D   C

C: I   IV$^6_4$ V$^6_4$ V$^4_3$ I

The A major triad is either V^6/ii or VI^6. The determining factors are *approach* and *resolution*. If the chord resolves as a dominant would in type one or type two fashion (root drops a fifth, or ascends a second), the chord is considered a secondary dominant. However, if the chord does not resolve in regular or deceptive fashion, but is approached and/or left in mediant relationship to another chord, it is a chromatic mediant. Therefore, the chord in question in example 16.02 would be classified as VI^6 since it is functioning as a chromatic mediant to the chords on either side of it.

The D major chord, although preceded by a chord in mediant relationship to it, resolves type one. The classification, then, is V/V. A similar progression is shown in example 16.03.

Example 16.03

C   A/C♯   F/C   D   B♭/D   G7/D   C

C: I   VI^6 IV$^6_4$ ♭VII^6 V$^4_3$ I

In this case, the D major chord does not resolve as a dominant would in type one or type two fashion. Most theorists consider it a V/V with type three (irregular) resolution. It is in chromatic mediant relationship to the chords it follows and precedes, and simply is not functioning like a dominant.

A case could probably be made for giving such a chord the designation II since it appears to be functioning more like a major supertonic than a dominant of dominant. In reality, however, the chord is functioning as neither a supertonic nor a dominant. It is its own entity—a chromatic mediant to the chords before and after it. There is no standard accepted analysis in these instances. It is generally considered acceptable to label the chord V/V (with irregular resolution), but alternate analyses, such as II, are worthy of consideration as exceptions to the rule "*the analysis symbol* II *does not exist*" (see page 307). If either designation (V/V or II) is used, it is ideal to *indicate the special circumstance* by including the parenthetical designation of chromatic mediant (CM) below the roman numeral analysis.

For the most part, it is only vital to know the designations of chromatic mediants *from the tonic*, as shown in example 16.01 at the beginning of this chapter.

The B-flat chord in example 16.03 is considered a chromatic mediant in this context. Under different conditions, this ♭VII chord would be a borrowed chord. Here, however, it is functioning in chromatic mediant relationship to the chords on either side. There is no harmonic analysis symbol to differentiate a chromatic mediant from a borrowed chord.

In the *Fundamentals* and *Diatonic Melody and Harmony* portions of this text (parts one and two), the elements of music were presented in so-called "black and white" detail. Once chromaticism becomes part of the musical texture, however, more "gray areas" surface. Opportunities arise for subjective, alternate analyses. Educated theorists enjoy discussing different ways of examining music, both aurally and visually.

In highly chromatic passages, enharmonic spellings of chords are abundant, as are modulations that employ the usage of accidentals rather than changing the key signature (see chapter 17). Understanding pitch classes is a crucial skill for the theorist. Analysts must always remember that *sound is more important than sight*. Aural effects take precedence over written spellings in composition and analysis.

At first glance, the chords in example 16.04 do not appear to be in mediant relationship. Although the roots of the two chords are an A2 apart, the aural perception is clearly a m3.

Example 16.04

C   D♯m

C: I

"If we were all determined to play the first violin we should never have an ensemble. Therefore, respect every musician in his proper place."
— composer Robert Schumann

As wrong as it appears, the correct analysis of the D-sharp minor triad is ♭iii. It is a doubly-chromatic mediant of the tonic triad, spelled enharmonically. Reasons for such enharmonic spellings will become evident in chapter seventeen on modulation.

A particularly challenging situation appears in example 16.05 on the following page. Care must be taken in analyzing *both* chords.

Example 16.05

"Music is the effort we make to explain to ourselves how our brains work. We listen to Bach transfixed because this is listening to a human mind."

— physician and educator Lewis Thomas

The analysis of the first chord is dependent on its relationship to the second chord. For the A major triad to be a V/ii, it would have to be followed by ii (type one) or vii° (type two), unless it is an irregular resolution (type three) as it appears to be. However, if the D-flat chord is considered enharmonically as a C-sharp triad, the chromatic mediant relationship is obvious. The ear perceives the interval between chord roots as a M3 (rather than the visual representation of d4). The proper analysis of both chords (using both spellings of the second chord) is shown below.

Example 16.06

C: VI   N⁶   C: VI   N⁶

Even though the analysis VI — N⁶ does not *appear* to indicate chromatic mediants, it *is* the correct analysis. By calling the A major chord VI, the *implication* of a chromatic mediant is made since a chromatic mediant is the only context where VI occurs (otherwise it would have been designated V/ii).[2]

In passages flush with chromatic mediants, the aural perception of tonic may become "lost." It is not unusual for analyses to vary from theorist to theorist in instances of ambiguous tonality. The analyst's responsibility is to use roman numerals to indicate *function* as clearly as possible. Because chromatic mediants are used as "color chords," providing variety and interest more than function, some theorists refer to them as *nonfunctional chords*.

In example 16.07, all the *minor triads* have only one possible designation each (iii, vi, ♭iii, and ♭vi). Every minor triad in mediant relationship to a given major chord is either completely diatonic (iii and vi) or doubly-chromatic (♭iii and ♭vi). There are no alternate analyses for those chords.

The *major triads* in chromatic mediant relationship to another major chord, however, are dependent on context to determine function. They are either chromatic mediants, secondary dominants, or borrowed chords.

---

[2] *If one desired to indicate the mediant relationship of the chord roots, the analysis would have to include the preposterous designation of #I⁶ for the second triad! Since the second chord is not functioning as any type of tonic, analysts must use judgment in choosing the best label (in this case, N⁶).*

Example 16.07

C MAJOR:

MEDIANTS BELOW — ONLY *DIATONIC* MEDIANTS — MEDIANTS ABOVE

DIATONIC: vi (below) → iii (above) — MINOR

CHROMATIC MEDIANTS *OR* SECONDARY DOMINANTS
TONIC TRIAD

CHROMATIC:
- VI or V/ii (below) ↔ III or V/vi (above) — MAJOR
- ♭VI (below) ↔ ♭III (above)

CHROMATIC MEDIANTS *OR* BORROWED CHORDS

DOUBLY-CHROMATIC — ONLY *DOUBLY-CHROMATIC* MEDIANTS — MINOR
♭vi ↔ ♭iii

When voice leading chromatic mediants (and chromaticism in general), it is important to avoid false relations if at all possible. A ***false relation*** (or *cross relation*) is a chromatic alteration in one voice immediately preceding or following an *unaltered* version of the *same note* in *another voice*. Chromatic alterations of a pitch should appear *in a single voice* whenever possible.[3]

Example 16.08

Left: C: I — ♭III, false relation E♮ — E♭ alto bass

Right: C: I — ♭III⁶, no false relation E♮ — E♭ alto only

This concludes the introduction to chromatic mediants. The roman numeral chart of chord identification is now expanded to include these chords, and appears on the following page in its completed form. Modulation will be covered in chapter seventeen.

---

[3] *It is not always possible to avoid writing false relations without breaking a law of voice leading. For example, there is a false relation that could not be avoided in the example provided in assignment 15.01 on page 371. This, along with the very awkward melodic interval of a diminished third, is a significant reason why Neapolitans rarely resolve directly to dominant—especially in voice leading.*

Example 16.09

Key of C	C	C#/D♭	D	D#/E♭	E	F	F#/G♭	G	G#/A♭	A	A#/B♭	B
Diatonic Triads	I		ii		iii	IV		V		vi		vii°
Natural Minor Diatonic Triads	*i*		*ii°*	*III*		*iv*		*v*	*VI*		*VII*	
Harmonic Minor Diatonic Triads	*i*		*ii°*	*III+*		*iv*		*V*	*VI*			*vii°*
Secondary Dominants	V⁷/IV		V⁽⁷⁾/V		V⁽⁷⁾/vi		(V⁽⁷⁾/vii°)			V⁽⁷⁾/ii		V⁽⁷⁾/iii
Secondary Leading Tones		vii°⁽⁷⁾/ii		vii°⁽⁷⁾/iii	vii°⁽⁷⁾/IV		vii°⁽⁷⁾/V		vii°⁽⁷⁾/vi		(vii°⁽⁷⁾/vii°)	
Borrowed Chords			ii°, ii°⁷	♭III		iv		(v)	♭VI		♭VII	
and their Tonicizers			vii°/♭III	V⁽⁷⁾/♭VI		V⁷/♭VII		vii°/♭VI		vii°/♭VII	V⁽⁷⁾/♭III	
Augmented Sixth Chords									It⁶ / Gr⁶₅ / Fr⁴₃			
Neapolitan Chords	vii°/N	N N⁶ N⁶₄			III				V⁽⁷⁾/N			
Altered Dominants								V⁺				
Expanded Dominants								V⁹ V¹¹ V¹³				
Chromatic Mediants				♭III / ♭iii					♭VI / ♭vi	VI		

Assignments and Drills

Assignment 16.01

The objective of this assignment is creation and identification of chromatic mediants in major and minor keys.

Instructions: Write out all diatonic and chromatic mediants for each tonic triad as indicated. Do not use enharmonic spellings. The first one has been done for you. REFER BACK TO EXAMPLE 16.01 IF NECESSARY.

		diatonic		chromatic				doubly-chromatic	
	tonic	mediant	submediant	mediant	submediant	mediant	submediant	mediant	submediant
1. Am:	i	III	VI	♭iii	♭vi	♯iii	♯vi	♯III	♯VI
2. G:									
3. F:									
4. Bm:									
5. A:									

391

Assignment 16.02

The objective of this assignment is identification of chromatic mediants in major and minor keys.

Instructions: Using pop-chord symbols, identify the six chromatic mediants for each chord name provided. Do not use enharmonic spellings. The first one has been done for you.
REFER BACK TO EXAMPLES 16.01—16.03 IF NECESSARY.

Chord: D.   Chromatic mediants: F#   B   F   B♭   Fm   B♭m

Chord: Cm.   Chromatic mediants: _____ _____ _____ _____ _____ _____

Chord: B♭.   Chromatic mediants: _____ _____ _____ _____ _____ _____

Chord: Em.   Chromatic mediants: _____ _____ _____ _____ _____ _____

Chord: E.   Chromatic mediants: _____ _____ _____ _____ _____ _____

Chord: Gm.   Chromatic mediants: _____ _____ _____ _____ _____ _____

Chord: A♭.   Chromatic mediants: _____ _____ _____ _____ _____ _____

Assignment 16.03

The objective of this assignment is harmonic analysis of chromatic mediants.

Instructions: Complete the harmonic analysis of the excerpt below.[4]

Assignment 16.04

The objective of this assignment is composition and voice leading of chromatic mediants.

Instructions: Voice lead the brief progressions below. Vary choices of key, meter, and harmonic rhythm for each one. Include inversions and nonharmonic tones if desired.

1. I—♭VI—iv—V—I.

2. I—III—I—♭VI—Gr$^6_5$—I$^6_4$—V^7—I.

3. I—VI—IV—♭VI—♭VII—I.

4. I—♭iii—V—♭VII—V/V—IV—V—I.

---

[4] Symphony No. 3, Opus 90, Second movement (Andante), piano reduction of final seven measures: *Johannes Brahms, 1883. Public Domain.*

Assignment 16.05

The objective of this assignment is proper roman numeral identification of diatonic and chromatic chords.

Instructions: Fill in the blanks in the chart below. Only refer back to example 16.09 to check your work when finished.

Key of C	C	C#/Db	D	D#/Eb	E	F	F#/Gb	G	G#/Ab	A	A#/Bb	B
Diatonic triads												
Natural minor diatonic triads												
Harmonic minor diatonic triads												
Secondary dominants												
Secondary leading tones												
Borrowed chords and their tonicizers												
Augmented sixth chords												
Neapolitan chords												
Altered dominants												
Expanded dominants												
Chromatic mediants												

Questions for Review

1. How many chords are in mediant relationship to any single triad? How many of those are diatonic? Chromatic? Doubly-chromatic?

2. What two factors make a chord a doubly-chromatic mediant?

3. How are borrowed chords and chromatic mediants differentiated when it appears that a chord could be classified as either one?

4. How are secondary dominants and chromatic mediants differentiated when a chord appears it could be classified as either one?

5. What are two challenges theorists face when analyzing chromatic mediants?

6. How do chromatic mediants function?

7. Define the term *false relation*.

Assignment for Use with Anthology

A16.01 Provide complete harmonic analysis of Chopin: *Prelude 9 in E Major*. Anthology pages 350-351, <u>entire composition (measures 1-12)</u>.

Chapter 17
Modulation

Modulation is a change from one tonal center (key) to another. For a modulation to take place, the tonic *note* must change. Movement from one key to its *parallel* major or minor is not considered a modulation; rather, it is a ***change of mode***. Movement from a key to its *relative* major or minor *is* a modulation because *tonic* is changing, even though the key signature is not.

This chapter explains two types of modulations: those to *closely-related keys*, and those to *foreign* keys. Each of these two types has three methods of achieving modulation.

Closely-related keys are those whose key signatures differ by no more than one accidental. In major, the closely-related keys to I are ii, iii, IV, V, and vi. Example 17.01 uses the key of C major to demonstrate closely-related keys.

Example 17.01

Key of C	C	D	E	F	G	A	B
DIATONIC TRIADS	I	ii	iii	IV	V	vi	vii°
CLOSELY-RELATED KEYS	(original)	Dm	Em	F	G	Am	
SHARPS/FLATS	0	1 flat	1 sharp	1 flat	1 sharp	0	

Each major key has five closely-related keys: the subdominant of that key, the dominant of that key, and the relative minor keys of I, IV, and V.

In minor, the closely-related keys to i are III, iv, v, VI, and VII. Example 17.02 uses the key of C minor to demonstrate closely-related keys.

Example 17.02

Key of C minor	C	D	E♭	F	G	A♭	B♭
DIATONIC TRIADS	i	ii°	III	iv	v	VI	VII
CLOSELY-RELATED KEYS	(original)		E♭	Fm	Gm	A♭	B♭
SHARPS/FLATS	3 flats		3 flats	4 flats	2 flats	4 flats	2 flats

As in major, each minor key has five closely-related keys: the subdominant of that key, the dominant of that key, and the relative major keys of i, iv, and v.

The first method of modulation to a closely-related key is the ***common chord modulation***. In this method, the chord *immediately preceding the chord containing chromatic alteration* is *diatonic* in both the old key and the new key. This "common" chord acts as a *pivot chord* to transition from the old key into the new key. Example 17.03 illustrates a common chord modulation.

Example 17.03

The chromatic alteration occurs in beat two of measure two. If the music were not modulating, the analysis would simply be V/V, resolving type one. However, a new tonic is clearly *established*, not just *suggested*. G is not merely tonicized; it actually does become tonic. The chord just prior to the chromatic alteration in measure two is common to both the old key and the new key. Analysis of a common chord modulation is done with a bracket at the pivot chord, indicating the roman numerals for the chord in both the outgoing and incoming keys. Analysis continues from that point only in the new key. The new key is indicated in front of the bracket.

Example 17.04

C: I   iii   IV   vii°6 ⸤ vi
G: ⸤ ii   V   I   I   ii   I^6 ii   V   V^7 I

Even though the key signature has not changed, the key has. The doubled ***B*** in both G chords in measure three would have been the leading tone in the original key, and could not have been doubled without the modulation. The ***B*** in the final chord of measure one is not doubled (even though doubling the soprano is usually the first choice in first inversion triads), because it is still the leading tone at this point.

The second method of modulation to a closely-related key is the ***phrase modulation***. In this method, sometimes called a *static modulation*, the beginning of a new phrase introduces the new key without warning. One phrase ends in the original key and the next phrase begins in the new key. Although it may seem that this method of modulation might be abrupt, the effect is usually rather smooth, simply because the two keys are closely related. In analysis, the new key is indicated (without a bracket) at the point of modulation.

Example 17.05

C: I   iii   IV   vii°6   I   V   I   G: I   vii°   I6   ii6   V   V7   I

The third method of modulation to a closely-related key is the ***chromatic modulation***. This modulation is characterized by mid-phrase chromatic movement in a single voice where the chord preceding chromatic alteration is not common to both keys. In analysis, the new key is indicated (without a bracket) at the point of modulation.

Example 17.06

C: I   iii   IV   vii°6   I   V   I   I   iii   F: V7   I   IV   V   I

The E minor chord on beat two of measure three is only diatonic in the first key (***C***), but not the second (***F***). The modulation takes place in the middle of the phrase, not immediately, and the chromaticism is not merely tonicization; it *establishes* the new tonal center (***F***), which continues onward from that point.

Modulations to foreign keys are more complex. **Foreign keys** are those whose signatures differ by more than one accidental. There are twelve pitches in the tonal system, and each one is the basis for a major and minor key, so there are twenty-four keys total (although some are duplicated due to enharmonic spellings). This means that excluding the parallel key (which is not available for modulation since the tonal center remains the same) and the five closely-related keys, *each key has seventeen foreign keys to which it could modulate*. There are three methods for reaching these seventeen foreign keys.

The first method of modulation to a foreign key is via **interchange of mode**. In this method, the modulation "goes through" the parallel key to reach the closely-related keys of the parallel key. Simply by changing mode to the parallel key, the composer now has access to five more closely-related keys. Example 17.07 uses the keys of C major and C minor to illustrate the new opportunities afforded by *interchange of mode*.

Example 17.07

Key of C	C	D	E♭ E	F	G	A♭ A	B♭ B
Diatonic Triads	I	ii	iii	IV	V	vi	vii°
Closely-related Keys	(original)	Dm	Em	F	G	Am	°
Closely-related to Parallel Key	(Cm)	°	E♭	Fm	Gm	A♭	B♭

Key of C minor (natural minor)	C	D	E♭ E	F	G	A♭ A	B♭ B
Diatonic Triads	i	ii°	III	iv	v	VI	VII
Closely-related Keys	(original)	°	E♭	Fm	Gm	A♭	B♭
Closely-related to Parallel Key	(C)	Dm	Em	F	G	Am	°

The second method of modulation to a foreign key is the most interesting and creative: **enharmonic pivot chords**. This method uses the same concept as the *common chord* modulation to closely-related keys. When used with foreign keys, the pivot chord is spelled in order to be interpreted the original key, but it is *functioning* as its enharmonic spelling in the *new* key.

The qualities of chords spelled enharmonically are diminished sevenths, augmented sixth chords, Neapolitan chords, and borrowed chords. For analysis, a bracket is used to indicate the pivot chord.

The diminished seventh chord is highly functional. It has been nicknamed the **Master Chord** [1] because of its ability to quickly and fluently transition to foreign keys. The diminished seventh chord is so versatile because each one is already diatonic in five foreign keys if simply spelled enharmonically.

Consider the B diminished seventh chord in example 17.08. In first inversion, it is identical to a D diminished seventh chord; in second inversion, it is identical to an E-sharp diminished seventh chord; in third inversion it is identical to a G-sharp diminished seventh. This single chord shares four spellings, and is not only enharmonic in multiple keys, but it is the *leading tone* in multiple keys. This is significant because leading tone chords, like the dominant chords for which they often substitute, progress naturally to tonic.

Example 17.08

It could be summarized, then, that $B^{o7} = D^{o7} = E\#^{o7} = G\#^{o7}$, in various inversions and spellings. Example 17.09 shows this concept another way.

Example 17.09

"Modulation: The cure for the common chord."
- Music theorist Holly Mirau

The analysis is left blank for the $E\#^{o7}/B$ chord, because this spelling is not functional in C major. Even though the D^{o7}/C-flat chord and the $G\#^{o7}/B$ chord *could* be encountered in C major, the aural effect is none other than simply vii^{o7}. Despite the spelling, this is how it would be best analyzed. If the $G\#^{o7}$ chord were to appear in C major as a leading tone of A, it would do so in *prime position*, not in inversion. In that case, it would be analyzed as vii^{o7}/vi.

---

[1] *A credit card company ran an advertising campaign for several years, proclaiming "It's everywhere you want to be." The company was Visa®, but a group of young theorists thought it would be more appropriate if it were Master Card®. Theorist Holly Mirau coined the adaptation of the slogan: "The Master Chord: It's everywhere you want to be." This makes reference to the diminished seventh chord which can easily get you to any new key.*

Example 17.10 diagrams all Master Chords. Because each chord is four notes (out of twelve in the tonal system), and is made up of only minor thirds, there are really only three distinct diminished seventh chords in existence. All the others are inversions/alternate spellings of these three.

Example 17.10

PITCH CLASS SET 1   PITCH CLASS SET 2   PITCH CLASS SET 3

$D°7 \quad E\#°7 \quad G\#°7 \quad B°7 \qquad D\#°7 \quad F\#°7 \quad A°7 \quad B\#°7 \qquad E°7 \quad G°7 \quad A\#°7 \quad C\#°7$

$D^{o7} = E\#^{o7} = G\#^{o7} = B^{o7} \qquad D\#^{o7} = F\#^{o7} = A^{o7} = B\#^{o7} \qquad E^{o7} = G^{o7} = A\#^{o7} = C\#^{o7}$

D F A♭ C♭   D# F# A C   E G B♭ D♭

The *prime* of *each* chord in each pitch class set above spells that same chord (in one of its four manifestations). Regarding modulation, the beauty of the extremely flexible function of the Master Chord lies in the fact that one single chord is not only the simultaneous leading tone chord of three other tonics, but that it can be used as a *secondary* leading tone chord.

For instance, if one wanted to modulate from C major to F-sharp major/G-flat major (a tritone away), the B^{o7} chord could be inverted, morphing into an $E\#^{o7}$, and the modulation is instantaneous. However, if one wanted to use the same Master Chord to get from C major to D major, none of the pitch class set 1 manifestations of the Master Chord lead to D. The B^{o7} chord could still be used, inverting into the $G\#^{o7}$ chord, which is vii^{o7}/A. Thus, it is vii^{o7}/V in the new key.

The Master Chord really is everywhere you want to be, creating simultaneous diatonic chords in multiple keys. Used diatonically, or as a secondary leading tone chord of any diatonic chord to which it resolves type one, *any diminished seventh chord can be used to get to any key*. Because of enharmonic spellings, the *prime* of *enharmonic pivot diminished sevenths* is considered the *lowest sounding note*, regardless of how the chord is spelled.

Examples 17.11, 17.12, and 17.13 demonstrate short modulations using the Master Chord. Each brief example establishes C as tonic and modulates to a foreign key.

Example 17.11

C: I   V   I⁶   ⎡vii°⁶₅
       E♭: ⎣vii°⁷   I   V⁷   I

Example 17.12

C: I   V   I⁶   ⎡vii°⁴₃
       G♭: ⎣vii°⁷   I   V⁷   I

Example 17.13

C: I   V   I⁶   ⎡vii°⁷/vi
       D: ⎣vii°⁷/V   V   V⁶₅   I   V⁷   I

Example 17.13 is particularly interesting because the enharmonic pivot Master Chord is a *secondary* leading tone chord in *both* keys. Ironically, it is an enharmonic spelling of a diatonic chord in the original key (vii°⁴₂).

Examples 17.14 and 17.15, on the following page, are re-voicings of example 17.13, illustrating that the *inversion* of the Master Chord is of little consequence. The exact same progression is used as in example 17.13, but spelled differently, and therefore analyzed differently. Note especially the analyses of the Master Chord in example 17.15.

> "I have my own particular sorrows, loves, delights; and you have yours. But sorrow, gladness, yearning, hope, love, belong to all of us, in all times and in all places. Music is the only means whereby we feel these emotions in their universality."
> – author H. A. Overstreet

Example 17.14

C: I   V   I^6 ⌈vii°$^4_3$/vi
        D: ⌊vii°$^4_3$/V   V^6 V^7 I   V^7 I

Example 17.15

C: I   V   I^6 ⌈vii°$^6_5$
        D: ⌊vii°$^4_3$/V   V$^6_5$ V^7 I   V^7 I

Another *enharmonic pivot chord* is the augmented sixth. The most common is the German sixth, since it has the enharmonic *quality* of a dominant seventh. Examples 17.16 and 17.17 illustrate how this chord is used as an enharmonic pivot.

Example 17.16

Am: i   V   i ⌈Gr$^6_5$
          B♭: ⌊V^7 I   V   I

"The goal of practice isn't doing something until you get it right. It's doing it until you can't get it wrong."

- *author and musician*
Bob Kauflin

Example 17.17

Am: i   V   i ⌈V^7
          A♭: ⌊Gr$^6_5$ I$^6_4$ V   I

The Italian sixth works just as well, because it is enharmonic with an incomplete dominant seventh chord (fifth missing).

Example 17.18

A: I V I ⌐ It⁶
Eb: └ V⁷/V   V⁷ V I V I

Notice how easily the augmented sixth chord transitions to extremely foreign keys. In the three previous examples, the tonal center transitioned from A to B♭, A♭, and E♭.

The Neapolitan sixth is another chord that can be used enharmonically when modulating. Example 17.19 illustrates one way that a chord can function simultaneously as a dominant and a Neapolitan.

Example 17.19

Am: i V i ⌐ V⁶
Eb: └ N⁶   I$_4^6$ V I$_4^6$ V⁷ I

Finally, borrowed chords may be used as enharmonic pivot chords. Example 17.20 shows a non-modulating progression using borrowed chords in the key of C major. In example 17.21 on the following page, the last chord of the progression is changed, creating a modulation and completely altering the function of the first borrowed chord.

Example 17.20

C: I V I V ♭VI ♭VII I

Example 17.21

C: I V I V ♭VI
          E♭: IV V I

"Music is the fourth great material want: first food, then clothes, then shelter, then music."
– author Christian Nevell Bovee

The last method of modulating to a foreign key is the **common tone** modulation. A particular single note that is common to both keys is emphasized in the transition to the foreign key. This note is held or repeated, much like a pedal tone, until the ear accepts the new tonality. The common tone may be spelled enharmonically in the transition. The most frequent common tone is the leading tone of the new key.

If a modulation up a half step were desired, for instance, the *tonic note* of the old key *is* the *leading tone* of the new key. Emphasis on that particular note makes the transition smooth and keeps it from sounding awkward. No bracket is used in the common tone modulation. The new key signature is inserted into the harmonic analysis at the point of chromatic alteration.

Example 17.22

tonic / tonic in old / leading tone in new

C: I IV^6 IV D♭: V I V vi V^6

Regardless of methods used, the primary matter of importance when modulating is the presence of functioning dominant and leading-tone chords of the *new* key. It does not matter whether the modulation is to a closely-related key or a foreign key. The appearance of a dominant or leading tone chord of the new tonic is the essential element. The types and methods of modulation outlined in this chapter seek to assist in understanding and creating smooth modulations that transition to new tonal centers in subtle fashion. Learning to modulate well takes practice, but the ability to do so is extremely rewarding.

This concludes the introduction to modulation and brings this book to a close. The *Postlude* to this text (found on page 421), provides a brief synopsis of subjects highly recommended for further study *outside* the scope of this text. Those who have successfully mastered the material presented in this volume and are ready to move on to further study should be congratulated as card-carrying theorists.

Assignments and Drills

Assignment 17.01

The objective of this assignment is creation and identification of closely-related keys.

Instructions: List the five closely-related keys to each key provided. REFER BACK TO EXAMPLES 17.01 AND 17.02 IF NECESSARY.

Key: D.   Closely-related keys: _____ _____ _____ _____ _____

Key: F.   Closely-related keys: _____ _____ _____ _____ _____

Key: G.   Closely-related keys: _____ _____ _____ _____ _____

Key: Cm.   Closely-related keys: _____ _____ _____ _____ _____

Key: B.   Closely-related keys: _____ _____ _____ _____ _____

Key: E.   Closely-related keys: _____ _____ _____ _____ _____

Key: D#m.   Closely-related keys: _____ _____ _____ _____ _____

Assignment 17.02

The objective of this assignment is identification of modulations to closely-related keys.

Instructions: Provide harmonic analysis for each brief excerpt below. Identify the *method* of modulation. REFER BACK TO EXAMPLES 17.03 — 17.06 IF NECESSARY.

Piano Sonata in B Flat Major *K. 333, first movement, measures 10-15. Wolfgang Amadeus Mozart, 1783. Public Domain.*

Invention No. 12 in A Major *BWV 783, measures 5-9. Johann Sebastian Bach, 1723. Public Domain.*

Assignment 17.03

The objective of this assignment is identification of modulations to closely-related keys.

Instructions: Provide harmonic analysis for the excerpt below. Identify the *method(s)* of modulation. REFER BACK TO EXAMPLES 17.03 — 17.06 IF NECESSARY.

Piano Sonata in A Major — K. 331, third movement, allegretto, measures 1-16. Wolfgang Amadeus Mozart, 1778. Public Domain.

Assignment 17.04

The objective of this assignment is identification of modulations to closely-related keys.

Instructions: Provide harmonic analysis for the chorale below. Identify the *methods* of modulation. REFER BACK TO EXAMPLES 17.03 — 17.06 IF NECESSARY.

Chorale: Zeuch uns nach Dir *J. S. Bach, circa 1725. Public Domain.*

Assignment 17.05

The objective of this assignment is creation of modulations to closely-related keys.

Instructions: Finish voice leading each exercise below as instructed. Include harmonic analysis.
REFER BACK TO EXAMPLES 17.03 — 17.06 IF NECESSARY.

1. Common chord modulation to G minor.

2. Phrase modulation to B-flat major.

3. Chromatic modulation to D major.

Assignment 17.06

The objective of this assignment is identification of modulations to foreign keys.

Instructions: Provide harmonic analysis for each excerpt of the Mazurka below. Identify the *methods* of modulation in each. REFER BACK TO EXAMPLES 17.07 — 17.22 IF NECESSARY.

Mazurka 33 Opus 56, No. 1 *Measures 1-6, 43-45, 74-82. Frédérick Chopin, 1838. Public Domain.*

Assignment 17.07

The objective of this assignment is creation of modulations to foreign keys.

Instructions: Finish voice leading each exercise below as instructed. Include harmonic analysis.
REFER BACK TO EXAMPLES 17.07 — 17.22 IF NECESSARY.

1. Enharmonic pivot chord modulation to A major.

2. Interchange of mode modulation to D minor.

3. Common tone modulation to D-flat major.

Questions for Review

1. Why is a *change of mode* considered a *mutation* instead of a *modulation*?

2. What is the difference between *closely-related* keys and *foreign* keys?

3. List and define the three methods of modulation to closely-related keys.

4. List and define the three methods of modulation to foreign keys.

5. How many distinctly different-sounding diminished seventh chords are there, and why?

6. How many distinctly different-sounding augmented triads are there, and why? (The answer is not found in chapter seventeen, but can be deduced based on the same rationale used to answer question five.)

7. Why does the Master Chord work so well in connecting seemingly-obscure keys?

8. Why do *phrase modulations* (to closely-related keys) not sound like abrupt shifts in tonality?

9. How does a *common chord* modulation work?

10. How does a *common tone* modulation work?

Assignments for Use with Anthology

For each assignment below, provide complete harmonic analysis, indicating both the *types* and *methods* of modulation.

A17.01   Bach: *March*, from *Notebook for Anna Magdalena Bach*. Anthology page 76, entire composition.

A17.02   Handel: Thy Rebuke Hath Broken His Heart (recitative), from Messiah (oratorio). Anthology page 95, measures 1-8.

A17.03   Haydn: *Piano Sonata in C Sharp Minor*, first movement (Moderato). Anthology page 145, measures 34-43.

A17.04   Haydn: *String Quartet in G Minor, Opus 74, No. 3*, second movement (Largo). Anthology page 152, measures 1-10.

A17.05   Mozart: *Piano Sonata in D Major*, K. 284, variation VII. Anthology page 175, measures 5-8.

A17.06   Beethoven: *Piano Sonata No. 8 in C Minor*, Opus 13, ("Pathétique"), first movement (Allegro). Anthology page 267, measures 133-136.

A17.07   Brahms: *Sonata in F Minor for Clarinet and Piano*, Opus 120, No. 1, first movement (Allegro). Anthology page 399, measures 25-38 (remember to transpose the clarinet).

A17.08   Gesangbuch: *So gibst du nun, mein Jesu, gut Nacht*. Appendix B of the anthology (page 639).

Postlude

Each chapter of *Practical Music Theory* presented *introductory* material to the subject(s) at hand. There is so much more to be explored. The goal of this book has been to familiarize aspiring theorists with concepts essential for a life-long exploration of music.

This postlude provides a brief synopsis of theory subjects highly recommended for further study *outside* the scope of this text.

Music of the 20th and 21st Centuries

A diverse abundance of music has been composed since the common practice era. New ways of perceiving, composing, and even performing elements of melody, rhythm, and harmony have emerged. A study of modern and recent music enhances the theorist's ability to comprehend and appreciate contemporary compositional techniques.

Form and Analysis

This book laid the groundwork for traditional analysis. Theory students who have successfully completed this text have a solid footing in foreground and middle-ground analysis. Study of musical *form* gives closer attention to middle-ground and background examination of compositions of all kinds. Further study of analysis introduces the theorist to diverse methods of understanding and analyzing music.

Forms:

- Strophic form (AAAA)
- Bar form (AAB)
- Binary (AB, AABB)
- Rounded binary (Aba, AABA)
- Ternary (ABA)
- Rondo (ABACA, ABACABA)
- Sonata
  ⇒ Exposition
  ⇒ Development
  ⇒ Recapitulation
- Theme and variations (A A' A'' A''')
- Through-composed (ABCDE...)
- Symphonic (multi-movement)

Alternative analyses:

- Shenkerian
- Mod 12
- Macro
- Nashville numbering system

Counterpoint

Counterpoint deals with advanced concepts of voice leading, exploring the relationships between simultaneous independent musical lines. There are three primary eras of counterpoint that are invaluable to the theorist's understanding of polyphony: Renaissance counterpoint (primarily 16th century), Baroque counterpoint (primarily 18th century), and Contemporary counterpoint (primarily 20th century). The most influential counterpoint, even in popular music, is that of the 18th century.

Soli Deo Gloria

Index

A Tempo 158
Accelerando 158
Accent Marks 44
Accidentals 12
Accompaniment 127
Active Tones 235
Al Coda 161
Al Fine 161
Alberti Bass 263
Altered Dominants 366
Alto Clef 8
Amplitude 3
Anacrusis 42
Anticipations 211
Appoggiaturas 211
Arpeggiated Bass 264
Arpeggio 128
Articulation 156
ASA System 15
Asymmetrical Meter 40
Augmented Dominants 366
Augmented Intervals 61
Augmented Sixth Chords 345
Augmented Triads 123
Authentic Cadence 237
Bar lines 12
Basic Conducting Patterns 43
Bass Clef 8
Beams 31
Beat 32
Block Chords 262
Blues Scale 98
Borrowed Chords 327
Borrowed Division 40
Broken Chords 263
C Clefs 8
C Instrument Chart 167
Cadence 164, 237
Caret (^) 235
Cantus Firmus 277
Change of Mode 399
Changing Tones 212
Chart of Roman Numeral Identification 390
Chorale Style 126, 264
Chord Charts 135
Chromatic Mediants 385
Chromatic Modulation 401
Chromatic Scale 97
Circle of Fifths (major only) 91
Circle of Fifths (major and minor) 92
Circle Progressions 241

Clef 7
Close Spacing 129
Closely-Related Keys 399
Coda Sign 161
Common Chord Modulation 400
Common Meter 42
Common Tone Modulation 408
Compound Intervals 59
Compound Meter 33
Concert Pitch 165
Consonances 85
Contoural Inversion 258
Contrary Motion 278
Contrasting Period 260
Cut Time 42
Da Capo 160
Dal Segno 160
Deceptive Cadence 238
Decibels 3
Decorated Suspensions 216
Diatonic Scales 83
Diminished Intervals 61
Diminished Seventh Chords 181
Diminished Triads 123
Direction of Inflection Principle 284
Dissonances 85
Dominant Seventh Chords 181
Dots 30
Double Dots 31
Doubling Principles 281
Doubly-augmented Fourths 65
Doubly-chromatic Mediants 385
Doubly-diminished Fifths 65
Downbeat 32
Duple Meter 32
Duplets 40
Duration 4
Dynamics 155
Dynamics 3
Eleventh Chords 367
Enharmonic Intervals 64
Enharmonic Notes 16
Enharmonic Pivot Chords 402
Escape Tones 210
Expanded Dominants 366
False Relation 389
False Sequence 259
Fermata 164
Fifths 62, 123
Figured Bass 188
Figured Bass Realization 191

First Inversion   129
Foreign Keys   402
Fourths   61
Free Tones   219
French Sixth   345
Fundamental   3
Gamut   14
German Sixth   345
Grand Staff   2
Grand Staff   9
Half Cadence   238
Half Step/Minor Second   10
Half-diminished Sevenths   181
Harmonic Analysis   124
Harmonic Intervals   59
Harmonic Minor   94
Harmonic Progression   127
Harmonic Progression   235
Harmonic Rhythm   242
Harmonics   3
Helmholtz System   15
Hemiola   44, 163
Hertz   1
Heterophony   261
Homophony   262
Homorhythm   264
Imperfect Authentic Cadence   237
Inactive Tones   235
Individual Note Durations   29
Individual Rest Durations   29
Inner Voices   193
Instrument Ranges/Clefs)   167
Intensity   3
Interhcange of Mode   402
Interval   10, 59
Interval Inversion   63
Interval Quality   60
Irregular Division   40
Italian Sixth   345
Jump Bass   263
Key Signatures   88
Keys   83
Laws of Voice Leading   279
Lead Sheets   133
Ledger Lines   9
Legend   159
Loco   10
Major Intervals   60
Major Second/Whole Step   10
Major Seventh Chords   181
Major Triads   123

Master Chord   403
Measured Tremolo   161
Measures   12
Melodic Intervals   59
Melodic Minor   95
Melody   127
Meter   32
Middle C   1
Midi Octave Designation   16
Minor Intervals   60
Minor Second/Half Step   10
Minor Seventh Chords   181
Minor Triads   123
Mixed Meter   162
Modal Mixture   328
Modes   83
Modified Sequence   260
Modulation   399
Monophony   261
Motif   255
Multiple Endings   161
Natural Minor   94
Neapolitan Chord   363
Neapolitan Sixth   363
Neighboring Tones   210
Ninth Chords   367
Note Components   13
Notes   2, 7
Oblique Motion   279
Octatonic Scale   98
Octave   10, 59
Octave Identification   14
Open Spacing   129
Order of Flats   90
Order of Sharps   89
Ornaments   157
Ottava Sign   10
Outer Voices   193
Overtones   3
Parallel Keys   93
Parallel Motion   278
Parallel Period   260
Partials   3
Passing Seventh   217
Passing Tones   209
Pedal Tones   212
Pentatonic Scale   99
Percussion Instrument Chart   167
Percussion Notation   159
Perfect Authentic Cadence   237
Perfect Intervals   60

Period   260
Phrase   260
Phrase Modulation   401
Phrygian II   363
Picardy Third   328
Pick-up Note(s)   42
Pitch   1
Pitch Class   97
Plagal Cadence   239
Polyphony   265
Pop-chord Symbols   132
Prime   284
Prime Unison   61
Quadruple Meter   32
Quintuple Meter   32
Rallentando/Ritardando   158
Range   1
Real Sequence   259
Regulations of Voice Leading   280
Relative Keys   93
Repeat Symbol   159
Resolution of Augmented Sixths   347
Resolution of Secondary Dominants   307
Resolving Seventh Chords   283
Rests   4, 30
Retardations   216
Retrograde Inversion   259
Retrograde Motion   259
Retrograde Repeat Symbol   160
Retrogression   242
Rhythm   33
Rhythmic Augmentation   259
Rhythmic Diminution   259
Rhythmic Patterns   42
Ritardando/Rallentando   158
Root   123
Root Position   129
Scale   11, 83
Scale Degree Names   84
Scale Degrees   11
Second Inversion   129
Second Inversion Triad Contexts   244
Secondary Authentic Cadence   308
Secondary Cadence   308
Secondary Deceptive Cadence   309
Secondary Dominants   303
Secondary Half Cadence   308
Secondary Leading Tone Chords   309
Secondary Leading Tone Resolutions   310
Seconds   63
Sequence   257

Seventh Chords   181
Seventh Chord Inversions   184
Similar Motion   278
Simple Meter   33
Simple Position   129
Solfège   14
Solmization   15
Sonority   181
Staff   7
Stem Length   13
Stretto   265
Substitute Notation   162
Suspensions   214
Syncopation   43
Tempo   35
Tempo Markings   158
Tenor Clef   8
Tetrachords   87
Textural Reduction   186
Texture   261
Thirds   63, 123
Thirteenth Chords   367
Ties   10, 13
Timbre   2
Time Signatures   35
Tonal Center   96
Tonal Sequence   259
Tonality   83
Tonic   83
Tonicization   303
Transposing Instruments   165
Transposing Instrument Chart   166
Transposition   87, 165
Treble Clef   7
Triads   123
Triad Charts   126
Triple Meter   32
Triplets   40
Tritone   64
Two-bar Repeat Symbol   159
Unaltered Intervals   61
Undulating Tremolo   161
Uneven Fifths   281
Unison   59
Unit   36
Vocal Ranges   168
Voice Crossing   280
Voice Leading   277
Voice Overlapping   280
Whole Step/Major Second   10
Whole-Tone Scale   97